GW00578626

THE POLITICS OF NEW LABOUR:
A GRAMSCIAN ANALYSIS

THE POLITICS OF NEW LABOUR: A GRAMSCIAN ANALYSIS

Andrew Pearmain

London Lawrence & Wishart 2011

Lawrence and Wishart Limited
99a Wallis Road
London
E9 5LN

First published 2011

Copyright © Lawrence and Wishart 2011

British Library Cataloguing in Publication Data.
A catalogue record for this book is available from the British Library

ISBN 9781907103254

Text setting E-type, Liverpool
Printed in Great Britain by the MPG Books Group,
Bodmin and King's Lynn

Contents

Introduction: Gramsci, History and New Labour

I'm not so bothered about hegemony,
I know that Gordon will look after me.

Model Worker, post-punk band Magazine[1]

This book is both general exposition and local application of the thinking of Antonio Gramsci, the Italian Marxist philosopher and communist leader. In particular it is an attempt 'to think in a Gramscian way' – the injunction of the leading British cultural theorist Stuart Hall – about the curious political phenomenon of New Labour. There is an extra layer of purpose in this enterprise, because elements within New Labour have cited Gramsci as a source of inspiration for their own 'project'. My central argument is that New Labour makes a far better object than agent of Gramscian analysis; specifically, as a 'transformist adaptation' of the far larger ideological force of Thatcherism. There is currently a pressing need to understand New Labour (even as it is being widely declared dead), and the ways in which it both fits into and diverges from the history of Labourism and the British left. Gramsci's key concepts – hegemony and historical bloc, coercion and consent, subalternity and pre-figurative struggle, war of position and war of manoeuvre, and, above all, passive revolution and transformism – can help us do that. As Labour retreats in electoral defeat to the places, people, institutions and 'values' of its heartlands, we need to salvage the Gramscian critique of Labourism that played some part in the formation of New Labour, and see what it says about the last sixty years of our history, and about the current parlous condition of the British left.

My opening chapters (1 and 2) outline the reception given to Gramsci's thinking in Britain, with its undisputed highlight the publication in 1971 of *Selections from Prison Notebooks*, brilliantly translated, edited and annotated by Quintin Hoare and Geoffrey Nowell Smith. Then in Chapter 3 I examine the key 'applied Gramscian' concept of Thatcherism, associated mainly with Stuart Hall, and its continuing relevance as the 'hegemonic' ideological dispensation or 'common sense' of our time. All political, cultural and 'moral' interventions in our society and economy, including (and perhaps above all) New Labour, have had to adapt to Thatcherism and to operate within the deep ideological parameters it set down. Without acknowledging and understanding what that involved – which some sections of the left have steadfastly refused to do – it is impossible to make sense of this last half-century. Chapter 4 looks at what I regard as abuses of Gramsci, specifically the 1980s and 1990s trends of 'post-Marxism', postmodernism and cultural studies. Then in chapters 5 and 6 I examine the record of the magazine *Marxism Today* (sponsored and subsidised by the Communist Party of Great Britain but increasingly independent as the CP approached its 1991 disbandment), and its signature themes and debates about the decline of the left and the dominance of the right. These culminated in the late-1980s debate about 'New Times', which, at a moment of global upheaval and disorientation, had a crucial (and largely unacknowledged) role in the transition from 'old' to New Labour. Finally, in chapters 7 to 11, I look in closer historical detail at the making of New Labour, what it took from both right and left (and chose to leave out), and its impact on British politics and society.

Antonio Gramsci

Antonio Gramsci (1891-1937) was a Sardinian hunchback, barely five feet tall, with a squeaky voice and an earnest, enigmatic manner. He was never entirely at ease with other people, spent much of his life alone, yet frequently complained in conversation and letters home that his family and friends were not making the effort to keep in touch. When he came to university on the Italian mainland in his early twenties, he was lonely and poor, cold and ill-fed, and would go for weeks on end without much to do with anyone else. His friend the revolutionary liberal Piero Gobetti, who wrote the fullest contemporary biographical sketch, observed in him the 'pessimistic solitude of a Sardinian migrant'. He dropped out without completing his degree in philology, much to the disappointment of his teachers, who had high hopes for his academic career. Instead, as war raged, he scraped a living with opinion pieces and theatre reviews for regional Italian socialist newspapers, or cadged off his older brother. In Turin's 'small world of intellectuals', a few hundred students and ex-students like Gramsci, he became known for his 'calmly destructive' writing style and his 'poisonous sarcasm'; he once described Marxism, his chosen outlook on life, as 'organised sarcasm'.[2] Gobetti declared that Gramsci was not an easy person to like, 'with his critical, destructive edge (and) a tyrannical logic which removes all trace of sympathy from his humour'. He was 'intransigent, a party man, at times almost ferocious; he even exercises his criticism on his friends, not as a personal or cultural polemic but through an insatiable need for sincerity'.[3]

Gramsci, now nearly thirty, was still hanging around Turin when the factory council movement emerged from the waves of industrial unrest at the end of the First World War. For the city's small circle of leftist intellectuals, the movement was a fortunate coincidence of their student politics and the Turin workers' syndicalism – the philosophy of revolutionary agitation in the workplace which was at that moment as influential in working-class politics as Marxism or labourism. The factory councils came very close to taking control of the city and the entire region, in what Andre Gorz calls 'the most striking example of a working class attempting to exercise unmediated power over production and to extend this power to society as a whole'.[4] This was the revolutionary syndicalist dream, with striking similarities to the model of soviets through which the Bolsheviks were seeking to disperse power to the Russian masses and construct a new state. It would never again be attempted with such fervour and purity, not least because of the lessons drawn from its failure and degeneration by later Communist leaders such as Gramsci.

But Gramsci's induction into Marxism was profoundly conditioned by syndicalism. The suspicion of 'voluntarism' – the overestimation of conscious human action and underestimation of objective circumstance – would dog him for the rest of his life. In 1918, Gramsci had written a notorious article on the October Revolution, 'The Revolution *Against* Capital', before he fully understood (or so he later claimed) its full ramifications. In a first flush of internationalist enthusiasm, he overstated the producer self-management of the Soviets and understated the military discipline of the Bolsheviks as driving forces in the revolution, not to mention the exhaustion of the Tsarist state. What he had meant, and in more circumspect language would stick by, was that the CPSU's decisive action had finally destroyed the Second International's social-democratic, positivist-scientific 'Marxist' notion of socialism as an inevitable consequence of capitalism, with no need for concerted struggle. What was needed was analysis *and* action, economics *and* politics, not to mention 'cultural forms from which a new civilisation could be consciously created'.[5]

Whatever the finer points of theoretical detail, the Turin Factory Councils were the closest the west would ever come to the creative upsurge of the revolutionary Soviets. Gramsci and his comrades put their obscure review, *Ordine Nuovo,* at the factory councils' disposal. The insurgent Turin workers adopted it as a principal source of direction, a prime example of what Gramsci later called '*irridazione*' or 'diffusion' of ideas; but they must have been at least a little bemused by its mix of tactical analysis, sectarian diatribe, sardonic humour, philosophical disquisition and cultural review. This was Gramsci's only experience of practical mass politics. The oddity of this funny-looking Sardinian intellectual hunchback addressing factory floor meetings was much commented upon at the time; he seems to have become a kind of mascot for the battle-hardened proletarians of the giant Fiat complex.

As far as we know, Gramsci had no intimate relationships until he met his wife Giulia in a Moscow sanatorium, where her sister Eugenie was recovering from TB and he was confined with 'nervous exhaustion'. A recent biography by Gramsci's grandson has revealed that his two sojourns in Russia were more eventful than long thought. He learnt Russian, grew a moustache, attended the momentous Fourth (Lenin's last) and Fifth Congresses of the Communist International, travelled widely outside Moscow to give speeches and lectures, and attempted to protect at least one Italian communist dissident from persecution. But the first visit lasted less than a year and a half (June 1922 - November 1923), including time in the sanatorium, and the second just a few weeks (March/April 1924).[6] Gramsci and Giulia had a brief and awkward courtship, and just a couple of years of married life – frequently interrupted by his political responsibilities, as fascism set about destroying the left (he spent much of the time across the border in Vienna) – until he was imprisoned and she returned to Russia. They never saw each other again. He was far closer to Giulia's sister Tania, who stayed in Italy and became his principal confidante, correspondent and prison visitor. He missed long periods of his first son Delio's infancy, and never actually met his second son Giuliano, who was born in Russia after Antonio's imprisonment.

Gramsci frequently shifted sides in the bitter disputes that heralded the break-up of the Italian Socialist Party and foundation of the Italian Communist Party (PCI). He had been an early admirer of Mussolini – another source of continuing suspicion – and he became leader of the PCI pretty much by default, when its other leaders had been imprisoned or exiled. Gramsci contributed just one major political statement (the 'Lyons Theses') on PCI and Comintern strategy, described by Paolo Spriano as 'the point of arrival for Gramsci's leadership', and an important but unfinalised theoretical analysis ('The Southern Question') on the historic inequality between the Italian regions. He was an MP for barely two years, before being arrested and imprisoned by the Fascists. He spent the remaining ten years of his life in squalid provincial jails, until he slowly and painfully declined and died in a clinic in Rome. For much of that time, he was ill and again alone, fastidiously keeping out of the ferocious political debates and theoretical discussions which preoccupied his fellow convicts, comrades and exiles during the 'Third Period' of the Communist International and the murderous faction fighting in the Soviet Union that confirmed Stalin's ascendancy. Vigorous debate persists among Gramsci scholars about his orientation towards Stalinism, but aside from an abiding commitment to democracy and open debate as the only sure way to secure deep and lasting change, there is little conclusive evidence of direct intervention in the controversies of the day.

Instead, Gramsci devoted himself to wide and systematic reading and to composing his notebooks – as much as prison conditions and his health allowed – in tiny writing, on ostensibly obscure themes of European history and philosophy, with much use of code and euphemism to avoid the attentions of the prison censor. The extent of self-censorship has also been the subject of much recent debate. The most famous example – the 'philosophy of praxis', for Marxism – is said to understate the originality of Gramsci's conception of 'the creative combination of thought and action'; while others may have been devised by his successor Togliatti to evade *Stalinist* censorship of his own writings.[7] Gramsci wrote to his sister-in-law that he was writing '*fur ewig*' – for posterity – determinedly unrelated to topical issues and events; the famous notes on 'Americanism and Fordism' were his only sustained commentary on the contemporary world, and were a decidedly unconventional take on it. What became known as the Prison Notebooks were composed over a period of little more than four years, between 1929 and 1934 – once his prison conditions had settled down sufficiently, and before ill health made work impossible.

In his letters and conversations, Gramsci complained frequently about loneliness and debilitating illness, and the appalling conditions in the Fascist prisons. He had constant trouble sleeping, which only exacerbated his health problems. A campaign was mounted for his release in the early 1930s, to his own considerable unease over the conditions that might be attached, but this was largely a vehicle for anti-fascist propaganda (a perennial campaigning technique of the left), and had no discernible impact on Mussolini. Gramsci died in 1937, barely noticed and 'not widely known in his own lifetime', either in Italy or the outside world.[8] He was 46, with no major political or professional achievements to speak of. The cause of international communism to which he had devoted his brief life was in abject retreat and internal disarray. He was penniless, out of contact with most of his own family, and effectively estranged from his wife Giulia, who herself spent much of her life in Russia undergoing psychiatric treatment (it had been going on for years before he found out). Only his sister-in-law Tania and one or two former friends and comrades – most notably the Cambridge economist Piero Sraffa – had kept in close touch. His notebooks survived because Tania and a couple of friends managed to smuggle them out of prison, into the vaults of the *Banco Commerciale Italiano*, then in the diplomatic bag to Moscow, where they stayed pretty much untouched until after the war.

The romance of Gramsci

Gramsci's life was eventful but brief and ultimately frustrated; 'tormented' according to Carl Levy. He was born, lived and died 'a person of the periphery', as Stuart Hall put it. While his 'inner life' was rich and deep, if his notebooks and letters are anything to go by, his relations with other people and his personal impact on the wider world were pretty limited. So why have Gramsci's story and writings exercised such a hold on the affections and imaginations of generations of left-wing intellectuals in Europe and America during the decades following the Second World War? The Gramsci 'foundation myth' was carefully promulgated and strategically deployed by Togliatti in his leadership of the postwar Italian Communist Party, but his appeal is also, at least partly, a matter of personal temperament. There is something about Gramsci that appeals to a certain cast of mind, especially among thoughtful younger men at odds with their social circumstances, 'outsider insiders' or 'gregarious loners' like the man himself, drawn by the romantic lure of enforced exile and incarceration, not to mention the lonely devotions of wilderness prophecy and inevitable early, largely un-mourned death. There is added appeal in posthumous acclaim and influence, which brings glory in fabled death without the blemishes of a real full life. There are obvious parallels in religious iconography, or in the short-lived 'bright stars' of the romantic tradition and our own popular culture; lonely suffering and early death can be a smart career move. Fittingly, Gramsci's ashes were deposited in an urn in the 'English' Protestant Cemetery in Rome where the poet John Keats was buried (with his beautiful headstone inscription: 'Here lies one whose name was writ in water'). But Gramsci's was not a self-willed confinement, or in any sense self-induced mortality. Besides, his sheer determination in conditions of spiritual, mental and physical adversity, which he seems if anything to have downplayed in his writings, seemed (and seems) truly heroic. For young lefties of the generally dispiriting 1970s, with our thwarted hopes and quasi-feminist openness to feeling, Gramsci was a sentimental inspiration.

There were other seductive historical parallels between our own time and Gramsci's, especially the cultural upheavals, actual and near-revolutions in and around 1917 and 1968, and their turbulent aftermaths. As it turned out, those parallels were quite misleading; the most obvious often are. The Soviet revolution was pretty much a one-off (albeit a mesmerising exception), and, as Gramsci himself concluded, the ruling classes of the western 'liberal democracies' were much better 'dug in' than we ever imagined. By the final quarter of the twentieth century, the organised industrial proletariat, the basic guarantor of the 'historic mission' of socialism, was rapidly disintegrating and dispersing, some upwards into the 'new middle class' and others downwards into the 'underclass'. But Gramsci (for Stuart Hall 'our foremost theorist of defeat') was especially helpful to understanding the depth and breadth of 'bourgeois hegemony', and to assuaging our political and personal disappointment. In a period during which the socialist left has been in constant retreat, 'international communism' has been utterly discredited, and most individual socialists and communists have withdrawn into private attitudes and consolations, Gramsci provides a model of emotional and intellectual endurance. 'Optimism of the will, pessimism of the intellect' runs the Gramscian 'motto' (actually coined by the French author Romain Rolland, but better known than any of Gramsci's own formulations).

Gramsci the real historical figure was well aware of his own charisma, and not averse to using it for personal and political ends; the most effective 'icons' usually are. After his death, and especially in the years of postwar 'democratic reconstruction', the Italian Communist Party assiduously cultivated an image of the lonely martyr. These most 'catholic' of communists conferred upon their founder a kind of secular canonisation. With the ascendancy of democratic perspectives within communism in the 1960s and 1970s, loosely known as 'Eurocommunism' and sharply contrasted with the abiding Stalinism of the Soviet model, 'Saint Antonio Gramsci' came into his own. His imprisonment and lofty detachment seemed to have left him untainted by the vicious debilitating factionalism of the 1930s, the horrors of Stalinism, and the long shadow cast over the communist, labour and socialist left by their gradual revelation.

Hamish Henderson, Gramsci's first translator into English, reported the painter Renzo Galeotti as remarking: 'By shutting him up, and keeping him shut up, Mussolini saved him'. The 'long prison Calvary' of Gramsci's incarceration conferred upon him the status of a secular 'martyr', or more precisely 'oracle'. These quasi-religious themes and images were given explicit expression in the Italian Communist Party's post-war iconography. They resonated widely on the international left, which has always liked to imagine itself as being secular, but has often incorporated religious elements into its own narrative mythologies of sacrifice, betrayal and redemption. A 1974 American article was even entitled 'The Martyrdom of Saint Antonio Gramsci'. If he had remained free, he would have been exiled in Russia and, with his distant but cordial relationship with Trotsky, would have almost certainly fallen foul of Stalin's purges or, like Togliatti, been forced into questionable compromise. As it was, the historical personality could readily be projected as selfless and incorruptible, visionary and principled, with leavening 'human' moments of doubt and anxiety; a classic hagiography.

Then there are the writings. Gramsci's prison letters are funny, engaging and profoundly moving. They won a number of literary prizes on post-war publication, and were beautifully translated into English by Hamish Henderson and Lynne Lawner.[9] Again, to a certain romantic, young (and mostly) male mentality, they represented a model of caring but measured sensibility; a thoroughly Marxist way of addressing your loved ones. But the prison notebooks were Gramsci's masterpiece, stuffed with extraordinary insights and reflections which to this day provide the most compelling and comprehensive explanation of the world by any Marxist after (and in some ways including) Marx himself.

The 1971 publication in English of the *Selections from Prison Notebooks* prompted an outpouring of what came to be known as 'Gramsciana' or 'Gramsciology', brilliant works of Gramscian history and analysis by contemporary intellectual heroes like Stuart Hall, Tom Nairn, Perry Anderson, G.A. Williams, Eric Hobsbawm and others. Suddenly everyone on the self-styled 'thinking left' seemed to be talking about hegemony, wars of position and manoeuvre, civil society, coercion and consent, subaltern mentalities and historic blocs. Every other issue of *New Left Review* and pretty much every session of the Communist University of London made some mention of Gramsci and his trademark themes. There was even a successful pop group, Scritti Politti, who took their name (roughly) from one of the published collections, and called their first single 'Skank Bloc Bologna', with the production details and costs modishly detailed on the cover. Another band, the Manchester 'post-punk' Magazine, used the term 'hegemony' in a song about industrial alienation (quoted at the beginning of this chapter).

I first encountered Gramsci in the mid-1970s, shortly after joining the Communist Party of Great Britain in a first fit of political engagement. A major part of the party's appeal was the buzz about Gramsci, who seemed to offer us a way into the 'mass politics' of the parliamentary democracies from which our older comrades had been largely excluded for their entire political lifetimes. Gramsci also made a handy moral equivalent to Trotsky, whose devotees continued to berate us with the horrors of Stalinism. Then there was the allure of Italy itself, the light and the heat, where people calling themselves communists got elected to councils and parliament and actually ran things, including the *Festa dell'Unita*, a programme of national and local events devoted to politics and culture that provided part of the inspiration for the CPGB's own popular festivals of the 1970s and 1980s. I identified deeply with Gramsci, the lonely, sharp-tongued, impecunious Sardinian among the toffs and toilers of Turin, then in austere monastic confinement. I still do, after all these years of 'internal exile' and 'enforced collusion' with the ideological dispensation of Thatcherism, which blew away most of our beliefs and organisations, and continues to blight the lives and careers of successive generations of idealistic, socially aware and politically engaged young people.

New Labour – what was all that about?

In the spring of 2003, BBC Radio 4 ran a profile of John Reid, MP for Hamilton North and all-purpose New Labour trouble-shooter. He had just been appointed as Minister of Health, his third or fourth such sideways shuffle in not many more months, and into the still warm cabinet seat of some other temporarily disgraced or displeased New Labour luminary. Dr Reid had been a member of the Communist Party of Great Britain (CPGB) in the 1970s, we were told, and still kept a copy of Antonio Gramsci's *Prison Notebooks* at his bedside. At the time, New Labour was pressing forward to war in Iraq, alongside the most right-wing US government in modern times. The uneasy anti-Tory electoral bloc of 'traditionalist' working class and 'progressive' middle class, which had carried New Labour into office in 1997 and again in 2001, was all too evidently breaking up. Millions of people were beginning to wonder quite where New Labour was heading, not just in the impending war but in its general approach to government.

Six years after the supposed death of Thatcherism, was this latest New Labour turn in actual fact some weird kind of resuscitation? Or even worse – with Blair's glib talk of 'liberal interventionism' – the use of cherished progressive traditions to legitimise actions no Tory government would ever have dared contemplate, let alone undertake? Was this assertion of what Dr Reid called 'Labour hegemony' simply a new and even more extreme twist on still hegemonic Thatcherism?

Listening to the radio that morning, I felt a very particular sense of outrage, having been an active and alert 'Gramscian' communist myself between 1975 and 1985. (John Reid's involvement was rather briefer, two or three years while he was at university in the early 1970s.) To hear Gramsci, to my mind the most original and creative left-wing political thinker of the twentieth century, and his trademark concept of 'hegemony', being bandied about as some kind of justification for this latest turn of events made me gag on my breakfast. I could accept that this communist revolutionary who spent the final quarter of his life in various fascist prisons, was primarily a theorist of left-wing defeat and of the resilience and regenerative capacities of capitalism; these were both key ingredients in the conceptual foundation and abiding temperamental mix of New Labour. But surely Gramsci would have had a lot more to say *about* than on behalf of the Blair and Brown (and self-declared 'Gramscian' Reid) project, and about its function in British politics.

Gramsci had a particular fascination for, if not always secure grasp of, British (or rather what he invariably called *inglese*) history. Like Marx, he saw English capitalism in its nineteenth-century heyday as exceptionally dynamic and innovative, its state machinery as highly efficient and enabling of the civil and political society around it, and its social structures as unusually adaptive and subtle. Indeed, he understood that the accommodating 'corporative' features of British state and society were partly responsible for Labourism's peculiar focus on ameliorative change through central government, the state reformism that formed its core strategic principle. Gramsci observed that Britain's ruling class was able to absorb political and cultural challenges that other national elites had brutally repressed or succumbed to, in large part due to its social permeability: 'the English aristocracy has an open structure'. This flexibility had allowed it to accommodate the emergent mercantilist, financial and industrial bourgeoisie within its ruling 'historic bloc', as well as, subsequently, leading elements of the socialist and trade union movement, with the rise of the essentially 'free trade' creeds of radical liberalism and Labourism. Throughout, the basic principles and impulses of the capitalist economy remained intact.

There is here, as in many of the more intelligent Marxist critiques of capitalism, an element of appreciation that threatens to totter over into outright awe, as well as deep practical insight into the way capitalist economies work. This is what brought Rush Limbaugh, the American right-wing 'shock-jock' of talk radio, to describe Gramsci as 'the left's secret weapon'. It is very hard to enforce political copyright over ideas, and no accident that many of the 'high priests' of neoliberal capitalism, from Alfred Sherman in the 1970s to Charles Leadbeater in the 1990s, were once committed Marxists and active members of the Communist Party. But – unlike Reid et al – the real historical figure of Gramsci remained for all his adult life a committed communist activist and leader, and a theorist and advocate of what he called Marxist 'historicism': a way not only of understanding history but also of changing its course in a more socialised, egalitarian, democratic and ultimately peaceful direction. Gramsci's life consciously echoes Marx's famous remark about philosophers describing the world and the point being to change it. He was and remained unmistakeably a figure of the revolutionary left.

What New Labour was now doing seemed to me a million miles away from what I remembered of my readings of the *Prison Notebooks*. In fact, the Thatcherism/New Labour nexus represented precisely the kind of right-wing political consolidation Gramsci had observed in the European context of his own time: specifically, the process of superficial change he identified as 'transformism ... the absorption of the enemies' elites' by the ruling class – which had occurred repeatedly in the political system of the newly unified Italian state of the late nineteenth and early twentieth centuries. Such subtle shifts occur within what Gramsci described as a 'passive revolution' ('molecular changes which in fact progressively modify the pre-existing composition of forces'), imposed upon a society 'from above'. They represent the historically characteristic outcome of an attritional 'war of position' ('a struggle ... involving all aspects of society') – such as the onset of fascism in Italy in the 1920s or of Thatcherism in 1970s/1980s Britain. On this reading, the New Labour 'project' is a 'transformist' accommodation, within the parliamentary political-electoral framework, to the deeper epochal shifts in our economy, culture and society engineered by the broader 'passive revolution' of Thatcherism.

So how on earth was John Reid able to cite Gramsci and 'hegemony' to justify this process, to turn Gramsci back on himself? What was it about New Labour, I wondered, which could admit and even proclaim such unlikely ancestry? What in fact is the ancestry of New Labour? Where on earth did this extraordinarily ill-defined and notoriously slippery political project come from – all 'windy generalisation' according to ex-British ambassador to Washington Christopher Meyer?[10] How did such an internally contradictory yet for the last decade and a half highly successful – if not truly 'hege-monic' in the properly Gramscian sense – body of politics keep going for so long? I wanted to understand this in terms not of the usual litany of personalities, media-spin and parliamentary and party machinations – what Gramsci, who was himself an MP for two and a half years in the mid-1920s, called 'the squalor of parliamentary life' – but of ideologies, cultures, interests and principles; terms which Gramsci himself would have deployed to gain an intellectual hand-hold on the phenomenon.[11] If we were unclear where New Labour was taking us, as the cacophony of propaganda and the dread of war mounted, were we any clearer where it had come from?

New Labour in history

The New Labour 'project' is now being airbrushed from history as thoroughly as its own origins in Labour history were obscured during its heyday (roughly 1994-2003). With its obsessive focus on the immediate and the novel, on today's 'policy initiative' and tomorrow's headline, New Labour showed nothing but contempt for the historical and the old – at least until the ultra-'neophyte' Blair's frantic last-days search for some 'legacy' other than Iraq. But 'the project' now has a history of its own, which heavily conditions (as history does) its present actions and future options, mostly for the worse. Not that you'd know it from Labour's running commentary on itself. During the run-up to the Labour leadership election, David Miliband felt able to blithely declare that it was now a matter of 'Next Labour', as if the New Labour chapter could be so easily closed. His brother's victory was widely touted as 'the death of New Labour', simply because union votes proved crucial. It's now some years since the term 'New Labour' has featured in Labour Party rhetoric or publications, though it made a brief and rather forlorn return during Blair's 'guest appearance' in the 2010 general election campaign. But the politics, personnel and practice of New Labour remain firmly entrenched at the top of the Labour Party; even if it manages (as Labour always has) to sound very different (and usually happier and more harmonious) in opposition than it ever did in government.

This is a work of 'contemporary history', a category I have found myself having to justify on several occasions, usually with other historians more securely rooted than me in the subject and in the past to which we are supposed to confine ourselves. It's simple really: contemporary history starts with the present, and seeks to work out how we got here. I have started with New Labour, which governed Britain for over a decade and 'made the political weather' for several years before and after, but all along remained a curiously slippery epiphenomenon. I have tried to identify where it came from, both in its own accounts and those of its observers and critics. I have also tried to be respectful and fair, difficult though that has often been, and to honour the project's intentions if not always its methods and outcomes. If my own occasional exasperation shows through, I might put it down to an earlier intellectual formation in times of greater political clarity and methodological rigour.

I hope all this serves to inform the post-mortem on New Labour in government. Labour has never been very good at understanding its own catastrophes. From its first unhappy experiences of government in the 1920s to Ramsay MacDonald's 'betrayal' in 1931; through the 'wilderness years' of the 1930s and 1950s (with the all too brief hiatus of the exceptional wartime and Attlee governments); to the depressing failures of the 'modernising' Wilson and Callaghan governments of the 1960s and 1970s; followed by the bitter factionalism of the 1980s, with the various shades of 'hard' and 'soft' left (not to mention the 'defectors' of the SDP and the 'stayers' of the Labour right), Labour has never been very good at explaining itself. Its 'inner life' has always featured more rancour than honesty, more insult than analysis, more blame than explanation. As a latter-day member of the party (1997-2002), I was always shocked by its lack of conviviality, as well as most members', councillors' and even MPs' almost total ignorance of its history.

The history of Labour's electoral post-mortems would make an interesting study in its own right. For all the rancour, some have clearly worked. 1950s 'revisionism' generated a truly innovative and expansive body of politics, the nearest Labour has ever come to a coherent modern social democracy. New Labour certainly felt like a renewal at the time, even if (like revisionism) it took a lot of agonising to get to and eventually collapsed into further rounds of failure and recrimination. Both of the periods of party history in which these 'modernising' projects took shape, the 1950s and 1980s, are usually characterised by mainstream political historians and commentators for their 'in-fighting', supposedly exhausting the party's activists and putting off the voting public. However, the very fact that they were eventually at least partially successful, and that Labour recovered sufficiently to win subsequent general elections, suggests that they were more constructive than destructive. The big difference between then and now was that the actual indices of the party's vigour – individual voluntary membership, the breadth and depth of debate, union affiliation, councils and councillors, the number and range of informal 'factions' agitating for influence and position, even (the 1983 'Alliance' election aside) voting figures – were far stronger. Perhaps the things that look from the outside like 'in-fighting' are actually signs of rude democratic health.

That may be why the latest post-mortem is proving notably less acrimonious, precisely because the Labour Party is in poorer political, programmatic and organisational shape than at any time in its own history (and don't let the advocates of the 'virtual party' convince you otherwise; Labour has lost its 'institutional presence' in most parts of the country outside Westminster). Even Westminster commentators picked up on this, through their own narrow parliamentary prism, when they complained that all the post-Brown leadership contenders looked the same: with the exception of Diane Abbott, all white, male, middle-aged ex-political advisers, with some of them even sharing the same parents. This simply reflects the 'hollowing out' of the Labour Party by the New Labour elite of career parliamentary politicians. Gramsci estimated that in the last days of the Italian Socialist Party, fully 60 per cent of its active membership depended on the party for their livelihood. A study of the contemporary Labour Party and of who does the actual work – its councillors, MPs and paid officials – would surely come up with a similar figure.

If you see New Labour as Labourism's last gasp, which I generally do, it's not easy to see what the party can do next. It's never been especially effective at marshalling opposition to capitalism, the political left's primary role, let alone its historic mission of creating a viable alternative. With its historic preoccupation with economic growth, it has very little feel for the big issue of our century, climate change and the need for a politics to contain it. And if the Labour Party's real historical objective is a parliamentary majority and government on its own (its coalitions and 'pacts' have always been expedient, unstable and short-lived), what happens when it can no longer realistically hope for either? A lot of people are asking 'What went wrong?' and 'What do we do now?' I may not have much of an answer to the second question, but I hope I can provide some help with the first.

Acknowledgements

Historical research is a generally solitary pursuit, but along the way a number of people have graciously given me lots of their time and attention. My thanks go to Andy Wood for his noble and hopefully successful attempts to turn me into a proper historian; to Pat Devine, David Purdy and Mike Prior for a hugely useful diversion into the work which brought about our co-authored *Feelbad Britain* (London 2009); and to all my interviewees (listed in the bibliography), but especially Stuart Hall, who was as inspiring in these 'newer times' as he was when I first heard him speak at the 1976 Communist University of London.

Notes

1. As sung live in London 2009 – the original version referred to 'Reagan'; see their CD *The Correct Use of Soap* (1981).
2. James Martin, *Gramsci Conference*, Senate House London, 28 May 2010.
3. P. Gobetti, quoted in G. Fiori, *Antonio Gramsci Life of a Revolutionary*, trans. T. Nairn (London 1970), p118; and in P. Spriano, 'Gramsci and Gobetti', *Antonio Gramsci Critical Assessments*, ed. J. Martin (London 2002), p68.
4. A. Gorz, *Farewell to the Working Class* (London 1982), p48.
5. A. Gramsci, *Selections from Prison Writings*, ed. Q. Hoare & G. Nowell Smith (London 1971), p167; hereafter referred to as *SPN*.
6. A. Gramsci Jr., *La Russia di Mio Nonno* (Roma 2008).
7. P. Thomas, *Gramsci Conference*, London 28 May 2010.
8. A. Carlucci, *Gramsci Conference*, London 28 May 2010.
9. A. Gramsci, *Prison Letters*, translated and introduced by H. Henderson (London 1988); *Letters from Prison*, translated and introduced by L. Lawner (London 1979).
10. C. Meyer, *DC Confidential* (London, 2005) p95.
11. G. Fiori, *Antonio Gramsci: Life of a Revolutionary*, trans. Tom Nairn (London, 1970), pp170, 219.

PART I: GRAMSCI AND HIS LEGACY

1. First Uses of Gramsci

This chapter explores the ways in which the writings of Antonio Gramsci were put to use in Britain from the 1950s to the 1980s. With passing time, Gramsci was subjected to 'readings' of very different tones, which broadly reflected the declining political health of the British left, as the post-war social-democratic consensus collapsed and what became known as Thatcherism began its ideological onslaught.[1] Against this backdrop, a distinctively British 'Gramscism' emerged, in several identifiable phases. Its first phase, a creative exploration of themes drawn loosely from Gramsci, was sponsored by the 'first New Left' of 1957 to 1962. The 'second New Left', associated with Perry Anderson's 'takeover' of the journal *New Left Review*, undertook closer study of his writings. Its third phase starts in the early 1970s, with the publication of Giuseppe Fiori's still-seminal Gramsci biography, and the first English edition of *Selections from Prison Notebooks*. The heyday of British Gramscism lasted until the 1980s, by which time the crushing defeat of the British political left became clear.

In 1977, the mid-point of this third phase, Cozens was able to write: 'Gramsci's theoretical work is now generally recognised to be of the utmost importance, particularly for the strategy adopted by the Communist Parties of Western capitalist countries'.[2] In the same year the English novelist John Fowles prefaced his book *Daniel Martin* with a Gramsci quotation, which summed up the prevailing mood in what was widely felt to be a country in steep decline: 'The crisis consists precisely in the fact that the old is dying and the new cannot be born; in this interregnum a great variety of morbid symptoms appears'.[3] A few years later, T.J. Jackson Lears described Gramsci as 'an intellectual cause célèbre and in some quarters a cult hero', and his

life and personality as 'a moral inspiration'.[4] This was plainly the
zenith of Gramscism, as well as of Western European communism.

Gramsci and the British left

Gramsci's writings were 'discovered' by the British left at around the
time of '1968', though there had been earlier isolated pockets of
interest. Gramsci seemed to offer plausible explanations for what was
seen as the social and cultural conservatism of the 'subaltern' working
class (for Nairn, this was 'Gramsci's most creative and distinctive
development of Marxism').[5] Gramsci's was a much more flexible and
suggestive Marxism than the other varieties then on offer, such as
Soviet-style, authoritarian Marxism-Leninism, or 'purer' but equally
doctrinaire and ultimately self-defeating Trotskyism and Maoism.
The first American-English translation was called *The Open Marxism
of Antonio Gramsci*, and this captured much of his growing appeal.[6]
At a time when British Trotskyism had been briefly reinvigorated,
Gramsci even provided a ready-made, contemporaneous critique of
Trotsky – 'the political theorist of frontal attack in a period in which
it only leads to defeats'; and of the Trotskyist 'general theory of
permanent revolution, which is nothing but a generic forecast
presented as a dogma, and which demolishes itself by not in fact
coming true'.[7]

The key Gramscian concepts of 'hegemony', 'war of position' and
'culture' seemed to provide a strategic, transformative purpose to left-
wing intervention in the established, traditional political processes
and institutions of 'advanced', 'late' or complex capitalist societies.
'Struggle' took on a self-evident and immediate point and a long-
term, constructive, 'pre-figurative' value, beyond the medium-term
defence of working-class interests within capitalism or the short-term
demonstration of the system's 'inherent' inability to satisfy them. If
revolution was a process, a protracted 'war of position' between
entrenched social coalitions, it could start right now and right here;
'hegemony' could be contested and gradually transferred from one
'historic bloc' to another. The process of revolution was not a one-off
event in which 'state power' would be 'seized' and used to impose
change. These were powerful arguments against both the cataclysmic
Leninism of the far left and Labour's more cautious central statism,
and they opened up a more promising 'terrain' between them.

Gramsci seemed to elevate the question of 'agency' – what political movements could actually do to bring about desired change in society – above the morass of base or sub-structural factors in which 'classical' or orthodox Marxism had got bogged down (primarily the 'economic', or 'historically inevitable', internally contradictory and self-destructive workings of capitalism). As a consequence, the cultural, social and ideological fields, in which many of us lived, worked and played, suddenly assumed value and importance in their own right. They were more than merely distant echoes of the titanic and somehow more 'fundamental' economic clash between classes.

At the same time, the classically defined economic 'class struggle' was revealed as, in itself, little more than a sordid squabble over the spoils of capitalism; what Gramsci dismissed as the 'economic-corporate' defence of established interests, still fawningly submissive to bourgeois hegemony. The exclusive focus on the 'wage struggle' became known in 'Gramscian' circles as the arch sin of 'economism'. 'Gramscian' economists argued that the working class was no longer the motor or 'protagonist of history' that Marx and Engels (and in his own day, Gramsci himself) had identified more clearly in Britain than anywhere else.[8] Worse still, for much of the time it was engaged in a competitive and inflationary 'sectionalist' scrap within itself, orchestrated by the trade unions, for a bigger share of the cake for particular sub-groups. This served to compound the poverty and oppression within capitalism of the already poor and oppressed, and hastened the stratification and fragmentation of the largest industrial proletariat in history. Other ancillary Gramscian concepts, such as 'the organic intellectual' and the 'modern prince', served to flatter the new left's emerging intellectual elite.[9]

As the British (and international) left retreated from its brief resurgence of the late-1960s and early 1970s, Gramsci was read less for offensive than defensive purposes. Those same concepts of hegemony and war of position, in which class domination was exercised and contested on a range of fronts – cultural and ideological as well as obviously political or 'economic-corporate' – found a new application, rigorously stripped of their 'offensive' (in every sense) vanguardist/Leninist origins. Gramsci now helped make sense of the resurgence of the right in its new, emboldened radicalism, as well as the application to the capitalist crisis of new socially conservative and economically liberal solutions. The term 'Thatcherism' was coined by

Stuart Hall and others associated with *Marxism Today*, and Gramscian concepts such as 'passive revolution' and 'transformism' were drawn upon to describe this new phenomenon of 'regressive modernisation' and 'authoritarian populism'. These concepts helped to describe the imposition of fundamental social change from the top down, and the remorseless and punitive destruction of the vestiges of the British 'labour movement' and its manufacturing, industrial base.

The publishing history of Gramsci in Italy

Gramsci's writings in Italian fall into four separate, successive categories (though this categorisation has been the subject of considerable continuing dispute in Italy and continental Europe). The first period – early academic, political and journalistic writings – is dated from 1910 to 1920. This period covers Gramsci's late adolescence in Sardinia, his student years at the University of Turin, his recruitment to the Italian Socialist Party in 1915 and his early journalism, and his early activism in left-wing and working-class politics. It culminated dramatically in his involvement in the factory council movement in and around Turin as a member of the *Ordine Nuovo* group, and the wave of factory occupations in 1919-21. This was undoubtedly his most formative experience of mass politics, and resonated through the rest of his public and intellectual life.

The second period – Gramsci's later political and journalistic writings – dates from 1920 until his arrest and imprisonment by the fascists in 1926. It includes his more mature reflections on the factory councils and on the Soviet revolution; his brief involvement in the affairs of the Comintern in Moscow and Vienna; the growing fascist repression and the imprisonment of many of its other leaders; and his two-and-a-half turbulent years as General Secretary of the Italian Communist Party. The final major work from this period, 'The Southern Question', anticipates many of Gramsci's later, more developed themes.

The third category – the prison writings – consists of 2,848 tightly packed pages in 33 notebooks written between 1929 and 1935. They were published in Italian by Einaudi in six volumes between 1948 and 1951, selected, annotated and re-ordered in a fashion that aroused much subsequent controversy. It was felt by some that the post-war PCI, led by Gramsci's friend, colleague and successor Palmiro Togliatti, were releasing only those materials which appeared to correspond to its own new strategy of pursuing a 'parliamentary road to socialism' and promoting a 'national culture'. For G. A. Williams, this amounted to 'a species of Gramsci cult of quite remarkable scope and intensity'; Gramsci became 'The Holy Ghost of Italian Communism'.[10]

A further, more selective but balanced anthology, edited by Mario Spinella and Carlo Salinari, was published by Editori Riuniti in 1963, as part of a corrective process that Williams describes as 'virtually unique' amongst Communist Parties: 'opening its archives to sympathetic but independently minded historians ... a magnificent historical enterprise which has successfully reconstructed the early history of the party but has thrown open the whole field to passionate, informed and principled controversy'. Finally, in 1975, a complete, definitive edition was published in four volumes, edited by Valentino Gerratana.

The fourth category – the prison letters – were addressed mainly to Gramsci's sister-in-law Tatiana, with whom he enjoyed a long-standing and curiously intimate relationship. The first Italian edition of 218 *Lettere del Carcere* was published by Einaudi in 1947, selected and amended for political purposes, most blatantly to delete friendly references to Amadeo Bordiga, who was (understandably) regarded as an ultra-leftist by the post-war PCI. This partial edition was superseded in 1965 by a new, comprehensive and definitive edition of 428 letters, annotated by Sergio Caprioglio and Elsa Fubini.

Since 1972, there have been over 20,000 works by or about Gramsci published in Italy (an annual average of over 500!), where he tends to be treated as an established historical figure, amenable to continuous re-evaluation and re-interpretation, rather than as a set of ideas subject to passing intellectual fashion.[11] In recent decades there has if anything been a 'second flowering' of Italian Gramsciana, with several further volumes of letters to a far wider circle of correspondents being published from the 1990s to the present, and a new complete edition of the Prison Notebooks published in 2007.[12] A massive Gramsci dictionary, with 600 entries contributed by over 60 people, was published in 2009.[13]

The publishing history of Gramsci in English

It has been argued that Gramsci, in translation, has had more impact on the British left than on any other political movement outside Italy itself. There have been two main British sources or 'centres' of Gramsci in English, which have each made very different claims on, and represented very different sides of, the Gramscian legacy. The first was associated with the *New Left Review*, mainly in its latter-day 'second' incarnation under the editorship of Perry Anderson. Though the earlier 'first' New Left, established in 1956 and loosely led by academic and political luminaries such as E.P. Thompson, Raymond Williams and Stuart Hall, were also interested in Gramsci, their interest was less focused than that of the 'second' New Left, which assumed control of *New Left Review* in 1962 and took it in a more theoretical, and generally leftist, direction. Close reading of Gramsci was particularly evident in the famous 1960s 'theses' on British history and society by Anderson and Tom Nairn, which made fertile use of Gramsci in the original Italian in their analysis of the construction, operation and limitations of British bourgeois hegemony.

The second and later Gramscian centre was the 'Euro-communist' wing of the Communist Party of Great Britain, whose publishing company Lawrence & Wishart put out the first of Gramsci's writings in English, and later published the most authoritative collections. This was itself a fraught process, part of the internal conflict that grew sharper as the party declined. Many CPGB intellectuals adopted Gramsci as their primary theorist in the 1970s, and sought to apply an array of Gramscian concepts to contemporary circumstances and events, in part for their own partisan purposes.

There have been overlaps and collaborations, as well as divergences and conflicts, between these two 'centres'. And there have also been quite separate and subsidiary sources of Gramsci material, including Pluto Press, which was associated (at least in its earlier years) with the International Socialists/Socialist Workers Party; the Institute of Workers Control and its publishing arm Spokesman, both connected to the Bertrand Russell Foundation; and Merlin Press's *Socialist Register*.

The first known English translations of Gramsci's work were a selection of prison letters prepared by the Scottish poet Hamish Henderson in 1948-50, though they were not formally published until 1974. A considerably different selection of letters from prison was translated and edited by Lynne Lawner and published by Jonathan Cape in 1975; and a complete edition of all the prison letters was published by the Columbia Press in America in 1985.

The first known publication of Gramsci in English was a translation by Louis Marks of his own selections from the prison notebooks, published as *The Modern Prince* by Lawrence & Wishart in 1957, but only after pressure from CPGB intellectuals in the aftermath of the Soviet invasion of Hungary the previous year; the first attempt at publication in early 1956 had been blocked because it was considered too heretical.[14] According to Malcolm McEwan, writing many years later, the PCI and its publisher Einaudi had to force L&W to publish by threatening to take it elsewhere.[15] In 1959 the *New Reasoner* published a small selection from the notebooks and a short selection of the prison letters. And in 1965 *New Left Review* published 'In Search of the Educational Principle', translated and introduced by Quintin Hoare. The next substantial appearance of Gramsci in English was a scattered collection of nine *Ordine Nuovo* articles from 1919/20, brought together under the heading 'Soviets in Italy' in *New Left Review* no.51 in 1968, and introduced by Perry Anderson with a burst of excited leftism. It was reprinted in 1969, without Anderson's introduction, by the Institute of Workers Control.

In 1971, Lawrence & Wishart put out *Selections from Prison Notebooks*, edited and translated by Quintin Hoare and Geoffrey Nowell Smith, who were loosely affiliated to *New Left Review*. This remains the definitive source of Gramsci's mature thought in English, and its publication marked the beginning of the second, Euro-communist 'centre' of Gramscian study and analysis. Two volumes of *Selections from Political Writings* were subsequently published by L&W in 1977 and 1978. *Selections from Cultural Writings*, published in 1985, is thought by many to have exhausted the archive of relevant and interesting Gramsci material. *The Gramsci Reader*, selected and edited by David Forgacs and published by L&W in 1988, included very little previously unpublished material. This reflected the demise within British politics of the Euro-communist or broader democratic left current. It also marked the shift of the *New Left Review* to other historical sources and pre-occupations (though *NLR* published in 1989 a substantial study by David Forgacs of Gramsci's impact in Britain). However, reflecting some continuing work in the academy, *Further Selections from the Prison Notebooks*, selected and edited by Derek Boothman, was published by L&W in 1995. More recently, in 2002, James Martin edited a substantial four-volume collection

Antonio Gramsci: Critical Assessments, which included most of the significant commentaries in English.

Gramsci and the New Left

The 'Open Marxism of Antonio Gramsci' resonated strongly with the new 'cultural' and historical preoccupations of the first New Left – people such as E.P. Thompson, Raymond Williams and Stuart Hall. Thus, for example, Michael Kenny observes that 'for Thompson, the economic sphere was always social', as a way of illustrating his determined anti-economism and anti-reductionism.[16] Raymond Williams argued for an analytical and political approach which acknowledged the 'social totality' of modern capitalism: 'If socialism accepts the distinction of "work" from "life", which has then to be written off as "leisure" and "personal interests", if it sees politics as "government", rather than the process of common decision and administration; if it continues to see education as training for a system and art as grace after meals ... if it is limited in these ways, it is simply a late form of capitalist politics.'[17] For Williams, patterns of domination and subordination in modern society had to be continually maintained and renewed, and invited resistance and subversion. This was inevitably an unstable and contradictory process, which created tensions and conflicts, and allowed subordinate groups and ideas the opportunity for challenge and contest. Several commentators, most notably Edward Said, have pointed out how closely this perspective resembles Gramsci's conception of hegemony.[18]

Younger members of the New Left such as Stuart Hall, drawn mainly from its *Universities and Left Review* source, were more inspired by Williams' 'culturalist' approach than Thompson's historical one, and subsequently used it (alongside Richard Hoggart's more traditionally social-democratic perspective) to create the basis for the modern academic subject of cultural studies, drawing heavily on Gramsci. According to Kenny: 'The similarities stemmed from their break with economism and reductionism, and more expansive conception of the importance of culture. The "culturalist" wing of the first New Left came close to Gramsci's influential notion of hegemony in its emphasis on the constant struggle for command of the moral, political and cultural worlds'.[19]

Gwyn A. Williams' essay 'The Concept of Egemonia in the Thought of Antonio Gramsci' represented the first concerted attempt in Britain at the kind of 'national-popular', historically and geographically specific project that Gramsci had urged upon every local section of the communist movement. According to Williams:

> The exhaustion of the Labour Movement's ethic and its electoral defeats coincide with the apparent establishment in Britain of a new form of 'managerial' and 'affluent society' based on active consent and clearly entering its 'moment of hegemony'. Confronted with this bleak prospect, increasing numbers of British Socialists are abandoning the apparently bankrupt orthodoxy of Fabian empiricism and seeking enlightenment, in modern terms, of their older and more fundamental traditions.[20]

This final sentence expresses the emerging tension, felt right across the British left then and ever since, between the impulses towards 'modernisation' and 'tradition'. In seeking to create a 'new society', do we look forwards or backwards for inspiration? This again is a recurring theme in Gramsci, a dilemma never entirely resolved, and may also help to explain his continuing resonance in ancient, complex societies like Britain and Italy.

G.A. Williams was also aware of contemporary Italian debates (and seems to have had ready access to Gramsci in Italian), especially on the relationship between the concepts of hegemony and the more formally Leninist 'dictatorship of the proletariat'. He insists on a rigorous distinction, 'throughout Gramsci's work', between political society or the state, with its predominantly coercive function of enforcing law and order, and civil society, where prevailing morality is generated and 'always associated with equilibrium, persuasion, consent and consolidation'. This creates the central Gramscian duality of directive force and hegemonic leadership, in which hegemony is the 'normal' situation, 'as opposed to the cathartic moment of force', which is rather held in menacing reserve. For Williams, too, the awareness of the creative capacity of the working class is perhaps the clearest differentiating factor in Gramsci's thought', distinguishing it from other conceptions that stress the destructive effects of revolutionary struggle. In particular, and in terms that clearly reflect Raymond

Williams' contemporaneous preoccupations, the aim must be 'the creation of a common culture'.

In 1964 Perry Anderson was describing Harold Wilson, newly elected prime minister, as 'hegemonic'. His grasp of Gramscian perspectives is evident in his description of how 'the present crisis of the governing class allows the Labour Party to split the Conservative bloc, detaching it from specific social groups in the population, first and foremost the technical intelligentsia'.[21] This early, narrowly party-political, take on 'hegemony' and the construction of 'historic blocs' comes dangerously close to New Labour's thirty years later – especially that of John Reid and Phillip Gould – and the politics of 'positioning'. Another source of left-wing responsibility for New Labour perhaps, alongside continuities in the intelligentsia's impatiently 'modernising' orientation towards Labourism. But to be fair, Anderson and his *NLR* collaborator Tom Nairn had bigger theoretical fish to fry, to do with the historical peculiarities and inadequacies of the British ruling class. This formed a central thread in the 'Nairn-Anderson theses'. Elaborated in a series of articles in *New Left Review* and subsequently published collections, their central argument was that the British ruling class had never been truly hegemonic because, unlike its counterparts in France and elsewhere, it had never undertaken a thoroughgoing bourgeois revolution. It remained therefore incompetent and inefficient in the management and direction of British capitalist society. This kept alive the possibility of classically Marxist proletarian revolution, a 'national-popular' modernising project to take British society onto its next historic stages.

But was this just a new, albeit highly suggestive, twist on the old left-wing *canard* of the inevitability of socialism? Specifically, was the British bourgeoisie so 'exceptionally' incompetent? And was the undoubted distinctiveness of Britain's class structure necessarily a source of weakness for capitalism? As E.P. Thompson, Henry Drucker and others would point out (with, in some cases, astute supporting use of Gramsci), broadly similar historical developments could be sponsored by quite different 'historic blocs' of social forces, depending on the balance of forces in any particular time and place.[22] The peculiarities of British capitalism, with its 'historic compromise' between bourgeoisie and aristocracy, and subsequent predominance of finance capital and land and other asset ownership, and the relative weakness of its manufacturing and mercantile branches, have not noticeably weakened its hegemony over British society. If anything, as Engels pointed out as long ago as 1892, they have made it more vigorous, adaptable and durable in the face of social dislocation and cultural upheaval.[23]

Britain's more complex class structure – not to mention its atypically 'internationalist' (more exactly imperialist) orientation – has generally managed to avoid direct confrontation between its two largest elements, the bourgeoisie and the proletariat, which the latter might well have won on numerical strength alone; and to placate or marginalise particular disgruntled groups. And to castigate British capitalists for their technical incompetence comes dangerously close to the 'arch sin' of economistic reductionism, divorced from political conflict, historical contingency and social relations. Do we have here a kind of high moral 'New Left' variant on the old Labourist habit of blaming individual capitalists for excessive greed and 'usury', while refusing to challenge capitalism as a system? A leftist social democracy perhaps, which *New Left Review* has regularly tended towards ever since.

What Nairn and Anderson were clearly (and honourably) looking for was some new basis for a reinvigorated and post-Labourist alliance between the industrial working class and the urban 'technical' intelligentsia, united in a new and deeper kind of technocratic progressivism and in the 'national-popular' cause of modernising an archaic society and creaking economy. There was indeed common ground here with early Wilsonism, most evident in popular, modernising, openly 'pre-figurative' initiatives such as the Open University. However, though they may have been addressing similar questions about the state of the country, the New Left were proposing very different answers; mainly involving popular, democratic, political mobilisation, as opposed to the technocratic, centralised, statist impulses deeply embedded in the Labour tradition and the quintessentially Labourist politics and politicians of the Wilson governments.

Following the familiar pattern of promised renewal, raised expectation and crashing disappointment – almost pathologically repetitious within the history of the British labour movement – the already tenuous connections between Wilsonism and the New Left were soon severed. By 1968's *May Day Manifesto*, composed by luminaries of the first New Left, Wilson's 'hegemonic strategy' had been transformed into what we would now recognise as a classically Gramscian 'passive revolution' – change imposed from above in order to re-stabilise the capitalist economy, justified by plainly ideological appeal to the 'national interest'. The *Manifesto*, edited by Raymond Williams, and mainly written by himself, E.P. Thompson and Stuart Hall, was pretty much the last collective gasp of the first New Left, though it clearly revealed the influence of subsequent developments by the second New Left. It is also, as Kenny notes, heavily imbued with Gramscian themes, and includes a still stirring challenge to the left to take 'as its starting point where people are living' – 'Not the abstract condition of a party or a government or a country, but the condition of life of the majority of ordinary people'.[24]

Gramsci in '1968'

By 1968, when *New Left Review* published 'Soviets in Italy', Perry Anderson was firmly in control of the journal. His introduction is written in the harsh light of recent May 1968 *evenements* in Paris, with a direct comparison between the French student occupations, the Turin factory councils and the revolutionary Soviets. Anderson's critique of Gramsci makes plain his conversion to the Trotskyist, Bolshevik/Leninist model of insurrection: 'It became clear that Gramsci had telescoped the problem of the Socialist state *after* the revolution with the problem of working class organisation *before* the revolution. The illusion of achieving dominant economic power prior to the seizure of national political power was dramatically exploded' (Anderson's italics). There is also here a bold universalisation of the very particular conditions in one country, Russia, at a very particular time, the exhausted final months of the First World War, and wilful neglect of the key Gramscian concepts of revolutionary process, cultural hegemony and pre-figurative struggle in more advanced and complex societies like Italy (and 1960s France).

Anderson's 'Introduction' can now be seen as one of the first British moves in dissecting Gramsci's experience and thought, and in particular in disconnecting his experience in the factory councils from his prison notebooks. This stands in marked contrast to Gramscian study and historiography in Italy itself, which, according to Forgacs, is marked by 'a strict line of continuity'.[25] There was at that time something of a fashion, of which this is a clear example, for thus dissecting the lives and thoughts of prominent Marxist theorists; most notably Althusser's distinction, enthusiastically endorsed and adopted by *NLR*, between the early 'humanist'/idealist and the mature 'scientific' theorist Marx, straddling what Althusser called an 'epistemological break'.[26]

The 'dissection' of Gramsci was partly prompted by attempts at the rehabilitation of Amadeo Bordiga, the first and determinedly 'intransigent' general secretary of the PCd'I, and one of Lenin's primary 'leftist' targets in early-1920s Communist International debate. Gwyn A. Williams' *Proletarian Order*, which accepts a more benevolent view of Bordiga's role in the foundation of Italian communism and of his relationship with Gramsci, nonetheless points out that this approach requires a 'dissected' Gramsci, who 'seems to stop somewhere just after April 1920'.[27] Pozzolini offers an only slightly less 'activist' Gramsci, but makes explicit the notion of a 'rupture' within his life and thought.[28] In 1970, *NLR* published the French leftist Regis Debray's 'Schema for a study of Gramsci', a short article attempting to 'reclaim his legacy from the stultifying embrace of official communism'.[29] The battle was on, to claim Gramsci for particular left-wing factional purposes, without at that stage much exposition, understanding or analysis of his life and body of work.

Notes

1. S. Hall, *The Hard Road to Renewal* (London 1988) contains the definitive, contemporaneous Gramscian analysis of Thatcherism.
2. P. Cozens, *Twenty Years of Antonio Gramsci: A Bibliography of Gramsci and Gramsci studies published in English, 1957-77* (London 1977), p1.
3. J. Fowles, *Daniel Martin* (London 1977).
4. T.J. Jackson Lears, 'The Concept of Cultural Hegemony', *American Historical Review* 90(3), 1985, pp567-593.
5. T. Nairn, in *Approaches to Gramsci*, ed. A. Showstack Sassoon (London 1982), p183.
6. *The Open Marxism of Antonio Gramsci*, translated and edited by Carl Manzoni (New York 1957).
7. *SPN*, pp238, 241.
8. B. Warren and M. Prior, *Advanced Capitalism, Backward Socialism* (Nottingham 1974); D. Purdy and M. Prior, *Out of the Ghetto* (Nottingham 1979).
9. R. Samuel, *The Lost World of British Communism* (London 2006), pp197, 207, argues with some force that the nearest the British left came to

'organic intellectuals' of the working class (or as Samuel puts it 'shop floor intelligentsia') were the militants of the earlier CPGB, the politically conscious and committed 'foremen' or 'labour aristocracy' of the 1920s/30s and 40s struggles against capitalism and fascism

10. G. A. Williams, *Proletarian Order* (London 1975), pp305/6.
11. *Bibliografia Gramsciana*, fondazionegramsci.org.
12. A. Carlucci, Gramsci Conference, London 28 May 2010.
13. *Dizionario Gramsciano* (Roma 2009).
14. D. Forgacs, 'Gramsci and Marxism in Britain', *New Left Review* 176, p73.
15. M. McEwan, *Congress Views 1*, CPGB 1990 Congress materials.
16. M. Kenny, *The First New Left* (London 1995) pp6/7.
17. R. Williams, *The Long Revolution* (Harmondsworth 1965), p113.
18. E. Said, *Foucault and The Imagination of Power* (Cambridge 1986), p154.
19. M. Kenny, *The First New Left*, p114/115.
20. G.A. Williams, 'The Concept of *Egemonia* in the Thought of Antonio Gramsci', *Journal of the History of Ideas* Vol. XXI Oct./Dec. 1960, pp586-599.
21. P. Anderson, 'Critique of Wilsonism', *New Left Review* 27, 1964.
22. E.P. Thompson, 'The Peculiarities of the English', *New Left Review* 1965; and *The Poverty of Theory and Other Essays* (London 1978), p283; H. Drucker, *Doctrine & Ethos in the Labour Party*, p9.
23. F. Engels, 1892 preface to the English edition of *Socialism: Utopian and Scientific*.
24. R. Williams (ed.), *May Day Manifesto* (Harmondsworth 1968), p14; Kenny, *The First New Left*, p17.
25. D. Forgacs, 'Gramsci and Marxism in Britain', *New Left Review*176, p76.
26. L. Althusser, *Reading Capital* (London 1970), pp119-145.
27. G.A. Williams, *Proletarian Order*, p338.
28. A. Pozzolini, Trans. A. Showstack Sassoon, *Antonio Gramsci* (London 1970), p153.
29. R. Debray, 'Schema for a Study of Gramsci', *New Left Review* 59, Jan/Feb 1970, pp48-52.

2. Optimism of the Seventies, Pessimism of the Eighties

> Gramsci neither wants to be idolised nor does he want to pontificate: he is too young to be resigned to the decorative and quackish function of a Pope and he really doesn't want to be an idol.
>
> Antonio Gramsci, writing about his own growing reputation in *Ordine Nuovo* 1919

The introduction to the definitive 1971 edition of *Selections from the Prison Notebooks*, written mostly by *New Left Review* associate Quintin Hoare, was the first detailed account of Gramsci's life and thought available to most of the British left. It would have also been their first account of the early history of the PCI, and its extremely complicated relationships to the Communist International, Italian socialism and fascism. Gramsci emerges as a real historical figure, reflecting, acting and changing over the course of his own lifetime, throwing up contradictions and revisions, but with certain connecting preoccupations. Hoare insists that there is no 'rupture' between Gramsci's experience of political activism and the reflections in the prison notebooks, which 'have an organic continuity with the political universe within which Gramsci had operated prior to his arrest'.

There are also, towards the end of this introduction, several salutary warnings about the use and potential misuse of Gramsci outside of his own historical setting. 'Gramsci has perhaps suffered more than any other Marxist writer since Lenin from partial and partisan interpretation, both by supporters and opponents; the Prison Notebooks themselves, read seriously and in all their complexity, are the best antidote to this.' The continuities of Gramsci's life and thought, first established in Marks' 1957 *The Modern Prince*, are reiterated – 'it is essential to understand the political experience upon which the Prison Notebooks are a comment and of which they are the fruit'. These warnings were frequently disregarded in the British appropriation of Gramsci's thought through the 1970s and 1980s within each of the separate 'camps' of Gramscian study and analysis. The real historical figure, and the human experience from which he emerged, tended to disappear behind competing dogmatisms.[1]

Gramsci goes continental – Althusser and Anderson

The French philosopher Louis Althusser published his most substantial remarks about Gramsci in an essay, 'Marxism is not a Historicism', in French in 1968 and in English in 1970.[2] It was enormously influential, as one of the first considered critiques of Gramsci from a rigorously Marxist perspective. Though Althusser, influenced by Gramsci, was interested in the ideological sphere – which was one of his main attractions for a left that was just beginning to turn away from the economic determinism of Soviet-style Marxism-Leninism – he always returned to the economic base 'in the last instance'. This meant that he had an appreciation of Gramsci's work on hegemony, and proletarian agency, but was critical of his lapses from communist orthodoxy as he saw it. Indeed, Althusser's Marxism now seems all too rigorously Marxist, based on a conception of 'absolute knowledge' and the 'science' of dialectical materialism that has not worn well, especially since the collapse of the 'real existing socialism' of the Soviet Union and Eastern Europe. The existence of nominally socialist states provided a kind of guarantee of authenticity to even those Marxist theoreticians who expressed reservations about the Soviet model. They might be 'degenerate workers' states' – 'state socialist', 'state nationalist' or even 'state capitalist' in other accounts – but at least they were *our* degenerate workers' states.

Althusser's treatment of Gramsci is oddly two-handed. It is routinely deferential and frequently inclined towards outright *hommage* towards 'his enormous political and historical genius', but of a kind which, within the rhetorical tradition of international communism, usually presaged denunciation – which is what follows here. Althusser sees Gramsci's 'humanism/historicism' as an understandable but misguided reaction against the economistic determinism of Second International-era, social-democratic Marxism, which had posited a form of socialism emerging naturally and inevitably from within capitalist development. The basis of Lenin's Third International Marxism, by contrast, was that socialism had to be actively fought for by the proletariat led by a consciously and systematically revolutionary party. Althusser argues that Gramsci took the issue of political and historical 'agency' beyond even Lenin's understanding, which was still (for Althusser) a recognisable 'dialectical materialism'; and Gramsci had gone several steps too far into the realms of an unacceptably anti-Marxist 'voluntarism'. Althusser's critique echoes criticisms made of Gramsci during his lifetime, that he was 'Bergsonian' in denying the 'real history' of 'absolute knowledge', and in arguing instead that Marxism itself is a historical phenomenon, which may be historically superseded. In Althusserian terms, this makes Gramsci a 'historical' rather than a 'dialectical materialist'. Perhaps we should have been forewarned by Althusser's prefatory declaration that 'I shall refuse to take Gramsci immediately at his word'.

When it comes to practical politics, Althusser reverts to 'Lenin's thesis … that Marxist theory must be imported into the proletariat', and opposes this to Gramsci's much more democratic, open and creative approach of dialogue and collaboration between the 'Modern Prince' of the revolutionary party and the masses. 'All the themes of spontaneism rushed into Marxism through this open breach: the humanist universalism of the proletariat' – as opposed to the single-minded vanguardism of the classically Bolshevik model.[3] Here we see most clearly Althusser's lingering reluctance, characteristic of the *Parti Communiste Francaise* of which he was a long-time and loyal member, to break with the Bolshevik model and the overriding interests of the Soviet Union. Althusser's abiding Leninism also rides roughshod over Gramsci's crucial distinction between the adaptable, established states of Western societies and the coercive, under-developed, pre-revolutionary, 'primordial and gelatinous' Tsarist regime in Russia.

Althusser's critique of Gramsci is ultimately a defence of Leninist orthodoxy, historically fixed at a moment in which Althusser's PCF, until then a truly mass proletarian party with an authority derived from its record of wartime resistance, was beginning to lose its way in increasingly complex circumstances and turbulent times. The PCF's relationship to the major events in the post-war history of the European left, '1968' and Euro-communism, was always ambiguous.

Their participation in the early 1980s 'Common Programme' government with Mitterrand's Socialist Party proved disastrous for both
their mass membership and their electoral base, mainly because they
were out-manoeuvred by their more 'modern', politically adept and
adaptable allies. (The PCF survives as a Leninist rump, a minor
adjunct to the Socialist Party. It scores popular votes in low single
figures, down from over 40 per cent at its post-war zenith.) Althusser
knew that understanding ideology was crucial, and understood the
need for the working class to make hegemonic alliances, but could not
ultimately move beyond the vanguardism of the old communist
parties.

Re-reading Althusser now, it is difficult to understand the scale of
interest in his work. He was a generally obscurantist, often pedantic
academic philosopher, most generously described now alongside the
sociologist Nicos Poulantzas as 'a structural Marxist'. In broader
academic terms, he provided something for French and western
European intellectuals to react against; their reaction took the form of
post-structuralism, post-Marxism and elements of postmodernism.
His theoretical musings happened to suit the largely unreconstructed
Leninism of the PCF and also, fortuitously, to offer a sophisticated
'continental' veneer to the largely unreconstructed, temporarily revitalised Trotskyism of the late 1960s/early 1970s *New Left Review*,
which introduced his work to an Anglophone audience alongside the
'student revolutionary' Gramsci of the 'Soviets in Italy'.

The next substantial commentary from within the *New Left Review*
stable was Perry Anderson's 'The Antinomies of Antonio Gramsci',
published in 1976.[4] This, in marked contrast to Anderson's earlier
introduction to *NLR*'s 1968 Gramsci selection, is a sober, insightful
account of the evolution of various key Gramscian concepts in both
Gramsci's own writing and among other earlier Marxist theoreticians.
Anderson's aim is to deflate the near-mythical status attaching to
Gramsci within the burgeoning Euro-communist movement: 'the
spread of Gramsci's renown has not to date been accompanied by any
corresponding depth or enquiry into his work'.[5] What's more,
Gramsci's is 'a work censored twice over', by prison conditions and by
his own prior intellectual formation, specifically 'the archaic and inadequate apparatus of Croce and Machiavelli', so there are inevitable
elisions and confusions. In this, Anderson's critique is not dissimilar
to Althusser's.

However, Anderson's account – clearly informed by the torrent of 'Gramsciana' or 'Gramsciology' over the previous few years – ends up much more appreciative than he might have intended. As Forgacs noted later, 'Gramsci (is) both more consistent in his concepts and closer to Anderson's own positions than he recognises'.[6] By far its most incisive sections trace the lineage of the concepts of hegemony and war of position/war of manoeuvre in the work of Lenin, Trotsky, George Lukacs, Rosa Luxembourg and others – to the extent that Anderson's article might have been better titled 'The Antecedents of Antonio Gramsci', though this would have blunted its polemical purposes. Anderson was deeply aware, at the time of writing, of the ascendancy of Euro-communism: 'the great mass Communist Parties of Western Europe – in Italy, in France, in Spain – are now on the threshold of a historical experience without precedent for them: the commanding assumption of governmental office within the framework of bourgeois-democratic states'. His primary concern, at least at the beginning of this long article, seemed to be that they had abandoned much of their Leninist legacy in doing so, in particular the concept of 'proletarian dictatorship … once the touchstone of the Third International'. Gramsci had provided the theoretical underpinning for this act of abandonment.

In these introductory remarks, we sense most clearly Anderson's conception of *New Left Review* as a kind of 'clergy' of the international left, keepers of the doctrinal flame, which at the time did not endear it to other less determinedly 'theoretical' elements. He rightly points out that *NLR* was instrumental in introducing Gramsci to Anglophone audiences, in the 'Nairn/Anderson theses' of 1964/65 that made much fertile use of the concept of hegemony in its analysis of the British state. *NLR* was indeed (disregarding Marks and Williams) 'the first socialist journal in Britain – possibly the first anywhere outside Italy – to make deliberate and systematic use of Gramsci's theoretical canon to analyse its own national society'.

Anderson then proceeds to lay bare various inconsistencies or 'antinomies' in Gramsci's conceptions of war of position/manoeuvre, the state, civil and political society. It does not seem to have occurred to Anderson that these shifts in category and priority might reflect real historical shifts amongst the institutions and structures of different societies at different moments of development; or that this precisely enables the application of Gramsci's thinking outside of its own time and place. This is odd, especially in the light of what comes next, a highly insightful account of the historical sources of another of Gramsci's conceptual trademarks. In Russia, 'The slogan of the hegemony of the proletariat was a common political inheritance for Bolsheviks and Mensheviks alike' as early as 1903. The only points of dispute were over the breadth and practice of 'proletarian hegemony' within a revolutionary movement, and to what extent it would have to accept a subordinate position within the intermediary stage of a bourgeois democracy. Thereafter, the concept can be found repeatedly in Lenin. In particular, Lenin considered the development of a 'hegemonic consciousness' critical to the prospects of successful proletarian revolution.[7]

At this point Anderson's critique of Gramsci reveals its basic character, as ultimately an orthodox and arid Leninism, with decidedly Trotskyist overtones within it. He is right to point to the various elisions and apparent inconsistencies in Gramsci, but in doing so he fails to appreciate that it is precisely the speculative and open-ended nature of the Prison Notebooks which makes them resonate so strongly in other times and societies, particularly our own. There is no doubting Anderson's technical proficiency as a Marxist, but he shows precious little feel for the emerging political realities of his own time; especially the neo-liberal revival of capitalist economy, state and society, which was just beginning when he wrote 'The Antinomies'. Least of all can he appreciate popular 'consent' to hegemony, its grudging acceptance by some and the active connivance by others, which at first sight appears to close off the prospect of revolutionary change. However this is also to fail to see the way in which it also opens up the fields of ideology, politics and culture to democratic contestation; this was the basis for the 'mass politics' of the post-war PCI and of Euro-communism in its 1970s ascendancy. And in one crucial aspect at least, Anderson takes Gramsci all too literally 'at his own word', when, like Gramsci, he understates what Karabel calls the 'transcendence of Lenin' inherent in Gramsci's far richer, multifaceted concept of hegemony.[8]

Ultimately both Anderson and Althusser, in seeking to fix Gramsci in the Marxist tradition and diminish his significance within it, failed to appreciate his most radical and momentous contribution to it: 'to recast the "base-superstructure" model of classical Marxism. He narrowed the economic base to include only the material and technical instruments of production; he broadened the superstructure to include political society, civil society and the state', as Jackson Lears put it in 1985.[9] There was the basis here for taking Marxist politics out of the factory, and into the broader community. To be fair, even Stuart Hall, writing in 1977 (the year after Anderson's 'Antinomies') on the 'base-superstructure' metaphor, conceded ground to Althusser and Anderson and their adjusted Leninism, but this was before he fully appreciated the power of the recently launched neo-liberal reso-lution of capitalist crisis by 'going global' and the decisive shift from productivism to consumerism in the west.[10]

The revival rather than demise of capitalism, and the defeat rather than impending victory of the working class, in both West and East, signalled the end of Anderson's orthodox Leninism, in just the same way that Trotsky's analyses had failed (in Gramsci's phrase) 'by not in fact coming true'. Neither could account for new, refreshed forms of bourgeois hegemony within the formally democratic societies of the West, with their relatively stable, constrained and accountable states and their complex and vigorous civil societies. Nor, even more point-edly, could they later account for the collapse of 'real, existing socialism' in the East, and the speedy restoration of a peculiarly rapa-cious capitalism. The end of 'state capitalism'/ 'degenerate workers' states' in the East posed just as much of a challenge to the Trotskyists as to the Stalinists of the West; still operating, as they all were, within the theoretical currents and schemas of orthodox Leninism.

Gramsci at the Communist University of London 1977-81

In contemporary political terms, Perry Anderson's critique of Gramsci was a barely concealed attack on the emergent phenomenon of Euro-communism, which at the time looked set to propel communists – at least those with an established parliamentary presence – into several Western European governments. In Britain there was never any elec-toral chance of this, but the new 'creative Marxism', heavily influenced by Gramsci, gave the Communist Party of Great Britain a new if temporary lease of life. The party had been in steady decline since its immediately post-war peak, but Euro-communism combined with the protracted after-effects of '1968' to draw a new generation of intellectuals into a quite distinct current within its generally (still) working-class 'militant labourist' membership. They used Gramsci to revitalise what had become a stuffy, isolated and doctrinaire organisation – a very large sect rather than an effective party, more of a subculture within than a political force upon British society.

There had been pockets of interest in Gramsci within the CPGB ever since the first editions and commentaries had begun to appear. Marks' semi-authorised collection *The Modern Prince* received a favourable review by George Thomson in the very first volume of *Marxism Today*, launched in 1957 as the CPGB's 'theoretical journal'.[11] During the heyday of new Gramsci publication in English, either side of the 1971 publication of *Selections from Prison Notebooks*, there were four substantial articles on Gramsci in *Marxism Today*, including one by editor-to-be Martin Jacques.[12] There was also a chapter on Gramsci in Franz Marek's 1969 semi-official *Philosophy of World Revolution*, and a CPGB Education pamphlet *An Introduction to Some Thoughts of Gramsci* was produced in 1976.[13]

The British Euro-communist current partly took shape at the Communist University of London (CUL), a kind of Marxist summer school which the party ran for a number of years through the 1970s and (just) into the 1980s. The new perspectives fed directly into the CPGB's internal debates of the time, most notably the 1977 revision of *The British Road to Socialism*, the party programme first composed in 1950 at Stalin's instigation, and the 1979 debate on 'Inner Party Democracy', which reviewed the party's classically Bolshevik model of policy formation and implementation and internal elections. There were three volumes of CUL papers published in those years: *Class, Hegemony and Party; Politics, Ideology and the State;* and *Silver Linings*.[14] There were not many plenary or workshop CUL sessions where Gramsci was not cited or quoted; he seemed to offer a new way to make sense of the wider non-left or even non-political world. After decades of sterile Stalinism, organisational decline and Cold War isolation, Gramsci offered the CPGB a new way into the political mainstream.

The first of Stuart Hall's contributions to the CUL papers goes some way towards defending the determinedly 'historicist' Gramsci, but is primarily a sympathetic exposition of Althusser's conception of the relationship between the economic 'base' and the ideological 'superstructures'; the central metaphor of classical Marxist theory.[15] In the process Hall attempts to reconcile the two, often opposed, currents of Gramscian historicism and the structuralism of Althusser and Poulantzas. In doing so, he reminds us of Althusser's central *motif*: an elaborate, broadly optimistic theoretical analysis of proletarian revolutionary prospects, which were in hard historical reality rapidly receding. However, in the concept of the 'ideological state apparatuses' Althusser did provide an insight of lasting value, to explain 'the reproduction of the social relations of production', or in other words, the ways in which the ruling class constructs and maintains a society supportive of a capitalist economy. Almost every social organisation or relationship, including education and trades unions, could be seen as an 'ISA' (ideological state apparatus), with a primarily repressive and exploitative function beneath a necessarily useful and supportive 'welfarist' veneer. These ideas would be taken further (perhaps too far, insofar as its all-encompassing embrace threatened to preclude any possible challenge or alternative) in the work of Michel Foucault, and have remained a central preoccupation of the surviving intellectual left.[16]

For Hall, 'The concept of the "ideological State apparatus", which has become a generative idea in the post-Althusserian analysis of the capitalist State, is a direct reworking of a few seminal passages on apparatuses of consent and coercion in Gramsci's "State and Civil Society" essay.' So even here, in a précis of Althusser's primarily coercive ISAs, the consensual nature of hegemony re-emerges. In the same volume, hegemony is given a practical application to Victorian Britain by the historian Robert Gray, who identifies active working-class consent to the hegemonic framework of the Victorian ruling 'historic bloc', and the specific role of the 'urban gentry', who performed a crucial, mediating, 'organic intellectual' function for capitalism, keeping the masses both in touch and in line.[17]

The second CUL volume from 1977 contains a paper by Anne Showstack Sassoon, 'Hegemony and Political Intervention', which provides a straightforward account of the basic Gramscian themes. In passing, it notes Anderson's then-recent 'Antinomies' article as an example of 'criticisms of common elements in the strategy of a number of Communist Parties, described as "Euro-communist", [which] have been made by criticising Gramsci's concept of the state'.[18] Anderson's article continues to cast a long shadow. Nearly thirty years later, one of the most recent substantial treatments of Gramsci, Michael Burawoy's 'For a Sociological Marxism', is scathing in its treatment of Anderson's 'Antinomies'.[19] Burawoy chooses to focus on Anderson's 'excoriation (of) the "Western Marxism" of Horkheimer and Adorno, Gramsci and Lukacs, Sartre and Althusser as ... detached from the working class and as lacking revolutionary vision. Anderson insisted that we return to the revolutionary road pioneered by Leon Trotsky.' Burawoy regards Trotsky as 'woefully adrift in the world of advanced capitalism', and Anderson's critique of Gramsci as 'written in a burst of revolutionary optimism.'

By 1981, after the publication of the final collection of CUL papers, the Euro-communist moment had also clearly passed. The Italian CP strategy of 'historic compromise' had died with the sympathetic Christian Democrat leader Aldo Moro, murdered in 1978 by the ultra-leftist Red Brigades.[20] In France, the Communists were losing ground to the Socialists within the 'Common Programme' government of Francois Mitterrand; and in Spain, Santiago Carrillo had reverted to older, pre-Euro-communist methods of party management when he himself came under challenge from younger, more aggressively Euro-communist elements in the PCE. In Britain, Thatcherism was taking firm shape following the 1979 election, and the reform drive inside the CPGB had visibly faltered. Geoff Andrews reports that the 1979 CUL attracted only '517 people, a 50 per cent decrease on the previous year'; and attendance in 1980 and at the final CUL in 1981 continued to decline.[21] Further, 'the low sales of [*Silver Linings*] provided another indication that the broad democratic alliance was not reaching the people it was principally addressing'. People were drifting away from the CP and the broader currents of left-wing politics. This represented a 'second exodus of leading intellectuals, following the departure of John Saville, Edward Thompson and others in 1956'.[22] But, as we shall see, it had nothing like the same regenerative effects for the broader political left.

Silver Linings itself contains only one paper explicitly concerned with Gramsci, Chantal Mouffe's 'Hegemony and the Integral State in Gramsci', an unexceptional piece of Gramscian exegesis. The other eight papers set out to explore various themes within the CPGB's developing strategy of 'broad democratic alliance' (BDA), and the various social forces who would form its main components as allies of the working-class movement: principally women, blacks and gays. Andrews may be right to consider the 1980 CUL and its volume of papers a rather forlorn 'attempt to widen the appeal of the BDA' by an ailing CPGB, but some of the *Silver Linings* papers retain their own intrinsic value and interest as examples of the growing integration of Gramscian concepts into contemporary political analysis.[23] For instance, Mike Morrissey's survey of the prospects for Northern Ireland, then at the height of 'the troubles', makes fruitful use of the term 'loyalist bloc' to explain the incorporation of the Protestant working class into the hegemony of the local, Orange ruling class, giving their 'active consent' to sectarian conflict and discrimination.

The most extensive application of Gramscian concepts to Britain, and in broader historical terms the most interesting paper in the book, is Bill Schwarz and Colin Mercer's 'Popular Politics and Marxist Theory in Britain: The History Men'. The use of Gramscian terms is by now customary, almost casual. Thatcherism, described here as 'populism of the right', 'displays its potential for articulating to its own programme elements of subordinate ideologies and winning consent'.[24] Schwarz and Mercer acknowledge the 'possibility of popular traditions becoming attached to a reactionary politics'; this was at the time a provocative position, at least on the left, and echoes Stuart Hall's delineation of Thatcher's 'authoritarian populism' in 'The Great Moving Right Show' and elsewhere.[25] Schwarz and Mercer advocate 'populism of the left' as a response, which they hope will go some way towards transcending the old and increasingly sterile confrontations between various old and 'New Lefts'. But they also caution – perhaps in anticipation of New Labour – that '(the term) "The people" has become the very cliché of the party political broadcast', which develops a point made by Gramsci that '[the term] "The people" is an abstraction', normally deployed for rhetorical, opportunist and populist purposes.[26]

1984: Post-Euro-communist Gramscian surveys and applications

Increasingly isolated Gramscian applications continued to appear in Britain through the 1980s. They drew upon the previous first, second and third-phase Gramscisms of the 1950s, 1960s and 1970s; and began to anticipate and overlap with the Gramsci of 'identity politics' and cultural studies of the 1990s, without yet wholly adopting this fourth-phase Gramscism's heavy emphasis on identity and culture, and its wilfully 'post-Marxist' rhetoric. As such, they represented a tentative transition, a defensive response to the harsher political and ideological climate of rapidly consolidating Thatcherism; a kind of 'hunkering-down' for the long haul, or step away from direct political intervention and towards the use of Gramsci in primarily academic settings.

David Forgacs' 'National-Popular: Genealogy of a Concept' was published in 1984, in *Formations of Nation and People*, alongside articles by people who had contributed to the Communist University of London volumes and continued to write for *Marxism Today*.[27] Forgacs' article, the only one in the collection to explore explicitly Gramscian themes, is primarily concerned with the application of the concept of the 'national-popular' in recent Italian history. He begins with a brief survey of the British political situation, 'where the tough and flexible ideological resources of Thatcherism have proved capable of mobilising a large popular base' and 'the weakly articulated ideological umbrella of the Labour Party' has proved incapable of effective resistance.[28] The concept of 'national-popular' provides at least part of the answer: 'A national popular alliance', which Forgacs equates with a war of position, 'is not merely a strategy against fascism in Italian conditions but the only form possible of struggle in the west under normal conditions':

> It recognises the specificity of national conditions and traditions. It valorises civil society as a key site of struggle. It emphasizes the role of ideological reorganisation and struggle. It identifies struggles common to more than one social class, fraction or group which can be strategically linked together. It recognizes that different social elements can and do act in terms not only of economic or ideological self-interest but also in terms of shared interests.

Forgacs argues that Togliatti's applications of selected Gramscian themes to post-war Italy represented the nearest the western left had come to a successful national-popular 'war of position'. The prospects for success of such a strategy depend on just how thoroughly the broad terrain has been prepared, and the outcome is never certain and always politically contingent: there is 'often a narrow distinction between class alliances that are effectively hegemonic for the working class, class alliances that are merely federative groupings around particular issues or at particular times (for instance elections), and class alliances that can be tipped the other way and reorganised under the hegemony of the bourgeoisie'. In the immediate postwar period the PCI was a mass party that embodied the national resistance to fascism, but by 1948 the PCI had already lost the momentum of political change by conceding 'the restoration of the old economic and political infrastructures and the maintenance of fascist personnel'. Much of the party's subsequent history was about attempting to regain the 'national-popular' initiative, with some notable local successes but ultimate national failure.

Geoff Eley's 'Reading Gramsci in English: Observations on the Reception of Antonio Gramsci in the English-speaking world 1957-82', initially a review of recent literature, amounts to a broader survey of British and American Gramscism in its first phases, rather like David Forgacs' later article in *New Left Review* in 1989.[29] Eley's assessment and periodisation of Gramsci is broadly compatible with mine: 'If 1967-75 was a phase of initiation, when notice of Gramsci was first properly taken, and 1975-7 one of consolidation when a range of essentially biographical studies started to appear, then 1978-82 was the phase of mature Gramsci scholarship'. A quite distinct 'Gramsciology' had taken shape. Gramsci, 'the arch-foe of economism' had come into his own as a contributor to 'the philosophy of defeat' rather than 'unrealized libertarian potentials', and in the process 'also attained academic respectability ... Thus, while a certain kind of knowing reference has become very fashionable, most Gramscian usages can remain very un-reflected and casual'.

Political applications in this period were (for Eley) more a matter of 'Gramscian traces' – 'the launching of the *New Socialist* and the Socialist Society, some intellectual cross-currents around Tony Benn, and talk of promoting "a general ferment of "socialist ideas"" – than of close, careful study. Gramsci had reverted to the status and function of an unacknowledged or only casually referenced source, rather as had happened during the very first 'New Left' phase of the late 1950s and early 1960s, but without that era's sense of new openings and forms of resistance. By the 1980s, the British left was in headlong retreat, especially in and around the Labour Party. *New Socialist* was a Labour Party-sponsored attempt to emulate *Marxism Today*. It was unusually lively and attractive, but survived only for a few mid-1980s years. The Socialist Society sought to give permanent organisational form to the Bennite hard left, which likewise did not survive the 1980s. For all their 'Gramscian traces', there was very little sign of Gramscian perspectives in the generally bitter debates and faction-fighting of Labour in opposition; the only substantial treatment was a three-page 'primer' on Gramsci in a pamphlet produced by the Labour Co-ordinating Committee in 1990.[30]

Eley laments 'how easily the potential value of Gramsci's concept [of hegemony] may be misconstrued without the necessary familiarity with both the texts of the *Notebooks* themselves and the larger Marxist discussions that have recently come to surround them. "Hegemony" must not be equated with straightforward ideological domination in [a] totalitarian sense'. As a corrective, he calls for closer attention to what Gramsci actually wrote, to the historical circumstances in which he was writing, and a more rigorously 'historicist' application of Gramscian concepts to other historical situations like our own: 'The philosophers have had their say. The historians should now take the stage.' Eley's appeal would remain, until recently, largely unanswered.

Gramsci on Channel 4

Finally, in 1987 Channel 4 broadcast a drama-documentary about Gramsci.[31] He is portrayed by the actor John Sessions as a clipped, terse and frequently sarcastic Edinburgh lawyer, dispensing pearls of wisdom to his fellow prisoners (most notably his fellow southerner Giovanni Lay), frequently wrapped up in proverbs and fables. The most memorable of these concludes with the advice to 'think of intellectuals as chicken shit'. There is much use of the painter Renzo Galeotti's stunning portraits of Gramsci in linking images and backdrops, and of extraordinary archive footage of Gramsci himself in Moscow, Vienna and Rome, passing quickly through blurry crowd scenes. The programme adopts a suitably reverential tone towards its subject, with far greater emphasis on the man's life than his ideas. While the Prison Notebooks are described as 'one of the 20th Century's greatest testimonies to human courage and endurance' – an investigation '*fur ewig*, forever' into 'everything that concerns people' – there is only fleeting reference to their key concepts, and then they are rendered rather superficially, for example 'political and cultural hegemony as the precursor of true democracy'. Otherwise the programme is a scrupulously unified account of

Gramsci's life – Sardinian childhood, university in Turin, anti-war agitation, *Ordine Nuovo* and the factory councils and occupations, the formation of the PCd'I/PCI and the initial, failed resistance to fascism, finally imprisonment and study and reflection – which traces the organic development of his thinking and the common threads throughout.

The drama-documentary was followed by a studio discussion, chaired by Trevor Haylett, who had made his name as a Granada TV industrial correspondent and was unusually attuned to the Euro-communist current in the CP and the 'new thinking' in the Labour Party associated with Neil Kinnock.[32] The four studio panellists were the Italian historian Lidia Curti (who makes the point that interest in Gramsci in Italy had for some time been steadily declining), Stuart Hall, Hamish Henderson and John Reid MP, with a rather fuller head of hair and a far more genial countenance than in his latter day New Labour incarnation. The discussion focuses on how Gramsci might be applied to contemporary Britain, in which all are agreed on the deepening hegemony of Thatcherism. For Reid, 'We may not like what Thatcher has done, but she has managed to establish a moral legitimacy in many parts of the country'. He cites as a primary example the extension of 'popular capitalism … almost nine million people own a share or two'.

Curti refers to Italy as an instance of 'the left working within hegemony to resist authoritarianism … to bring about huge civil society victories like the legalisation of abortion and divorce, very difficult in a deeply religious country'. She pointed to the 'ways in which the left had been able to establish a presence in everyday life', for example in the *Feste dell'Unita* organised nationally and locally by the PCI to promote popular culture.[33] Stuart Hall, when asked specifically how a new anti-Thatcher hegemony might be constructed, responds 'If I knew that, I'd be in business!' All he can say is that it requires something beyond 'old-style Labourism'.

The primary historical interest of the discussion, at least for my purposes, is of course Reid's contribution. Recruiting a serving (and rising) Labour MP to a discussion of Gramsci would have felt like a real achievement for the programme-makers, while Reid would have welcomed the chance to contribute to the general 'ferment of socialist ideas'. He adopts a demeanour of slightly bemused condescension throughout, especially during Hall's customarily incisive contributions, and persistently mispronounces Gramsci's name: the Slavic-sounding 'Gram-ski' rather than the properly Italian 'Gramshi'. Amongst other plainly self-serving observations we hear that 'Gramsci came to regret being a founder-member of the Communist Party'. What Gramsci actually wrote in 1926, in one of his last explicit political commentaries as a free man, was that 'we should certainly have separated ourselves from reformism (the Socialist Party leadership) and maximalism (the Socialist left) … But afterwards, and without giving up our ideological and organisational struggle against them, we should have attempted to build an alliance against reaction'.[34] There is absolutely no evidence, *contra* Reid, that Gramsci at any time regretted his part in the foundation of the Italian Communist Party. Perhaps Reid had some difficulty in grasping the concept of separate parties entering freely into long-term alliances. Labourism, with its rhetorical stress on 'principle' and practical preoccupation with its own exclusive electoral prospects, has always been resistant to the politics of open, negotiated alliance with separate political forces. Regarding *itself* as a 'left alliance', it sees no need for another one.

But Reid's contributions at this stage in his career do reveal a familiarity with Gramsci that suggests recent, generally attentive and retentive reading; or at the very least receptivity to the 'general ferment' of Gramscian ideas. He has a strong grasp of the distinctions made by Gramsci between East and West, and their ramifications for political action: 'it's probably common sense, but it's good socialism as well'. He shows a better grasp than the others of the 'subalternity' of provincial cultures, with their 'enclaves of Thatcherism', which points to the need for some kind of rapprochement with the dominant south of England. Another nascent New Labour theme is evident in his observation of 'the beginnings of thought-processes inside the Labour Party [posing the question] what are the values of Labour? They may be the same as those of Keir Hardie in the 1880s, but how do we apply them in the 1980s?'

The discussion only really gets going towards the end, when it moves on to what the left might learn from Thatcherism in constructing some kind of practicable alternative, some kind of 'counter-hegemony'. A brief but fascinating exchange about 'tactical voting', as a way to combine Labour and Lib/SDP Alliance votes to dislodge the Tories, finds Hall broadly endorsing the idea and Reid arguing against it, on the basis that hegemony is a much bigger issue than elections. 'You cannot reduce Gramsci to a mechanism at the polling booth', Reid says, an interesting position in the light of his (and Phillip Gould's) later reduction of the concept 'hegemony' to parliamentary party electoral machinations. What he is really arguing for, of course, is the Labour Party's historic tendency (claimed as a kind of right) to go it alone, which tends to override other political considerations.

Interestingly, Haylett then inverts the question, to ask 'How could Thatcherism penetrate the hostile territory of Scotland?' To this the panel, including Reid, choose to respond in solely electoral terms. 'There is no hope,' declares Henderson 'of a Tory revival in Scotland!' Reid argues that to extend 'Thatcherism into the periphery, she has to abandon the free market', as previous 'one-nation' Tories had been partially prepared to do. Further, Scottish nationalism in its various political shades offers a bulwark against it. Finally, Hall cautions that 'nothing is permanent … there is a touch of self-interest, a little bit of Thatcherism, in all of us'.

Gramsci in Britain: some conclusions

The thirty-year period between the first publication in English of Gramsci's writings and the Channel 4 documentary saw the slow absorption of his thought into the mainstream of British left-wing political discourse. It plainly informed the first New Left's attempts to broaden its appeal through new cultural and historical associations, and to overcome the horrors and accretions of Stalinism. It allowed the post-'1968' left to connect the Marxist tradition with the emerging themes of personal liberation, cultural struggle, consumption and identity politics, and to see beyond an anachronistic, dogmatic, narrow, sectionalist, 'economistic' and 'productivist' politics of class. 'Gramscism' briefly revitalised the Communist Party of Great Britain, and attracted and enthused a new generation of intellectuals, both 'traditional' and 'organic' (in the properly Gramscian sense of thinking 'organisers' or activists).

Through Gramsci and the first phase of 'Euro-communism', the British left caught glimpses of a body of political thought and practice which might enjoy both popular support and long-term, strategic, transformative potential in the advanced capitalist, liberal-democratic West. Into the 1980s, those same insights enabled discussion and understanding of the gathering storm of Thatcherism and of what it might mean for left-wing politics. In retrospect this thirty-year period, 1957-87, looks like the heyday of British 'Gramscism'; measurable in the sheer volume of 'Gramsciana' or 'Gramsciology', the books and articles of material published in English by and about Gramsci, and palpable in the sense of excitement and creativity generated by his 'open Marxism'. These features would be noticeably lacking in later uses, and abuses, of Gramsci. Before examining those, we need to take a more practical and historically specific look at the concept of Thatcherism, by far the most important to arise from the creative application of Gramsci's thinking to British circumstances, not least because, in its own way, Thatcherism was just as preoccupied with rallying 'national-popular' support for a new 'common sense', mobilising 'consent' with more than a hint of 'coercion', and reconstituting a 'historic bloc' for the greater cause of re-establishing 'hegemony'.

Notes

1. A. Gramsci, *SPN*, ppxi, lxviii, xciv, xvv.
2. L. Althusser, 'Marxism is not a Historicism', in *Reading Capital* (London, 1970), based on a series of seminars delivered in 1965.
3. L. Althusser, *Reading Capital*, pp129, 130, 126, 141.
4. P. Anderson, 'The Antinomies of Antonio Gramsci', *New Left Review* 100, January 1976.
5. P. Anderson, 'Antinomies', *NLR* 100, p5.
6. D. Forgacs, 'Gramsci and Marxism in Britain', *NLR* 176 ft.17, p79.
7. P. Anderson, 'Antinomies', pp6, 7, 17.
8. J. Karabel, 'Gramsci and the Problem of Intellectuals', in J. Martin (ed.), *Antonio Gramsci: Critical Reassessments Vol. 3* (London 2002), p.18
9. T.J. Jackson Lears, 'Concept of Cultural Hegemony', *American Historical Review* 90 (3), p571
10. S. Hall, 'Rethinking the Base-Superstructure Metaphor', in *Class, Hegemony and Party*, ed. J. Bloomfield (London 1977); and personal interview, 12 January 2004.
11. G. Thomson, 'Gramsci, the first Italian Marxist', *Marxism Today* vol.1 no. 11, Nov 1957, pp 61-64.
12. J. Harvey, 'Antonio Gramsci', *Marxism Today* vol. 11 no. 4, April 1967, pp114-20; M. Jacques, 'Notes on the Concept of Intellectuals', *Marxism Today* vol. 15 no. 10, Oct. 1971, pp307-317; J. Harvey, review of *SPN*, *Marxism Today* vol.15 no. 12, Dec. 1971, pp360-66; R. Simon,

'Gramsci's Concept of Hegemony', *Marxism Today* vol.21 no. 3, March 1977, pp78-86.

13. F. Marek, 'Intervention from Behind Prison Walls', in *Philosophy of World Revolution* (London, 1969); S. Riva, *An Introduction to Some Thoughts of Gramsci*, CPGB Education Dept. pamphlet 1976, cited in P. Cozens, *Twenty Years of Antonio Gramsci*, p7.

14. J. Bloomfield (ed.), *Class, Hegemony and Party* (London, 1977); S. Hibbin (ed.), *Politics, Ideology and the State* (London, 1978); G. Bridges & R. Brunt (eds.) *Silver Linings* (London, 1981).

15. S. Hall, 'Rethinking the "Base and Superstructure" Metaphor', in *Class, Hegemony and Party,* pp 43/72.

16. See Slavoj Zizek, 'Resistance is Surrender', *London Review of Books,* 2 November 2007, for an interesting if ultimately dispiriting recent example.

17. R. Gray, 'Bourgeois Hegemony in Victorian Britain', in *Class, Hegemony and Party,* p73.

18. A. Showstack Sassoon, 'Hegemony and Political Intervention', in *Politics, Ideology and the State*, p9.

19. M. Burawoy, 'For a Sociological Marxism: The Complementary Convergence of Antonio Gramsci and Karl Polanyi', *Politics and Society* vol. 31 no. 2, 2003, pp193/261.

20. T. Jones, *The Dark Heart of Italy* (London 2003), p28; and the 2006 feature film *Romanzo Criminale*.

21. G. Andrews, *Endgames and New Times*, p193.

22. G. Andrews, *Endgames and New Times*, p195.

23. G. Andrews, *Endgames and New Times*, p195.

24. B. Schwarz & C. Mercer, 'Popular Politics and Marxist Theory in Britain', in *'Silver Linings'*, p143.

25. S. Hall, 'The Great Moving Right Show', *Marxism Today*, January 1979.

26. B. Schwarz & C. Mercer, 'Popular Politics', *Silver Linings*, p.144; A. Gramsci, *Prison Letters*, quoted in 'Gramsci', Channel 4 TV 1987 (see below).

27. D. Forgacs, 'National-Popular: Genealogy of a Concept', in *Formations of Nation and People* (London 1984), pp.83-98.

28. A. Pearmain, 'England and the National Popular', *Soundings* 38, Spring 2008, attempts just such an application of the Gramscian 'national popular' to contemporary English circumstances.

29. G. Eley, 'Reading Gramsci in English: Observations on the Reception of Antonio Gramsci in the English-speaking World 1957-82', *European History Quarterly* Vol. 14 (1984), pp441-78.

30. N. Lawson (ed.), *New Maps for the Nineties – A Third Road Socialist Reader* (London 1990).

31. 'Gramsci', *Channel 4 Television*, directed by Mike Alexander, scripted by Douglas Eadie, and narrated by Brian Cox.

32. Haylett is now a sports journalist for the *Sunday Telegraph*.

33. Curti had, with Iain Chambers, contributed an essay on 'A Volatile Alliance: Culture, Popular Culture and the Italian Left' to the 1984 collection *Formations of Nation and People.*
34. A. Gramsci, *L'Unita*, 24 February 1926, collected in *Selections from Political Writings 1921-26*, p380, and quoted in G. Fiori, *Antonio Gramsci Life of a Revolutionary*, p153

3. Iron in Our Souls: the Hegemony of Thatcherism

Everything's a version of something else ... from 20 years ago'
Patrick Marber, *Closer*

Margaret Thatcher was elected leader of the Conservative Party in 1975 but the concept of Thatcherism did not take full shape until well after the 1979 election victory of the Conservatives, and the elevation of Thatcher herself to the position of prime minister. For some time still, most of the left thought it was dealing with the same old enemy, the political party of the high bourgeois interest in capitalism, and that the same old response, 'one big heave' by the industrial working class against the bosses, would soon get us back on the British road to socialism. In fact, Thatcherism turned out to be very different from traditional Conservatism, in both its paternalistic and 'one-nation' guises, which have both been among its most notable victims. As a form of 'authoritarian populism', with a primarily petit bourgeois social base and crucial linkages to the 'respectable', 'aspirational' upper working class or 'labour aristocracy', Thatcherism has more in common with earlier right-wing currents like fascism and Poujadism. It is not, however, equivalent to them; it has some shared characteristics, but these are set within a wholly distinctive and historically specific English 'national-popular' context.[1]

It wasn't really until the mid-1980s, after the Falklands War and the miners' strike, and well into the process of 'closure' of the mentalities, procedures and institutions of the post-war social-democratic consensus, that it was widely appreciated that something qualitatively and substantially different was happening here. But there were earlier premonitions on the left of a right wing backlash as far back as 1978, when *Marxism Today* published Eric Hobsbawm's masterly 'The Forward March of Labour Halted?', which set about clinically dissecting the illusion of a unified, inherently socialist British working class inexorably headed towards the overthrow of capitalism.[2] Hobsbawm took as his rough historical framework the hundred years following 1870, when the manual working class had constituted an actual majority of the British population, at around 70 per cent. This had meant, amongst other things, that 'from the point of view of the ruling classes, it was absolutely essential to gain or maintain the political support of an important section of the working class'. This created the economic imperative for the labour interest in capitalism, and for the emergence of a 'labour aristocracy' within this huge, heavily stratified and multiply fissured working class. Since 1870 there had been a steady decline in the manual working class but a commensurate growth in the wider 'proletariat', as classically defined by their wage-labour, because of the growth of white-collar clerical or supervisory jobs. However, manual labour was for a long time still relatively important to British industry, which remained under-automated and technologically primitive compared to other industrial societies. For example, in 1914 a quarter of a million men were employed as coal miners, equipped with little more than picks and shovels and their own brawn. This reinforced the importance in the British workplace of craft (or trade) unionism, heavily dominated by separate sections of the labour aristocracy, as compared to the general, industrial or political unionism developed elsewhere. There were all kinds of social and cultural consequences.

An entire proletarian 'style of life' had emerged in Britain, based around the dominant preferences and habits of male manual workers, such as football as a mass spectator sport, fish and chip shops, and Blackpool and other seaside resorts. It was this social and cultural complex which served to unify the British working class, rather than any strong sense of common economic or political interest or purpose. Coupled with the growing defensive strength of Labourism as an electoral force within the established parliamentary and municipal framework, and the tendency of state and private enterprise towards monopoly, this came to mean that 'the factors which determine the workers' conditions are no longer those of capitalist competition'. Classically liberal 'free trade', in labour as well as goods, was being increasingly managed. This was the economic and industrial effect that after some decades of social conflict and the cataclysm of the Second World War came to be known as the 'social democratic consensus' or Butskellism. But even as it took hold in the 1940s and 1950s as official government policy and prevailing 'common sense', Hobsbawm argued, the post-war settlement between capital and labour was being undermined by changes in the composition of the working class itself.

Firstly the proportion of women in the workforce, doing what were called 'white-blouse' jobs as well as menial assembly, was growing rapidly. Secondly, ethnic, regional or sectarian differences might always fracture social unity, and frequently did, in London, Liverpool and other urban centres. But thirdly and above all, sectional differences (always inherent in a craft-based system of labour) between different groups of workers and their trade unions had pitted them against each other, especially in the sphere of 'wage struggle', where large temporary gains by some groups were offset by price-inflation for everyone else. Most recently, with the rapid growth of the public sector as a feature of 'state monopoly capitalism', sectionalism had found new expression in forms of industrial action whose strength 'lies not in the amount of loss they can cause to an employer, but in the inconvenience they can cause to the public'. Furthermore, the large minority of the population defined as poor were mostly beyond the embrace of the labour movement altogether, but especially vulnerable to the economic consequences of sectionalism, price-inflation and the growing cost pressures on the public services that housed, treated and schooled them. The upshot of all of this was to be seen in static or decreasing levels of trade union membership, a Labour vote in steady decline from its historical highpoint of 1951, and a palpable withering of 'socialist consciousness' amongst the working class. This was ameliorated, but not ultimately offset, by the 'radicalization of students and intellectuals' during the cultural upheavals around 1968. Various waves of 'economistic militancy', most notably between 1970 and 1974, served not to reverse but to hasten this decline.

The ensuing debate about 'The Forward March of Labour Halted?' did not shed a great deal more light on the subject, and like many of the 'great debates' in and around *Marxism Today* tended to get bogged down in the internal conflicts beginning to engulf the fast-declining Communist Party of Great Britain. Most contributions represented various shades of what Geoff Andrews calls 'militant labourism' – the dominant 'industrial strategy' with which the CPGB was attempting to maintain its working class base and stave off its own demise.[3] They seem wholly preoccupied with matters of trade union procedure, tactics and leadership. Others, from outside the CP, attempted a broader critique of the 'Gramscian' thesis then taking shape. Most of them interpreted the historical and statistical evidence differently, to make the case that things were not as bad as Hobsbawm had argued. In retrospect, Hobsbawm seems if anything to have understated his case; in the thirty years since his article, trade union membership has almost halved, from its historical late-1970s peak of 12 million to less than 7 million today, with a large majority of them (around 5.5 million) in the public sector and formerly public utilities. 'Union density' in private industry is at a modern historic low. The British labour movement, and its various left-wing political agencies, were in rapid retreat.

The only exception to the preoccupation with the nuts and bolts of trade unionism and the mood of over-optimism running through the 'Forward March' debate came in Raymond Williams' contribution, in broad agreement with Hobsbawm. For Williams, the venerable cultural theorist and founding father of both *New Left Review* and the academic subject of cultural studies, the primary fault of the British labour movement was its 'militant particularism', a focus on immediate, localised industrial disputes, which forestalled attempts to construct a socialist 'general interest' either on a national scale or internationally. 'There are millions of marginal and beyond-the-margin poor in our own country, but also in far greater numbers in many very poor countries with which we trade.' Clearly anticipating developments towards globalisation, Williams noted how 'capital can pick up and move faster than any worker'.[4]

Hobsbawm was clearly startled by the scale and ferocity of the debate his article provoked. What is clear now is that he had hit upon a number of serious fault-lines within the labour movement which its activists and advocates were loath to recognize. In his initial (somewhat defensive) response, published in late 1979, Hobsbawm was able to deploy the evidence from that year's momentous general election, most notably (and still a little incredulously) that 'a third of trade unionists appear actually to have voted for the Tories'. This fundamental shift in working-class political allegiances was 'not offset by the good showing of Labour in Scotland, by the immigrant vote, by the resistance of women to the appeal of the Tories (their swing was only 3% compared to 9.5% among the men), and by the interesting fact that the Labour vote actually rose significantly among the smallish professional and managerial group'. These electoral consolations also offer a foretaste of some of the regional, ethnic and social tensions which Thatcherism would highlight, exacerbate and exploit.

Hobsbawm argued that other responses demonstrated forms of syndicalism or workerism in equating political progress with industrial unrest largely inspired by sectionalist wage-demands (his later response to the 1984/5 miners' strike was based on this critique of syndicalism, which he detected as the central feature of Arthur Scargill's politics), or with the survival of mass working-class 'styles of life' or cultural forms (again a major theme in the miners' strike). In total, what was happening amounted to a steep 'decline in the *political* class movement'. This theme of left-wing decline became one of the foundations of the *Marxism Today* critique of 'old' Labourism, which took shape during the 1980s. It took rather longer for the corollary of right-wing resurgence to be spotted, and labelled as Thatcherism. In Martin Jacques' 1981 preface to the Verso collection of contributions to the *Forward March of Labour Halted?* debate, the rise of the right was still being seen as a symptom of capitalist crisis, rather than a far-sighted attempt at its resolution. In Hobsbawm's initial response to the debate, the Tory election victory was described as 'Mrs. Thatcher's and Sir Keith Joseph's proposal to turn the economic clock back to about 1865.'

It was Stuart Hall who began to delineate what 'Thatcherism' might be trying to achieve as a positive political project, with what he called its 'regressive modernisation'. Within reactionary forms there was always and necessarily a 'modernising' impulse, such as Gramsci had detected in Italian fascism. Likewise, Thatcherism sought to resolve capitalism's latest crisis and impose a new economic and political settlement. Hall's essay 'The Great Moving Right Show' first appeared in *Marxism Today* in December 1978, three months after Hobsbawm's piece, and six months before Thatcher's election victory in 1979. It contains, as far as I am aware, the first mention of 'Thatcherism' and the first attempts to analyse its ascendancy.[5] Though it acknowledges the economic and social dimensions of recent British history, as outlined by Hobsbawm, its focus is very much on this emerging right-wing ideology. Thatcherism had grown out of a backlash against the cultural revolutions of the 1960s. It was initially identified as Powellism (after the similarly ideologically adept Tory/Unionist politician Enoch Powell) and was only temporarily slowed by the industrial upheavals of the 1970-74 period. But it was crucially aided by Labourism's loss of nerve and its conscious abandonment of the corpo-ratist-integrationist, social-democratic post-war consensus. Left-wing responses to Thatcherism – that it represented a 'sharpening of contradictions' within capitalism, a traditional 'economic cyclical downturn', or, for the Labour right, 'mere ideology' and for the left 'false consciousness' – were woefully inadequate. They failed to explain 'how a capitalist economic recession (economic), presided over by a social-democratic party with mass working-class support and organised depth in the trade unions (politically), is "lived" by increasing numbers of people through the themes and representations (ideologically) of a virulent, emergent "petty-bourgeois" ideology.'

Hall describes Thatcherism as 'the recession's condition of existence', which is the first hint that 'the crisis' might represent a solution for capitalism rather than a collection of problems; as such it represents a significant development of Hobsbawm's 'Forward March' thinking. It was not the same as 'fascism', which some of the left had attempted to resurrect as a comforting historical bogeyman, in a fit of 'mere name-calling', but a form of 'authoritarian populism'. Unlike fascism, at least in its more mature and consolidated forms, it was prepared to retain 'formal representative institutions' and to seek 'active popular consent'. To equate Thatcherism with fascism was to ignore their fundamental differences in (amongst other aspects) their orientations towards the state and the economy. In positive terms, the 'swing to the right' was an attempt to construct a new 'historic bloc' to address capitalism's crisis, and to deploy a 'radicalism of the right'. It was, crucially, a new turn for the Conservative Party, superseding the 'Heath course', which had retained some of the statist, corporate elements of 'Butskellism', and 'directly engaging the "creeping socialism" and apologetic "state collectivism" of the Heath wing ... It destroys that form of consensus in which social democracy was the principal tendency.'

Just as crucially, Thatcherism was able to exploit the primary internal contradiction of Labourism: that it entered the political fray representing the economic interests of the 'subaltern' working class, but was forced to govern in the 'national interest'. This created repeated conflicts of purpose and interest, most recently and most notably between the trade unions and the mass of the population. Labour had attempted to manage and overcome this contradiction by the use of the interventionist state in every aspect of national life, but in the context of economic crisis and cuts in public spending, the actual experience of many people was of diminishing, demeaning or disciplinary state services. This provided the ideology of Thatcherism with the material and experiential basis for popular grievance against an oppressive state. Its anti-statism elided into anti-collectivism, and enabled 'the translation of a theoretical ideology into a populist idiom' through devices like 'the emotive image of the scrounger: the new folk-devil' and 'the colonisation of the popular press', and later the 'nanny state', poking its nose into every aspect of our lives:

> Thatcherite populism is a particularly rich mix. It combines the reso-
> nant themes of organic Toryism – nation, family, duty, authority,
> standards, traditionalism – with the aggressive themes of a revived
> neo-liberalism – self-interest, competitive individualism, anti-
> statism.

Freedom is equated with the free market, and the state is to be made strong but minimal, a lean and mean machine to enable 'Britain to be made Great again', 'to tear society up by the roots and radically recon-struct it!'.[6]

The lived experience of Thatcherism[7]

Premonitions and suspicions

Mike Prior and David Purdy are professional economists, with an intellectual perspective on this period which reaches back to their 1977 collaboration on *Out of the Ghetto*, originally published as a contribution to the CP's *BRS* revision debate and amongst the first assessments of the possibilities of populist reaction. Mike now remembers 'the first few years of the 1970s (as) a period of cata-strophic decline of capitalism. The rate of profit in British companies had declined almost to zero. There was no sense of crisis on the left, the crisis was in capitalism'.[8] According to David:

> This was more than just a cyclical downturn … Keynesian social-
> democratic, elite macro-economic management was visibly failing.
> Inflation was going through the roof, and no one seemed to have any

alternative but the radical right, who were saying the whole thing
was wrong from the word go … The post-war consensus had been
utterly misconceived and had opened the floodgates to disorder all
around you, stretching from inflation and its various malign effects
to, in the eyes of rather more politicised people, sexual permissive-
ness and so on. There were real linkages to the cultural struggle.
Thatcher and the Tory right gained new confidence, born of desperation, because the game was almost up. British capitalism was in
desperate straits by the mid-1970s, easily the worst crisis it had had
since the war.[9]

Stuart Hall himself recalls how:

the settlement of the welfare state was reaching the limits of what
could be extracted from the system itself without changing the
system. There was a long period when mass labour movements could
extract the welfare state from capitalism, and leave it still relatively
intact, but there was always a limit to how far that could go …
Capitalism would have to go elsewhere to get round it, to sustain its
capacity to manage the working class and the rest of society. That it
did by going global. The mid-1970s was the moment when contemporary globalisation really begins to take off, as the response of
capitalism to the welfare state.[10]

For David Purdy, this was a zero-sum game. 'What was at stake was
the whole post-war settlement.' Hall, Purdy and Prior readily
acknowledge that this was hardly if at all understood at the time, by
themselves or anyone else, and that their contemporary accounts
benefit heavily from hindsight. John Chapman joined the Labour
Party in 1979 because, he says, 'I had a gut feeling that this Tory
government under Thatcher would be a different order of things. It
would be a radical, right-wing departure, and we'd probably be
looking at a slash and burn of the working class'.[11] However, he could
see that on the back of widespread disillusionment with Labour, it was
'very difficult to make the argument that this time the Conservative
government you're going to vote for will be very different and very
damaging to you as a working class person.'

In a certain crucial sense, Thatcherism was predicated on the
decline of Labourism, and actually continued much of the economic

strategy adopted by the failing Labour government. Alan Lawrie, then a CP activist, was 'most conscious that Labour social democracy had failed':

> The Callaghan years were a disaster really. When Thatcher was elected, people were not so aware of her radical agenda. It became clear that she was able to relate to a lot of working class people on issues like trade union democracy, personal freedoms, the sale of council houses. She had pulled that agenda in, while we had been off talking amongst ourselves.[12]

Peter Molyneux was a member of the Conservative Party at the time, because compared to Labour, 'the Tories seemed like a breath of fresh air. Thatcher was very attractive'.[13] Echoing Alan Lawrie's perception, in an interesting convergence between Euro-communism and the traditional Tory perspective which Thatcher would subsequently deride as 'wet', Peter says: 'There wasn't much engagement with her economic policies, but a disengagement from Callaghan.' For Alan Lawrie, looking for something to join, 'The Labour Party just wasn't an option … It had no political organisation as such, it seemed like an old man's, dead party.' At this stage, the prevailing mood was more about the decline of Labourism than the ascendancy of Thatcherism.

For a while, the Tories were buoyed up and united by electoral success. Peter Molyneux continues:

> In '79, I wasn't aware of any major schism. I remember the misogynists and people on the Tory left saying it was the revenge of the lower middle classes, we'll have her for one term. Never mind, really. Willie and Peter and Jim and Francis are running the show, which of course they weren't. In 1980, it became really stark. I was at a Conservative conference where there were people doing Nazi salutes. Baroness Cox at a private meeting said that the Tories had to tackle the whole issue of segregation of schools. We couldn't continue to have black children in the same classes as white children. I stood up and complained that this was racist and outrageous. I think I was sitting next to the only black person in the room, which I think had spurred me on … I got thrown out of the meeting for showing discourtesy to a guest. I left the Tory Party that day.

From a later generation, and a very different political position, the hard left of the Labour Party, Andy Wood still 'felt that if we were a real socialist party, then we would really win elections. That's cobblers, self-evidently, but I wasn't prepared to accept the structural changes that were occurring in the economy, the growing prosperity of Britain, when all I could see was the poverty of inner city Manchester'.[14]

The economic impact of Thatcherism

We are beginning to see some of the ground from which Thatcherism emerged. Everyone seems to agree that a large part of its root system was economic; even Stuart Hall, who has been derided by some for an overly 'culturalist' view of history. 'Marx said capitalism always has to go forward – it always seeks to raise the level of profit, and maintains its capacity to manage, to extend the opportunities for profit making, and globalises more of the world territorially or more of the person. Whatever it does, it's a revolutionary force; everything dissolves.' For Pat Devine, another CP-member professional economist, a key element of the economic impact of Thatcherism was the changing role of the state from the promotion of welfare to the promotion of business:

> I don't think we thought at the time that the role of the state could be changed. We thought it was a requirement of capitalism, at the stage to which it had evolved. We then saw that the role of the state was indeed being changed very fundamentally, though interestingly the 'weight' (i.e. the general level) of public spending didn't really change. We hadn't made that distinction, between the weight and the direction of public spending.

Furthermore, the anti-statist rhetoric of Thatcherism served to mask this shift, from the welfare to the business state.[15]

John Chapman, increasingly active in the (generally left-wing, with pockets of old right-wing Labourism) London Labour Party, recalls the prevailing economic strategy on the left at the time:

> The idea was the revolution was just around the corner, because the working class was going to bring capitalism to its knees by ever-

increasing wage demands. It didn't happen of course! There wasn't a profit squeeze, there was a labour squeeze, and people started to lose their jobs instead, which came as a great surprise to most people on the left.

It is a testimony to the hegemonic depth of the post war social democratic consensus, at least in the thinking of the left, that it assumed the continuation of policies of full employment, and that it had such little sense of the historic role of mass unemployment in economic restructuring and social discipline. The 1930s, less than fifty years before, represented a kind of forgotten Labourist 'pre-history'.

The social basis of Thatcherism

If we accept that politics bears some relationship to the economic interests of particular social groups, what or rather who did Thatcherism represent? In 1987, Stuart Hall put it plainly enough: 'The hard-faced, utilitarian, petty bourgeois businessmen are now in charge, not the grouse-shooting, hunting and fishing classes'.[16] This is what Peter Molyneux called 'the revenge of the lower middle classes' (the sociologist Richard Sennett has used the same terminology of 'vengeance' to describe the primary impulse of Thatcherism).[17] Peter goes on to talk about his mother, who espoused a 'very right wing, working class Conservatism, which she was completely unaware of':

> So every time she opened her mouth, bless her, she thought she was being part of the middle class. But what she was doing was showing that she wasn't part of the middle class at all, partly by talking about politics – which wasn't done in polite society – and partly by expressing it in a very working class way. There was a long list of hatreds – black people, Americans, Churchill. She didn't like men very much, so most politicians were spineless, until 1979.

Peter's family history also illustrates the connection in British society, crucial to an understanding of the social basis of Thatcherism and the shifting political allegiances it sought to exploit, between the lower middle class or petty bourgeoisie and upper working class or labour aristocracy. This latter sector, 'relatively comfortable and ideologically moderate, and drawing disproportionate benefits from the world monopoly of British industrial capitalism' (for Hobsbawm), had been at its historical peak in late Victorian times, with its whole 'style of life' and what Friedrich Engels at the time called its 'respectable prejudices'.[18] This comfortably 'subaltern' mentality is still deeply embedded in British national-popular consciousness and mythology. It echoes through many of our mass cultural forms, such as soap opera, memoir and 'popular' social history, football or the tabloid press, albeit twisted into novel shapes by the imperatives of unrestrained commerce. Peter Molyneux's grandfather had grown up on the Mile End Road:

> … again quite aspirational. He always voted Labour, but he never discussed it because it was too controversial. He had seen real poverty, and his driver was that at least Labour had put an end to poverty. He could stomach Wilson, because at least Labour had delivered everyone into the middle class. I'm not sure he had that much awareness of working men, because his path had been different; he was clerical.

In other words he was part of Hobsbawm's burgeoning non-manual, stiff white-collared but still wage-labouring proletariat.

We also have here a clear illustration of the transference of aspirationalism, the desire for upward social mobility, from 'old' Labourism to Thatcherism. In this case, the step up from working to middle class has taken place within one generation; which means, of course, that its achievement is not particularly secure. This insecurity provides another social (or more exactly psychological) basis for the appeal of Thatcherism to the many 'ordinary' British people who live in this indeterminate space between working and middle classes, estimated by Ross McKibbin at around ten million at any stage in recent British history.[19] There is also a view, which helps explain the apparent ease of this ideological transference between aspirational vehicles, that there is a thick seam of social conservatism running through British society, at pretty much the point where lower middle class meets upper working class. John Chapman, an American resident in this country since 1972, feels 'the UK is a very conservative country, and it's very hard to make a breakthrough. There is a deep conservatism and an in-built fear in the British electorate.'

Within what Stuart Hall called its 'authoritarian populism', there were particular novel ideological devices with which Thatcherism sought to appeal to this heady national-popular brew of respectability, hatred, aspirationalism and fear. Foremost among them was individualism, expressed through Thatcher's famous epithet 'there is no such thing as society, only individuals and their families', and coupled with the moral argument that not only was there nothing wrong with becoming rich, but that it was laudable and desirable for everyone to attempt it. Looking back, Janice Robinson (then a CP activist) says 'what Thatcherism did was unbelievable. It was a social revolution, like the right to buy (council houses), and the impact that's had on society. It brought a ton of practical problems, but it freed people up. The left could only sit there and watch in amazement.' Janice, herself a successful professional from a solidly working-class background, and now something of a self-confessed elitist, contrasts this with the way 'Labour do level down, concentrating on the many not the few. Standardisation, bringing everybody down, is still a very big part of the Labour instinct'.[20]

Thatcherism's appeal to individualism could take surprising forms. Sally Davison, then working as a teacher in East London, remembers 'talking to young black boys, and they'd say it doesn't matter about my exams because I'm going to set up a business. What do you say to them? You can't say come off it, because you don't want to undermine them'.[21] Stuart Hall might be talking about these young boys ten years on, or perhaps their older brothers, when he says that 'Thatcherism undoubtedly opened up some intermediate spaces, and allowed for hustling as a survival strategy. Black people hustled their way into music, into fashion, in a way that a steady increase in equal opportunities programmes would never have done.'

Many understood at the time, and were appalled by, this hosanna to selfishness and greed, supposedly characteristic of the 'me-decade' of the 1980s. What was less immediately apparent was that it also served as the device which placed our ordinary daily lives of work and family, of earning a living and making a life, beyond the reach of democratic collective politics, most obviously but not only by its assault on trade unionism. Thatcherism reified and commodified and inserted personal experience into the nexus of consumer capitalism. Principles and identities transmuted into choices and labels. If the 1970s left had declared that 'the personal is political', it was trumped by capitalism's 1980s shift into higher, turbo gear. 'The personal' still mattered – indeed it was all that mattered – but it had less and less connection to any version of 'the political' associated with the left. There is a troubling connection here with the politics of personal identity, which mobilised a lot of the 'new social forces' emerging from the cultural upheavals around 1968, and laid heavy emphasis on individual freedom. This is the route, for example, from gay liberation to the pink pound, via the politics of homosexual law reform, community, scene, lifestyle choice, and now, niche marketplace.

Stuart Hall acknowledges this historical thread, but insists that there is no necessary political connection

> A degree of individuation has happened, which did bring questions of personal identity, of subjectivity, of 'the personal is political', of the subjective dimension of political action. Both Thatcherism and the left would have had to address that shift. It doesn't mean that only Thatcherism can flow from it. I have always felt that we needed to occupy the same world that Thatcherism does, but provide different answers.

This at least keeps alive some sense of possible alternatives. Sally Davison makes a similar point about her early-1980s North London feminist, communist, squatting lifestyle, and particularly its free-wheeling 'promiscuity' – 'We thought we were being moral, but we had a different morality. We didn't think do what you like, but that sticking to one person is so bourgeois.' As the 1980s wore on, this kind of self-contained, 'alternative', predominantly left-wing 'politics of personal identity' would be ideologically encapsulated in the terms 'loony left' and 'political correctness' and held up to public ridicule. Such lifestyles provided another key ideological target for Thatcherism's social and political counter-mobilisation, most dramatically in Section 28 of the 1988 Local Government Act, which forbade the 'promotion of homosexuality' by local authorities. For Janice Robinson, this backlash was facilitated by Ken Livingstone's Greater London Council:

> It was like the emperor has no clothes, but none of us could stand up and say we're talking bollocks here. We're not engaging with anybody ... I remember one incident in the British Youth Council. It was the Scouts, who were just beginning to slough off their image

of being predatory paedophiles, and they were being forced to include in their charter something about gay rights!

The Left disorientated and split

The left in Britain was not only defeated electorally by Thatcherism; it was politically disorientated, socially disconnected, culturally fragmented, and organisationally stilled. This had massive implications for what has followed, in particular for what we might call the New Labour adaptation. The political disorientation of the left was partly caused by the confusing novelties of Thatcherism itself, which for Stuart Hall (talking specifically about its relationship with black people) was a 'deeply contradictory formation':

> When it was talking on its state, nationalist, English side, it regarded black people as an alien wedge. When it's talking in market terms, there's no reason why black people shouldn't play the market like anyone else! So it had two languages.

Historically, there have been other, apparently internally contradictory, right-wing political formations, which have also confused the left and been seen as temporary aberrations, or even as precursors to socialist revolution. David Purdy sees 'a certain analogy between the late 1970s and the Nazi accession to power in Germany in 1933, when the German CP took the view "Hitler today, us tomorrow", as if this was just another temporary Weimar-type government. A lot of people on the left had a similar attitude towards Thatcher in 1979; it'll just be a short-run thing and then we'll be back.' There was, perhaps, an understandable reluctance to acknowledge that things were quite as bad as they would turn out.

By this time, the left as a community of people was increasingly isolated from the rest of the population, or perhaps more exactly insulated. Sally Davison says 'if you live inside the left, and you live in London, it's quite easy to blot out the fact that there are all these other people that are Tories and right-wing and racist'. The differences between the metropolitan left and what we might call 'outer England' are not only articulated politically. Mike Rustin has written elsewhere about how it was possible by the late 1980s to lead an entirely self-sufficient, 'alternative' lifestyle, with forms of employment,

consumption, leisure and recreation, housing and household arrangements, clothing, childcare and sexual orientation – all amounting to
distinctive and novel 'subcultures' – which were almost wholly
different from the mass of the British people.[22] Despite much excited
talk on the left and elsewhere about cultural diversification and the
fragmentation of the whole population into discreet if overlapping
minorities, the majority continued to think and behave – and more to
the point, to see themselves – as if they belonged to a unified whole,
partially but increasingly identified by hostility to any brand of left-
wing politics.

Within the Communist Party (as well as in the pages of *Marxism
Today*) there was some understanding that something epochal was
going on, especially on its Euro-communist or Gramscian wing; and
that it might require a quite different kind of politics in response. For
Alan Lawrie, 'there was now a realisation that this wasn't just about
working harder. It required a different alignment, and really the
labour movement was a bit of an irrelevancy.' This kind of thinking
had been going on in and around the CP since at least the mid-1970s,
but it had failed to become 'hegemonic' even within the party, never
mind the broader left and the wider world. The CPGB's own history
of sectarian isolation had caught up with it. Looking back, and with
an eye towards the deep social and cultural shifts already detected by
Hobsbawm, Pat Devine now feels it was probably too late for the CP:

> the prospect of turning the party into an effective Euro-communist
> force, with a Gramscian hegemonic approach, was lost. If it had
> happened in the early 1970s when the forces on the ground were
> there, we might have succeeded, but by the end of the 1970s these
> forces had already dispersed.

The Labour left response to Thatcherism was rather different. John
Chapman says 'What we traditionally do in the Labour movement
when we lose, of course, is set amongst ourselves and start a good old
in-fight. The 1980s was no exception, with the left blaming the right
for losing the election because there wasn't enough socialism in the
programme'. In response, the Labour right (by which is generally
meant the upper echelons of the parliamentary party or the trade
unions) either hunkered down for the long haul back to electability –
the approach favoured by what Hayter calls 'the stayers' – or departed

to the newly founded and briefly blooming Social Democratic Party. The right was no longer much in evidence among Labour's active, local membership. David Purdy describes the experience of being in the Labour Party between 1980 and 1983 as 'simply awful ... I naively thought that I would be joining some kind of mainstream, and actually it was full of Trotskyists and nutters, and even the non-aligned members were in a state of denial. They simply didn't understand what had hit them, and were living in a real ghetto. It was extremely leftist [and at the same time] there was no conception of a party that would do anything other than fight elections.' It felt like the worst of all possible political worlds.

During the early 1980s, the dominant political strain within the Labour Party was what came to be known as Bennism, associated with Tony Benn's narrowly defeated campaign for the leadership of the party. Benn himself, in a contemporaneous interview with Eric Hobsbawm, said that 'the role of the socialist critic of a Labour government must be to work within the party, within the constituencies, within the trade unions, at Conference and in the National Executive and its study groups'.[23] As Hobsbawm later pointed out, 'the best and most left-wing party is not enough, if the masses won't support it in sufficient numbers' – as indeed they would not do for many years yet, by which time it had changed pretty much beyond recognition. To many on the left at the time, Bennism – with its almost complete fixation on internal intrigue and manoeuvre for policy and positional advantage – felt like a curious attempt to turn a mass party into an insular sect.

A broader historical view might suggest that these elements – a vigorous tradition of sectarian debate and activism superimposed upon a largely passive mass base – have always been part of the Labourist mix, most obviously for successive generations of Trotskyist 'entryists' but also other more respectable attempts to take control of the party, such as those of the 1950s revisionists, and more recently New Labour. What was most historically significant about the early 1980s Labour Party was the palpable withering of that mass base, expressed in the decline in its individual membership and (most dramatically) in its share of the popular vote. Individual Labour Party membership fell from 348,156 in 1980 to 276,692 in 1981. Labour's vote in the 1983 general election was down by over 3 million from 1979, from 11,532,148 to 8,457,124.[24]

John Chapman sees Bennism as another example of left-wing detachment: 'Benn's leadership bid was important to the left, but seemed to pass everybody by outside of the Labour movement.' Neal Lawson 'was a Bennite for a while, and always loved the rhetoric and the communicative power, but even at 16 or 17 I knew there wasn't really a programme here'. Sally Davison 'saw Bennism as leftism, and I was never attracted to that.' Pat Devine, deploying the four-cornered political model of left, right, radical and conservative favoured by the Euro-communists, feels that 'what we saw with the hard left, and Benn, was a reaction to right-radicalism, and a fallback to left-conservatism'. Andy Wood, himself a Bennite at the time, deploys similar language to express a rather different perspective:

> What we wanted was a kind of Thatcherism of the left, with the same political bravery. Benn seemed to represent a commitment to the peace movement, democracy, the alternative economic strategy … Anti-corporatism was part of the Bennite mix … Benn developed a not dissimilar critique of the post-war settlement to that of Thatcherism. He arrived at a different set of conclusions over what's to replace it, but had a similar sense that the corporatism that had emerged post-1945 was consciously disempowering and paternalist.

What is historically most noticeable about Bennism is that its expansive rhetoric of democratic alliance with other popular movements, with appreciative nods towards grass roots democratic insurgencies like the Lucas Aerospace Alternative Plan or the Meridan Cooperative, did not match its practice of internal party manoeuvring for positions of power. Benn himself unconsciously illustrated this when he bemoaned to Hobsbawm the fact that 'a lot of people who should be in the Labour Party (have) *disappeared* into community groups' (my italics).[25]

For a while, the entryist faction Militant appeared to be an important part of the Labour left (Benn resisted their and other 'Marxists' expulsion). The early-Kinnockite or 'soft' left was in part a response to their unsavoury politics, and the expulsion of Militant from the Labour Party in 1985 was a key moment in Neil Kinnock's own inner-party ascendancy. For Neal Lawson, 'the crucial thing about the [soft left, then New Labour] leadership mindset is that it was forged in that deeply, darkly, depressing late 1980s/early 1990s period, when all the hope, all the life, all the ambition of the Labour Party was just sucked out of it.' Andy Wood talks about the cumulative effect of successive electoral defeats:

> It was obvious that the 1983 election had been an absolute catastrophe. I couldn't understand in those days why we lost the 1987 election, because we had a leader who was presentable, with a social-democratic agenda offering sops to the right. I still think the 1992 election was a clerical error, and we actually won it!

The only remaining issue to examine in this survey of the effect of Thatcherism on the left is whether it represented a serious setback or a terminal defeat. This apparently fine distinction matters profoundly because it affects the subsequent orientation of New Labour, and the prospects or otherwise of a genuine revival of the left. For Martin Jacques, the left was exhausted and 'Labour was really a bust flush'.[26] He freely admits that this central theme of the magazine contributed to the early development of New Labour. Stuart Hall, however, says he never said the left was dead:

> I thought that it had to get out of this notion that the electoral cycle would swing Keynesianism and Fabianism back into power; that we might be submerged but if we held our breath long enough we'd go back to 1975 ... I wanted to disconnect the automaticity of 'society is changing, therefore socialism is dead'. It was Thatcher's objective to get us to think there is no alternative.

Moments within Thatcherism

Whether we think that Thatcherism seriously wounded or actually killed off the British left, there were certain key moments when especially effective blows were delivered. For many the first sign that the tide of public opinion had been turned decisively was the Falklands War in 1982. Until then, the hegemony (in its full, Gramscian meaning of 'common sense') of Thatcherism had not been fully established, and there was still widespread popular resistance to its neo-liberal or monetarist economics. Mass unemployment was still being seen as a mark of government incompetence – under the criteria of the social-democratic consensus – rather than a necessary, restructuring, disciplinary tool for a capitalist economy. The Falklands war, and Thatcher's subsequent comfortable re-election in 1983, changed all that. But again the left was largely oblivious to the momentous shifts in popular feeling. Sally Davison was then working at CND. 'We set up an ad-hoc anti-Falklands war campaign. A friend in Labour CND told me that, canvassing for the 1983 general election, if people said they supported the war you didn't say anything because it was such a vote-loser.'

The next significant moment for Thatcherism was the miners' strike of 1984/85, which can now be clearly seen as the last gasp of old-style industrial militancy (Hobsbawm's 'syndicalism') in Britain. It was also the most significant, classically 'conjunctural' moment in recent British history – to deploy Gramsci's analytically fertile distinction between the 'epochal', the deeper permanent shifts within a society, and the 'conjunctural', the day-to-day to-and-fro of political and cultural discourse, some of which contributes to the formation of the epoch but much of which disappears with little trace. At this moment class-based political conflict briefly shifted into higher gear.[27] At the time, it felt like a genuinely unpredictable confrontation between the 'authoritarian populist' state and important and potent (both numerically and mythologically) sections of the population. It could still 'go either way', which is what made the actual conduct of the strike so important.

Alan Lawrie remembers 'at the time realising that there were a whole load of people who were passionately for the miners, and a whole load who were passionately against, but a big majority in the middle who were undecided, and didn't feel at all connected to the issue.' It was at this point that Thatcherism moved from its normal stance of 'war of position', a kind of civil trench warfare, to a more overt and active 'war of manoeuvre', most graphically represented by the violent invasion and occupation of the pit villages by the semi-militarised and nationally co-ordinated police. Most of my interviewees were heavily involved in solidarity and fund-raising for the strike, but had a deep sense of foreboding and a particular concern about the NUM's refusal to hold a national ballot, which they felt deprived the whole movement of wider democratic legitimacy. Janice Robinson remembers 'buckets out at Ridley Road market, donating food. That was up front. Behind the scenes there was consternation. What the fuck is going on? Why isn't there a ballot? They would have won it initially. It could have turned out completely differently.'

Andy Wood maintains that the infrastructure of support for the strike was 'built on the organisational structures of the Labour Party', despite official Labour Party ambivalence towards the strike. 'The Labour left weighed in very strongly on the side of the miners, and in those days we ran the constituencies. The idea that the organisational structures of the party might lend themselves to an industrial struggle against the state was quite logical.' It is some measure of the scale of the left's political defeat represented by the miners' strike that this 'might seem wholly bizarre today'. Actual involvement in support for the strike itself is nonetheless remembered fondly, and as an occasion for personal and collective discovery and creativity. Sally Davison was involved in 'a holiday scheme in South Essex for miners' kids, and it was so enjoyable. It was just for four weeks but it was very intense. You could think this is great, all these people helping out, but you knew it was going to lose, so it was also very depressing.'

One source of consolation for the defeat of the strike was the continuing 'municipal activism' of the Greater London Council under Ken Livingstone and in other councils, notably Sheffield. But not everyone felt positive about the GLC. Janice Robinson recalls that 'some people in the (Communist) Party gravitated towards Ken Livingstone, and others were repulsed by him. I thought the GLC was ghastly … the loony leftism was wrong, it was alienating people, but it was like a fast-moving train, and nobody could pull the communication cord'. When Thatcher abolished the GLC, Janice 'was pleased to see it go because I hated Livingstone so much'. This third moment of high Thatcherism, the abolition of the GLC (and just as significantly and perhaps more tragically the abolition of ILEA, the pioneering education authority), could be seen as the final blow to the British political left, and to the organisational foothold in municipal government it had sought to establish as a 'base' of resistance and revival following successive national electoral defeats. Following on from the quasi-imperial adventure of the Falklands, and the re-assertion of national 'authoritarian populist' order after the defeat of the miners, it represents the final, symbolic and actual, closing-down of the left's political space and options, and the entrée to Thatcherism's rampant, late-1980s, full bloom.

The international context – Thatcherism goes global

Stuart Hall argues that the onset of Thatcherism in the mid-1970s can now be seen as the beginnings of globalisation on a neo-liberal model, an attempt to transcend the limitations imposed upon capitalism by the Labourist welfare state, and in strictly economic terms, a resolution of its latest crisis of profitability. In this sense, Thatcherism always had an international purpose, especially when allied to the privatising, deregulating crusade of Reaganomics in the USA, and drew upon a range of wholly un-English inspirations, most notably the American economist Milton Friedman and the Austrian philosopher Friedrich Hayek. We should also note in passing that the 'defeat of communism' was an explicit foreign policy objective all along. This was given a symbolic boost by the Soviet invasion of Afghanistan in 1979, and subsequent jihadist Mujaheddin resistance, which gave the young Thatcherites a quasi-internationalist cause and a set of 'freedom-fighters' all of their own. These people – many now Tory MPs and grandees – were often to be found masterminding 'ultra-libertarian' causes like the legalization of prostitution and drugs. They seized control of the Federation of Conservative Students from the 'wets' in 1980/81, casting themselves quite consciously and explicitly as 'militants of the right' (one of them, Brian Monteith, has 'bluetrot' as his e-mail address). In the late 1980s, these long-held cold war policy objectives appeared to come to pass with the collapse of the Berlin wall, and of the 'actual existing socialist' regimes in Eastern Europe, and two years later the end of the Soviet Union.

What is interesting, from the point of view of left-wing history, is the way this international triumph of the right exposed the deep, long-established fault-lines in the British left's attitude towards the Soviet Union. Pat Devine – then embroiled in the three-sided dispute within the dying Communist Party of Great Britain between long-time Euro-communists like himself, the central (and centrist) leadership, and those few 'Leninists' remaining – recalls that the leadership 'were not fully-fledged Euro-communists, and they hadn't really thought through the positions like we had'.

For Andy Wood in the Labour Party, 'Obviously, the really shattering experience was what happened in 1989, with Tiananmen Square and the end of the Berlin Wall …'. Again, this caused divisions on the left, some of them surprising. Andy recalls being 'delighted' by it:

I remember having a massive bust-up with a friend of mine who was in the (orthodox Trotskyist) International Marxist Group, who described the 1989 revolutions as the worst defeat for the working class ever. I thought it was great, because I'd been influenced not by a classical Trotskyist Marxism but something closer to the SWP. Given the choice, I'd rather have bourgeois capitalism than state capitalism. It took everyone by surprise, and all the more in 1991, when the Soviet Union collapsed.

New times, new contingencies

If the story so far is one of left-wing division and disorientation, and the closing down of political space and options, we should also note that like any destructive force Thatcherism opened up new, and in some cases, honourable political possibilities. Sally Davison echoes Stuart Hall: 'The thing about Thatcherism was that it was a politics that artic- ulated itself to the new times, but you could also develop another kind of politics that gave you another way of relating to new times. Thatcherism was a very smart response, but it wasn't the only response.' This refers to the 'New Times' analysis, which was championed by *Marxism Today* in the late-1980s, and drew heavily on 'cultural' analysis of such phenomena as post-modernism, the shift towards consumer and service capitalism, and above all, theories associated with 'post- Fordism'.[28] This notion, derived from and supposedly superseding the Gramscian term 'Fordism', posited a move away from mass, automated, industrialised forms of production and towards a decentralised, partici- patory and potentially liberating 'knowledge economy'.[29] There was also an argument, closely allied to new developments in sexual politics, that there were pleasures to be had in the new forms of consumption and ostentation, and that if the left was to regain any popular credi- bility, it had to recognise 'the politics of fun'.

Stuart Hall now feels this went too far: 'there was that odd moment, when the critique went overboard, when we almost hero-ized consumption and designer capitalism, in an effort to get in with the new forms'. A repeated criticism of *Marxism Today* throughout the 1980s was that in attempting to delineate what Thatcherism was, it became mesmerised and on occasions plainly excited by what Martin Jacques still calls its 'power and strength'. Pat Devine feels 'there's no doubt that the radicalism of Thatcherism was something Martin found quite exciting, possibly even appealing, and you can see why!' This excitement is not too far removed from Karl Marx's sense of awed, horrified wonder at the ruthless dynamism of British capitalism in its most adventurous, mid-Victorian phases. For Neal Lawson:

> The upside of *Marxism Today* was that it defined Thatcherism, as this different sort of beast with some sort of hegemonic project. The downside was that it destroyed the left even further. We had to adapt to Thatcherism, rather than think we could ever take it on. Having to face up to something which wasn't just the normal swing of the pendulum of British politics, but was something qualitatively different, was both helpful and devastating.

He goes on to paraphrase the *MT* 'New Times' thesis, especially the version espoused by Geoff Mulgan and Charles Leadbeater, as 'Isn't capitalism changing and developing in interesting ways, and aren't there spaces in that for doing interesting things?' This recognition of change within capitalism, not all of it bad, coupled by some with a certain sense of political realism, gave rise to a search for new alliances and forms of cooperation. Some of this drew inspiration from the Euro-communist notion of 'the broad democratic alliance', first advanced in the 1977 revision of the CPGB programme *The British Road to Socialism.*

Stuart Hall attributes at least some of the improvement in the social status of women, black people and homosexuals to the 'new times': 'There is a sense in which Thatcherism enabled these things to happen, in breaking down some of the bureaucratic nature of the Labourist welfare state, with its clientism, its Fabianesque approach of the middle classes doing good to the working class.' For Peter Molyneux, our token ex-Tory, political choices were directly influenced by sexuality – 'I knew it was easier to be gay in the Tory Party than the Labour Party. It was easier then to be gay on the slightly far left (which is where he went next), and I've always hated beards, so how could I join the Labour Party in the 1980s?' Of course, and deeply ironically, one of the most prominent casualties of this anti-Labourist historical thrust was the ('militant labourist') Communist Party itself, still underwriting *Marxism Today*, and by 1989 adopting 'New Times', albeit half-heartedly by all accounts, as the theme of its own latest, short-lived programme.

Janice Robinson, who let her CP membership lapse in the late 1980s, sums up the gains and losses of Thatcherism for women as follows:

> Women are doing incredibly well now. I know there are still barriers. I don't really like what I see. Capitalism has incorporated it all. I like the fact that some of the more austere elements of feminism have gone, like not being allowed to wear make-up or shave your armpits. For some women who needed to shave their legs, it was miserable! When I look at some of the things girls wear now, I think that feminism devastated my teenage years, having to wear such horrible clothes.

Perhaps this gives us some clue to the way capitalism has now closed off some of the political possibilities or 'contingencies' of the 1980s/90s 'New Times', and, as Janice says, 'incorporated it all'. When I interviewed David Purdy, I read to him a quote from his own 1977 book co-written with Mike Prior, *Out of the Ghetto*: 'Capitalism can offer a perspective of private material prosperity. Yet accompanying this perspective is its twin, a set of social relationships whose poverty and fragmentation matches the increasing levels of private affluence'.[30] David now feels this view …

> has been spectacularly vindicated, with commodification. Capitalism's relentless expansion has completely distorted the other three sectors, the public sector, the household sector and the voluntary sector. This is 'crowding out' by capital of social possibilities, and that has to do with people's freedom. The societies we live in now are very stifling, even compared with 25 years ago. One can almost talk about a kind of market totalitarianism.

The continuities and discontinuities of Thatcherism

If we accept that the ideological apparatus of Thatcherism is still largely intact, we need to identify the threads of continuity over these last thirty-odd years. How have we got from Thatcher's election as Tory leader in 1975, through her unceremonious deposing in 1990, up to the inglorious New Labour episode and beyond, which finds the political left even more disorientated than ever? We also need to note the discontinuities of Thatcherism, the ways in which it has had to adapt and mutate, as must all successful 'hegemonic' political/ideological projects and 'historic blocs' (Gramsci's beautifully malleable concepts of how social groupings construct and maintain dominance and directive leadership). For Stuart Hall, 'Thatcherism is the opening of the neo-liberal transformation of British politics, insofar as neo-liberalism becomes the dominant discourse. Thatcherism is the orientating moment, and in that sense, there's continuity.' However:

> I'm not entirely sure that neo-liberalism fully expresses what's happening now. I mean the marketisation of everything, privatisation as the only efficient form of economic organisation, markets as the only test of value, the complete demolition of the notion of the public as an independent realm, of the public interest as a value which can be given effective force in how society is organised. We live in a one-dimensional world. Everybody believes that is how the world works; the BBC believes that, critics believe that, the *Guardian* believes that. It is the common sense, and the New Labour project is intrinsically part of that.

There is a conscious, theoretical design in this 'project', Hall says: 'New Labour was "Hayeked" as thoroughly as Thatcherism was. Hayek said you can't measure the public good. All you can know is what markets produce out of individuals. That's what Blair believes.' For Sally Davison, Thatcherism 'has been kept alive and nurtured by Blairism … if you spend all your time in office pushing the market, denigrating institutions of any sort, people are swayed. There's nothing to challenge people's look-after-number-one attitudes.' This is hardly surprising if we accept, with Martin Jacques, that New Labour was founded on the assumptions that 'the left is exhausted and Thatcherism is hegemonic'. These continuities derive partly from New Labour's timidity, what Jacques calls 'the politics of pessimism, that it's never really tried to do anything apart from hyperbole … they say they'll do what will work, which is of course almost always an argument in favour of the private rather than the public'.

Neal Lawson on the extant Labour left uses the same term – 'they have an essentially very pessimistic view of the electorate, of what middle England will tolerate … I've always equated New Labour with people who gatecrash a party, then stand in the kitchen waiting to be thrown out.' For Lawson:

the crucial thing about New Labour is that it's bought globalisation, decided there's nothing you can do about it. Social Democracy is about making markets the servants of people … what New Labour has done is inverted that, and tried to make people the servants of markets. You can't control this global beast, so what you try to do is equip people to operate in a global market. You make them competitive and employable … Let's renew and revive the state, not to provide welfare, but to provide employability.

The orientation of Thatcherism was summed up at the time, by Andrew Gamble and others, in the formula 'free economy/strong state'.[31] Perhaps now we should look at it a little more closely, and differentiate between the functions of the state, at least into a two-part 'hard/soft' polarity, to reflect the duality of Gramscian hegemony: dominance and leadership, coercion and consent. It was clearly the 'hard state' which Thatcherism strengthened and, at key strategic points like the miners' strike, enthusiastically deployed, while the 'soft state' of health, education, social services and social security was steadily pared back to its directive and disciplinary essentials (always of course a part of their Fabianesque 'welfare state' conception, but until then offset by social-democratic egalitarianism, liberal mutualism, still vigorous 'productivism' and trade unionism). It is this 'soft state' which has been rehabilitated by New Labour with large amounts of money and 'managerialist' rhetoric, 're-grafted' onto the social relations fundamentally altered by Thatcherism, and used to regain popular consent for the 'common sense' of neo-liberal market capitalism, which had faltered in the last years of Tory government, especially after the enforced withdrawal from the ERM on 'Black Wednesday' in 1992.

But this is a New Labour state with its disciplinary, 'dominant-coercive' role kept intact and in some crucial ways enhanced, especially in their 'New Deal' and 'Welfare to Work' initiatives; and its 'old Labour' redistributive, equalising and enabling role kept firmly in its pre-Thatcher, historical closet (public spending was massively increased in the New Labour years, in order to retool and re-energise a range of state institutions, but much of it simply disappeared in increased staff salaries and arcane accounting manoeuvres). The extensive involvement of just these market forces in the provision of 'soft state' services, under the aegis of Public-Private Partnerships and the Private Finance Initiative (PFI), or more bluntly 'outsourcing' and 'cherry-picking', completes this circular process and the refreshment by New Labour of neo-liberal hegemony. The 'welfare state' has been increasingly colonised by the 'business state', partly as a source of new profits but also as a way of imposing 'market discipline' on the public sector.

Stuart Hall has detected the same adaptation of 'hard' Thatcherism to a more viscous and penetrating New Labour form of 'soft' statism. This transmutation consists of the historical shift which begins with Thatcher's withdrawal of the state from the economy to enable 'freedom of enterprise, and of the play of market forces', with a residual and reinforced coercive power to counter any popular resistance from the 'enemy within'. It culminates in use of the state to enlist all sections of the population into the new consumer-led and service-orientated capitalist economy. The diminished and refocused national state in Britain and much of the rest of 'the west' now intervenes merely to populate globalisation with local (and loyal) consumers and service-providers. Its employees are all now, to some degree, globalisation's emissaries and functionaries.

Hall says:

> In the Thatcher/Reagan period, neo-liberalism meant the minimal State. It doesn't mean that any longer. It means no state interference in the economy, but lots of state interference in everything else. It's the rediscovery of 'active government', which comes from other sources, the whole transformation of public policy in the States, which mimics the market. It's part of managerialism, to bring to the management of the state the same techniques which work when you're managing a small firm. There's the term 'governance', which means active government at a distance ... taking responsibility for the overall scene within which government is operating. Government is literally what the administration actively does, and governance is spin, the softening-up of the general terrain.

We might call this hybrid 'State Thatcherism' – a consolidation, stabilisation and institutionalisation of Thatcherism's revolutionary impulses – and observe its effects across the whole field of New Labour government policy. This is what united the supposedly different visions of Tony Blair and Gordon Brown, from Sure Start

and the New Deal for Communities, through ASBOs and the drive
to neighbourhood policing, to crackdowns on 'asylum-seekers' and
'terrorists', and the marketisation of higher education and other
public services. It also accounts for New Labour's determination to
reform the financing and administration of the public services,
usually in ways which create new opportunities for private finance
and service industries; what Will Hutton called 'privatisation by
stealth'.[32]

There is some residue of Labourism in all this, which has required
what Hall now calls further 'modifications' to Thatcherism:

> The fact that New Labour is coming from the social democratic
> tradition does mean that its politics is different, because it always has
> to address that part of its constituency which hasn't locked into the
> new message. Thatcherism could fight them to a standstill, and fully
> intended to break the unions. New Labour is a different politics,
> what Gramsci called transformism of a passive revolution, the slow
> re-making of one thing into something else. It's part of Clintonian
> triangulation, you borrow from everything, you create a mish-mash
> Third Way, which is neither one thing nor the other. Elements of
> that programme are what has forced New Labour to take on the
> reforms of the public sector as a central issue, but then they think
> about it in a neo-liberal way, so reform becomes marketisation, but
> they can't leave the public services behind.

Other odd strands of Labourism abide, even into the supposedly post-
New Labour era, which Hall describes as 'habits of compromise with
the existing system. Labourism had a continuous habit of being
obliged to let capitalism work, and seeing what you can get out of it
– a certain, subaltern perspective'. Another of these continuing habits
of Labourism is 'loyalism to whatever the leadership is doing. New
Labour certainly has that, for example the abject obeisance of the
backbenchers!' There are also strong, lingering elements of Fabian
paternalism and moralism in New Labour social policy, most obviously in the drive to get single mothers and incapacitated men from
Welfare to Work (still 'the emotive image of the scrounger', Hall's
1978 'new folk devil'). Overall, however, the admonition of the poor
has remained relatively incidental to the main thrust of New
Labourism, and serves more as a warning to the still comfortably off

majority. That main thrust is an accommodation to the supposed realities of globalisation and an instructive or disciplinary approach to the British people represented by the concept of 'State Thatcherism'. Ironically, this analysis of recent British history lends itself to a highly traditional Marxist account of dialectical development, with Labourism posited as the thesis, Thatcherism as the antithesis, and New Labour as the synthesis. 'Con-Lib'-ism, which so far consists of a slightly more vigorous and unrestrained New Labourism, with Cameron and Clegg simply doing more quickly what Brown and Darling would have done, represents a further 'transformist' adaptation, another link in the chain.

There is one final, long-term effect of Thatcherism to note, if we are to understand what has happened to British politics, and gain some sense of what might yet supersede New Labourism. This is the effect on the Conservative Party itself of being used as the base for such a powerful, petty bourgeois, neo-liberal campaign of 'regressive modernisation' and 'authoritarian populism'. The effects on party membership are plain enough, declining rapidly, actually as well as figuratively aging and dying; the average age of Conservative Party members was reported in 2005 to be 69 and still rising (Labour Party membership has, under New Labour, taken an even steeper dive), for all Cameron's widely publicised but highly localised attempts at 'modernisation'.[33] As Simon Jenkins argues, Thatcherism represents an ideological as well as organisational blow to the Conservative tradition.[34] For Martin Jacques, still working from the *Marxism Today* couplet of exhausted left and hegemonic Thatcherism, a central factor in the rise of New Labour was

> the crisis of the Tory Party ... What Thatcherism did, by her victory and defeat of the traditional Tories, meant the Tory Party had nowhere to go after she became deeply unpopular and went. It couldn't go back to One Nation Toryism. It had become a strangely ideological party, and it's taken all this time for them to discover that they should be entirely pragmatic and ruthless about electability. Until this point, ideology has always been put ahead of it, which is extraordinary when you think about it.[35]

Again, there is an instructive contrast between Thatcherism and New Labour, if we still view them as separate, albeit successive, political projects. For Mark Perryman, 'Thatcher offered a political ideology, which then disorientated the right when she was no longer leader. All Blair has done is disorientated the left, he hasn't offered a political ideology which you could then be part of, or even in some ways critique.' [36] Another way to put this might be that while Thatcherism hegemonised British society, New Labour has merely hegemonised the Labour Party. This then raises the question of what follows New Labour. Martin Jacques asks 'After the defeat of Blair, where is New Labour going to go? How will it recuperate? What will it be? What remains of the Labour Party? What are its well-springs? How much is it still in touch with what it was? Can it draw on that? I don't know, but I do profoundly believe that New Labour was the defeat of the Labour Party.'

There is only one surviving, vigorous ideological strand in British politics, culture and society, beneath the competing managerialisms, spin and rhetorical froth which takes up much of the daily, party political shouting match; and that is Thatcherism. Most of my interviewees, when asked for their view of the future, anticipate some kind of Tory revival, most probably on the basis of some sort of new, rejuvenated Thatcherism; what Stuart Hall anticipated in 1987 as 'lots more third, fourth and fifth generation Thatcherites, dry as dust, sound to a man, waiting to take her place'. It will be driven not so much by the spirit of vengeance which Richard Sennett detected in Thatcherism first time around, but a desire for retribution which picks up on the popular mood of shame and distaste for the 'binge' of consumption and acquisition associated with the New Labour years, underpinned by a certain taste for austerity which has always been part of the story the English like to tell about themselves.

These dust-dry Thatcherites have been waiting quite a long time now, patiently or not so patiently, within or beyond the Conservative Party, in their mansion flats, suburban villas and country houses. They are culturally offended by some of Cameron's New 'Notting Hill' Conservatism – specifically the gloss and the spin and youthfulness borrowed from New Labour – but, like a proud but bemused uncle, they are prepared to indulge the youngsters if it provides electoral success and lets them 'get on with business'. If it doesn't, they will look for, and help to create, a more congenial vehicle, which will be even more antithetical to the principles and objectives of the political left; even if only an electorally resurgent Conservative Party which no longer needs its Lib Dem coalition partners. New Labour is widely being declared dead; in the grand sweep of British political history, it's more as if it never really happened.

Notes

1. S. Hall, *Hard Road to Renewal*, passim.
2. E. Hobsbawm, collected in *The Forward March of Labour Halted?* (London 1981).
3. G. Andrews, *Endgames and New Times*, passim.
4. R. Williams, *The Forward March of Labour Halted?*, pp142, 152.
5. S. Hall, 'The Great Moving Right Show', collected in *The Hard Road to Renewal.*
6. S. Hall, 'The Great Moving Right Show', *Hard Road to Renewal*, p38.
7. This section is based on contemporary interviews with around 30 people who were involved in politics in this period; they are not in any sense 'representative', just interesting.
8. M. Prior, personal interview, 18 June 2004.
9. D. Purdy, personal interview, 6 January 2004.
10. S. Hall, personal interview, 12 January 2004.
11. J. Chapman, personal interview, 22 April 2004.
12. A. Lawrie, personal interview, 17 June 2004.
13. P. Molyneux, personal interview, 16 April 2004.
14. A. Wood, personal interview, 28 April 2004.
15. P. Devine, personal interview, 6 January 2004.
16. S. Hall, 'Gramsci and Us', collected in *The Hard Road to Renewal*, passim.
17. R. Sennett, interviewed in S. Gunn & R. Bell *Middle Classes* (London 2002), p178.
18. E. Hobsbawm, *Forward March of Labour Halted?*, p13.
19. R. McKibbin, *Ideologies of Class* (Oxford 1991), p182.
20. J. Robinson, personal interview, 25 July 2004.
21. S. Davison, personal interview, 13 October 2004.
22. M. Rustin, *Out of Apathy – the first New Left* (London 1989).
23. T. Benn, interviewed by E. Hobsbawm, *The Forward March of Labour Halted?*, p84.
24. H. Pelling, *A Short History of the Labour Party*, pp199, 200.
25. T. Benn, interviewed by E. Hobsbawm, *Forward March of Labour Halted?*, p86.
26. M. Jacques, personal interview, 12 December 2003.
27. *SPN*, p177; R. Samuel (ed.), *The Enemy Within* (London 1986); H. Beynon (ed.), *Digging Deeper* (London 1985); B. Fine & R. Millar, *Policing the Miners Strike* (London 1985); D. Peace *GB84* (London 2004).

28. S. Hall & M. Jacques (ed.), *New Times* (London 1989).
29. *SPN*, 'Americanism and Fordism', pp217/316.
30. D. Purdy & M. Prior, *Out of the Ghetto*, p37.
31. A. Gamble, *The Free Economy and the Strong State – the Politics of Thatcherism* (London 1988).
32. W. Hutton, 'How Big Money is Stitching up the NHS', in *The New Labour Reader*, eds. Chadwick & Heffernan (Cambridge 2003), p155.
33. *Daily Telegraph*, 20 April 2005.
34. S. Jenkins, *Thatcher and Sons*.
35. M. Jacques, personal interview, 12 December 2004
36. M. Perryman, personal interview, 12 April 2005.

4. The Abuses of Gramsci: 'Post-Marxism', Postmodernism and Cultural Studies

The undisputed pinnacle of British Gramscian scholarship was the *Selections from Prison Notebooks*, published in 1971. A few years later Tom Nairn wrote: 'What counts therefore is following Gramsci's example within our own society, employing the innumerable clues and implications of the Prison Notebooks to do so'.[1] *SPN* editor Geoffrey Nowell Smith wrote at about the same time: 'There can be no point in trying to "apply" Gramsci's description of a historically remote situation to situations such as ours today'.[2] This dissonance between Gramsci's own writings and their contemporary application has cropped up regularly in modern academic Gramscism. The most recent attempt to resolve it was Adam Morton's elaboration of Gramsci's 'absolute historicism': 'historicists reject any claim to absolute or transhistorical values by demanding that ideas must be analysed in relation to historical circumstances and assessed in terms of the particular context in which they arise'.[3] In this reading, an attempt to rescue Gramsci from both the arid 'structuralism' of Althusser and the pop shine of 'culturalism', history provides thematic continuity and a final guarantee of authenticity and relevance.

Political conflict over Gramsci was rather less measured. During the 1970s, British debates around Gramsci began to divide between contrasting political claims to his legacy, made by competing sections of the notoriously fractious British left. So we got the 'revolutionary' Gramsci of the factory council years set against the 'reformist' Gramsci in prison. The 'activist' Gramsci was most strongly promoted by Pluto Press, then still the publishing arm of the Socialist Workers Party, which was beginning to lay claim to the 'true revolutionary' legacy of the early 'pre-Stalinist' Communist Party. Pluto's most prominent and substantial Gramscian title was *Proletarian Order* (1975) by Gwyn A. Williams, who by this stage was dismissing his much more rounded and balanced earlier work on Gramsci as 'wrong-headed and in a sense irrelevant'.[4] The book itself contains much fascinating and insightful material, especially on the factory council movement, but it is heavily conditioned by its contemporaneous political overlay. For the more esoteric neo-Trotskyists, Alex Callinicos supplied a deeper duality in Gramsci's thought, between its early Crocean idealism and later hard-nosed Leninism; Callinicos drew heavily on Althusserian critiques of Gramsci's 'historicism'.[5]

The 'reformist' (or perhaps more accurately, 'defeatist') Gramsci was represented by the Communist Party of Great Britain, which found in the Prison Notebooks a rich theoretical basis for the 1977 revision of its programme *The British Road to Socialism*, its creative accommodation with liberal democracy, and its broader Euro-communist reorientation. Though Thompson argues with some force that the revised *BRS* represented 'a modification of outlook rather than a fundamental alteration', and it did indeed retain much of the party's traditional perspectives, the document did at least indicate an underlying process of change with considerable if short-lived momentum, powered in large part by Gramsci.[6] This included the abandonment of previously sacrosanct formulations such as 'the dictatorship of the proletariat' and any prospect of violent overthrow of the state; and a critical acceptance of parliamentary democracy and a range of objects and sites of 'pre-figurative struggle' previously derided as 'reformist'.[7] In large measure this dissection of Gramsci – into revolutionary and reformist – simply expressed the opposing readings of the contemporaneous political situation and its prospects for the extra-parliamentary activist British left, and furnished it with a new source of (often artificially) counter-posed rhetorical flourishes, slogans and mantras. The far left retained their subjective faith in proletarian revolution – 'optimism of the will' – while the CPGB had objectively accepted – 'pessimism of the intellect' – that in an advanced capitalist democracy like Britain it was practically impossible.

The Gramsci represented in *New Left Review* – by that stage closely aligned with the more thoughtful 'Fourth International' Trotskyism of the International Marxist Group – was a quite different character to the one that stalked the corridors and columns of the Communist University of London and *Marxism Today*, or for that matter the factory picket lines and student occupations of the SWP. The *NLR* Gramsci was recast as a 'continental Marxist' alongside Lukacs, Benjamin, Adorno and Arendt, partly venerated and partly dismissed.[8] *NLR*'s interest in Gramsci was book-ended by 'Soviets in Italy' and eight long years later Anderson's 'The Antinomies of Antonio Gramsci' (see p40). Anderson's later critique was taken by CPGB intellectuals as an attack on Gramsci's novelty and distinctiveness, and hence on their own 'Euro-communist' analyses of the contemporary world. The most curious aspect of this uneasy intellectual standoff between the CPGB and *NLR* over Gramsci's corpus was that Hoare and Nowell Smith, the editors of the classic *Selections from Prison Notebooks* published by the CPGB's publishing house Lawrence and Wishart, were themselves longstanding *NLR* associates and regular contributors.

The 1970s plethora of competing 'Gramscisms' is hardly surprising given the 'fecund but cryptic' nature of much of his writings, especially the prison notebooks, which lend themselves readily to differing and sometimes conflicting interpretations.[9] The circumstances in which they were being digested, thirty years the other side of the Second World War, were dramatically different from the circumstances in which they had been composed between 1929 and 1934. Gramsci himself had warned that 'the content of posthumous works [which is what the *SPN* were, with their tortuous history of selection, editing and interpretation] has to be taken with great discretion and caution, because it cannot be considered definitive but only as material still being elaborated and still provisional'.[10] While this process of elaboration was taking place within a vigorous and relatively healthy political left, textual authenticity and theoretical discipline could be imposed by the prerogatives and lessons of practical action. But once the British left began its precipitous decline and withdrawal, from the mid-1970s onwards, reading Gramsci himself rather fell out of fashion and 'Gramscism' in all its varieties lost its moorings. On into the 1980s, Gramsci was appropriated by the burgeoning academic discipline of cultural studies. The Marxist (and arguably Leninist) 'historical materialist' Gramsci seemed to disappear altogether.[11]

Was Gramsci a Leninist?

Gramsci's relationship to Lenin, at least on a theoretical basis, had been a central issue in post-war debate in Italy itself, especially within the resurgent PCI, which was much troubled by its relationship with both the Soviet Union and the new social democratic settlement across Western Europe. Was Gramsci a Leninist? From this historical distance, the question doesn't seem to matter quite so much. For what it's worth, the Prison Notebooks contain numerous complimentary references to 'Ilich' or 'Vilich' – as Gramsci called Lenin to evade undue attention from the prison censor – and his political theories and principles. Meanwhile Lenin, at the Second Congress of the Communist International, explicitly endorsed the judgement of Gramsci's obscure *Torinese* publication *Ordine Nuovo* on the 1919/20 Red Years in Italy, to the considerable chagrin of more exalted, both rightist and leftist, rivals.[12]

But Gramsci was forcibly removed from active politics before 'Leninism' solidified into a fixed body of dogma following Lenin's death – and largely for factional and successional purposes. Stalin ultimately triumphed over Trotsky because in the straitened circumstances of late-1920s Russia he made the more convincing Leninist, before proceeding to destroy most of Lenin's surviving comrades in the purges of the 1930s, culminating in the horrific show-trials, executions and mass deportations of the year of Gramsci's own death far away in Italy.[13] By the onset of the Second World War, the impulses and personnel of the Bolshevik revolution were pretty much exhausted, but Leninist dogma and practice were now deeply rooted in the communist and socialist left; especially so in Britain, where the elitist, anti-democratic approach of 'Marxism-Leninism' suited the small sectarian groups that made up the non-Labour left.

Gramsci and Lenin were contemporaries, communist activists and theoreticians during one of the most turbulent periods of recent history, so they would inevitably share many principles and preoccupations, but Gramsci himself was clear (at least by the time he composed the Prison Notebooks) that conditions in Russia and the West were fundamentally different. Most famously, civil society in the east was comparatively 'primordial and gelatinous', and the state brutally coercive.[14] This accounts for his much broader and richer conception of hegemony, which Lenin and other earlier communist theoreticians had used to denote the more straightforward domination or coercion or dictatorship they confronted and sought to overthrow in their own societies. Gramsci was aware of 'the concept of hegemony in Lenin' but laid much greater emphasis on hegemony as the exercise of leadership or 'direction', enlisting the active consent and limited participation of the led.[15] As Burawoy puts it in one of the most recent sustained considerations of Gramsci's Marxism: 'he thematizes the significance of society – a concept entirely absent in Lenin – for the prosecution of revolution'.[16]

On the other hand, the real historical Gramsci was a committed and consistent Marxist revolutionary from his early adulthood until his death. This helps us resist the tendency to incorporate his thought into other (especially liberal) traditions. He was unusually open and respectful to them – hence his reputation as a 'libertarian' Marxist and his friendly collaboration with the 'revolutionary liberal' Gobetti – but only insofar as he acknowledged their historical place in the intellectual and cultural tradition of the Renaissance and the Enlightenment: 'The working out of the present cannot but continue the past by developing it, cannot but graft itself onto "tradition"'.[17] What he called 'the philosophy of praxis' was the pinnacle of that 'progressivist' tradition so far, because it afforded the means to understand how and why it had developed, and to take charge of the historical process itself.

Marxism was a 'modern historicism', both a guide to action and 'a moment of modern culture', linked conceptually and chronologically to other philosophies. It 'presupposes the cultural past', but those other philosophies had remained the preserve of the ruling elite and their intellectual servants, while the masses remained mired in ignorance and superstition. The 'absolute historicism or absolute humanism' of Marxism could, unlike its philosophical antecedents, become a 'mass philosophy', primarily through the efforts of the 'organic intellectuals' of 'the modern prince' (always, in Gramsci's mind, understood as the revolutionary party).[18] But in doing so, it would incorporate other bodies of thought, 'residues of a philosophy that may have "moments of renewal" and "fresh intellectual splendour", linked to "a dead past that is at the same time a long time dying"'.[19] It may of course be argued that Gramscism is just such a 'residual' philosophy, as Gramsci readily conceded 'the philosophy of praxis' could one day become; such is the occupational risk of 'absolute historicism', whose continuing value can only be tested by its practical relevance to any particular historical situation.

Gramsci's politics can be hard for non-Marxists to digest, not least because they resist populism and espouse a certain hard Rationalist elitism. This has been the focus of both liberal and leftist critiques. Nowell Smith's valiant attempt to argue that Gramsci manages to avoid 'the ideological snares of the elitist/populist dichotomy' notwithstanding.[20] Gramsci's 'humanistic historicism' was also of course the basis for posthumous leftist critiques, most famously Althusser's but also in Italy during the period in the 1970s of what G.A. Williams called 'a quite massive rehabilitation of Bordiga and an equally massive diminution of Gramsci'. Indeed, in some quarters, 'historians go so far as to deny that Gramsci was a Marxist at all'.[21] Gramsci would not be the first or the last Marxist thinker to be subjected to essentially the same critique from the liberal right and the far left.

The turn to Cultural Studies: was Gramsci a Marxist?

Through the 1980s and 1990s, the 'historical materialist' Gramsci only really survived (and then only just) in the writings of Stuart Hall. Throughout this period Hall was applying Gramscian concepts to contemporary circumstances and in the process alerting the rest of us to the truly 'epochal', 'passive revolutionary' character of Thatcherism. He was uniquely attuned to its ideological shape-shifting, its 'translation of a theoretical ideology into a populist idiom', and its instinctive refinement of popular mood into political programme; in this instance, the journey from Hayek and Friedman's originally obscure neo-liberal market utopianism, through an anti-statism derived from popular experience of a bureaucratic, demoralised, ultimately oppressive late-Labourist welfare state, and on into a more wide-ranging anti-collectivism which underpinned the wholesale privatisation and deregulation of late-1980s high Thatcherism.[22] However, Hall's later work was rarely about Gramsci himself, and more often (as Gramsci himself insisted was necessary in every era) sought to make analytical sense of present hard reality through a Gramscian prism. In the meantime, Gramsci was increasingly being deployed in academic rather than political settings, disconnected from his own practical revolutionary experiences and impulses, institutionalised and domesticated, rather like much of the post-1968 political and intellectual left. Stuart Hall himself was making his living and primary reputation in the burgeoning academic field of Cultural Studies, firstly at Birmingham University and then as Professor of Sociology at the Open University.

'Cultural Studies' had begun life as an offshoot of the academic subject of sociology, which by the later 1970s was looking rather tired and stale. The injection of Marxist and other forms of radical theory into the more empiricist and positivist 'study of society' in the 1960s, which had made sociology newly fashionable, had fallen away with the decline of 'class politics'. Initially at least, Cultural Studies was an attempt to revive and re-apply class perspectives, specifically through study of how groups within the working class created their own 'sub-cultures' in order to make sense of their historical experience and mount some kind of resistance – however ineffectual and 'subaltern' – to capitalist exploitation, ideology and control. Its institutional locus was the Centre for Contemporary Cultural Studies at Birmingham University, founded by Richard Hoggart and by the 1970s under the directorship of Stuart Hall. According to Bennett and Kahn-Harris:

> its seminal account of post-Second World War British working class youth (was) *Resistance Through Rituals* (1976). Drawing on the cultural Marxism of Gramsci and Althusser, the CCCS interpreted post-war youth subcultures such as the Teddy boys, mods and skinheads, as pockets of working class resistance to the dominant hegemonic institutions of British society.[23]

The CCCS in the 1970s functioned as a kind of year-round Communist University of London (at CUL's more innovative, *outré* end), pulling together concepts and trends that had never before been combined, and dignifying elements of popular experience that had previously been seen as marginal or superficial. Paul Willis' book *Learning to Labour* was a particular inspiration, as an attempt to explore through the techniques of 'participant observation' how working-class boys were inducted into the mentalities and routines of Labourism and manual work, and how they attempted through humour and petty delinquency to assert their individuality, and condition or at least defer their induction into adulthood drudgery.[24] At that stage, Cultural Studies was fiercely focused on the categories and realities of class. It helped to take the working class beyond both the abstractions of traditional Marxist 'class analysis' and the exclusive focus of labourism on material conditions in the workplace and on electoral routine, and into the far more engaging terrain of style, banter and personality, the 'everyday lives' we all lived and recognised and enjoyed.

However, some of its practitioners were already noting the transformative limitations of subculture, deploying the Gramscian conception of 'subalternity' within its original setting of the capitalist economy; for Clarke et al: 'Subcultures "solve", but in an imaginary way, problems which at the concrete material level remain unresolved'.[25] Others were beginning to see how ruling class hegemony might be refreshed and deepened by sub-cultural challenge; for Hebdige, 'the resistant qualities of any given sub-cultural style are ultimately compromised because of its incorporation and commodification by the fashion industry'.[26] From within the CCCS itself emerged a powerful feminist critique, questioning the applicability of the available sub-cultural theory to the experience of girls and women, which was necessarily more focused on home and family than the workplace or public space. Even within the working class, there were major gender differences in patterns of consumption, cultural expression, interpersonal relationships and behaviour. And some elements of those were themselves reactions against male oppression: McRobbie and Garvey found in 'Teenybopper' culture 'a meaningful reaction against the selective and authoritarian cultures which control girls' lives'.[27]

Later, as the traditional working class was dispersed and class itself fell away as a category of social analysis, the notion of sub-cultural resistance came under fresh fire: it 'rests on the essentialist notion that members of sub-cultures were indeed exclusively or even predominantly working class'.[28] Rather, (for Bennett) 'it could be argued that post-war consumerism offered young people the opportunity to break away from their traditional class-based identities, the increased spending power of the young facilitating and encouraging experimentation with new, self-constructed forms of identity'. Youth culture offered an escape route from class allegiance as well as class oppression. Frith suggested that membership of subcultures might just be a matter of adolescence, passing phases or affectations, and no more significant in themselves than any other source of identity.[29] It could just be 'a bit of fun', a period of pleasure and indulgence before adult responsibility and restraint sets in; or even, within an increasingly consumerist society, a department store of available styles and accessories to be adopted and discarded at will (or rather, whim).

In a more traditionally Marxist critique of cultural studies, David Harris argued that Gramscian applications had facilitated just this shift 'from class struggle to the politics of pleasure'. Harris' critique is largely drawn from the earlier SWP-style 'activist' Gramsci, and downplays conceptions of culture and hegemony in favour of a more Leninist perspective of class domination. He has a point about the steady disappearance of considerations of class within cultural studies, and its displacement by the other categories of the emerging 'identity politics', but in making it he misses the ways in which cultural studies can enrich our understanding of class society. Cultural studies academics cannot be blamed for finding Gramsci interesting and useful, or for the rising popularity of their subject in a period of wide-spread disillusionment with politics and with more traditional academic subjects. The real problems arise when Gramsci is removed from history. With their 'de-historicised' deployment of many of his concepts, in ways and settings very far removed from their origins, cultural theorists eventually moved a long way away from his 'absolute historicism'.

This later, strongly 'culturalist' take on Gramsci began in earnest in 1985, with the best known work of Ernesto Laclau and Chantal Mouffe, *Hegemony and Socialist Strategy*.[30] In retrospect it signifies the decline of applied political Gramscism, the end of its thirty-year heyday. Its famous 'post-Marxist' reading of Gramsci is little more than the wearily familiar sound of academics retreating behind their institutional walls and wrapping themselves up in ever cosier layers of technical, essentially hollow jargon, invariably 'signified' by pompous quotation marks or *announced* in italics. As the American Gramscian T. Jackson Lears observed in the very same year, its 'post-Marxism' was part of a current which looks 'less like part of a satisfactory theory and more like part of a fashionable ideology'.[31] Its lofty dismissal of the importance of class as a social category seems frankly bizarre at a time when the ultimate class-warrior Thatcher was delivering the *coup de grâce* to the tattered remnants of the post-war social democratic consensus and the labourist traditions and institutions of the British working class.

The question raised by Laclau and Mouffe was not simply was Gramsci a Leninist, but was he a Marxist of any kind? Even a cursory reading of what he actually said and wrote, taking the texts of any period after Gramsci's 'Sardist' youth pretty much at random, would establish that he was (Sardism was a Sardinian, anti-Italian nationalism widespread in Gramsci's youth, when he famously wrote a school essay calling for 'the mainlanders to be thrown into the sea!').[32] Gramsci had an abiding awareness of the shaping of historical development by material forces and social relations, and of the 'economic nucleus' to all aspects of human interaction, not to mention a recurring concern with the prospects for a socialist revolution powered by a radicalised and constructive working class; but after reading *Hegemony and Socialist Strategy* you would be forgiven for thinking otherwise. As Burawoy put it many years later, its 'interpretation is that the working class cannot develop an ideology of its own but has to work within the existing ideologies, expanding, elaborating and valorising those that are most consonant with its interests'.[33] If the working class is wholly trapped within capitalism, the left might as well abandon any form of class politics. This is not so much pessimism as fatalism of the intellect.

The then-Trotskyist academic and *NLR* luminary Norman Geras said pretty much the same thing soon after publication.[34] But it didn't stop Laclau and Mouffe's book becoming one of the various 'linguistic turns' into structuralism and post-structuralism and ultimately the arid wastes of postmodernism, where much of our contemporary academic and intellectual 'discourse' takes place. More recently, Peter Ives' *Language and Hegemony in Gramsci* pretty well nailed Laclau and Mouffe. Ives reminds us usefully that Gramsci was himself a linguist and philologist; that many of his historical and political concepts (most importantly hegemony) were partially derived from linguistics, and that language is a vitally important terrain of social conflict. But – and this is what saves us from the obsession with 'text' of structuralism and post-structuralism – it is not the only one, and only attains 'meaning' insofar as it relates to experience, which is profoundly conditioned by the exercise of power and subordination. However, by the time of Ives' publication in 2004 the damage was thoroughly done.[35] The 'post-Marxist' Gramsci was well suited to the 'New Times' of the late 1980s and early 1990s, as the British left became ever more desperate to dislodge or mount any kind of challenge to the truly hegemonic 'project' of high Thatcherism. A 'de-classed' Gramscism found a new appeal and function in a setting of headlong retreat by the traditional left and the onslaught of the revitalised right.

What Hay calls the 'politics of catch-up' required some pretty drastic measures, including widespread 'over-compensation' by the left in jettisoning previous approaches and grasping at new ones.[36] The positive appeal of 'post-Marxism' was that it seemed to offer the basis of a new 'modernising' project, and the prospect of progressive social and political alliances beyond the discredited certainties of an outdated class-centred politics. These were seized upon by professional politicians of the left. Charles Clarke was Neil Kinnock's chief of staff for much of his time as Labour leader. At a chance encounter in 2006 Clarke was keen to stress the importance of Gramsci to the Kinnock 'project'. Quite coincidentally, the *Guardian* reported at around the same time (in yet another profile of John Reid) that Kinnock's advice to any aspiring acolyte at that time was 'Polish your shoes and admire Antonio Gramsci'. The *Guardian* assured us that Reid at least 'devoured the Italian philosopher's writings'.[37] A certain Gramscian 'affectation' was an important part of the Labour modernisers' self-image and sense of purpose.

It is now arguable that the 'centre-left' New Labour never had any recognisably left-wing political content, and that Kinnock's main achievement was to jettison Labour's 'socialist' baggage. For Hay, it 'had moved some time before the 1997 election to a position significantly to the right of the median voter', leaving it the pretty hollow centre of a narrowly electoral project to launch a small group of men and women into successful parliamentary and ancillary careers. In shameless pursuit of 'floating voters in marginal constituencies', they had turned the Labour Party into little more than 'an opportunistic instrument of vote maximization'.[38] A familiar left-wing critique perhaps, with antecedents at pretty much every stage of Labour history, but gaining force as the institutions, culture and social base of Labourism hollowed out, withered and dispersed. Once that process had been completed, with the elevation of New

Labour into government, there was very little further practical use for Gramsci, even as a name to drop.

A 'neo-Gramscism'?

In recent times there has been a small revival of interest in the historical and political Gramsci, at least in academic and intellectual circles, sufficient for the emergence of a distinctive and self-proclaimed 'neo-Gramscism'.[39] In particular, Gramsci has been used to make sense of neo-liberal expansionism and triumphalist 'globalisation'; and just as importantly, of the fact that it has apparently been conducted with the active and enthusiastic connivance of the consuming 'western' masses. Even within 'developing', ex-colonial societies, it requires the active consent and (especially in its manufacturing arm) willing participation of the producing 'subaltern' masses.[40] The search for understanding of this process has provoked a new wavelet of interest and study into the detailed exercise of 'bourgeois hegemony' on a multi-national basis, and the ideological, political and cultural construction of the 'common sense' of contemporary capitalism. These themes have been creatively explored by the School of South Asian Subaltern Studies, whose main thesis 'claims struggles against colonialism were fought on the unseen marshes of Western ideology. The choice between National Liberation and the National Bourgeoisie was an illusory choice, formulated in a moment of decolonizing euphoria'.[41] This approach also draws fruitful inspiration from Frantz Fanon, whose work explored French colonial society and its multiple layers of racism from a decidedly (but almost certainly unknowingly) 'Gramscian' perspective.[42]

In North America, much modern Gramscism derives from the work of Joseph Femia, whose *Gramsci's Political Thought* (1981) was a philosophical work of continuing academic interest but limited immediate political impact.[43] As such it inadvertently set the tone for the period ahead. Femia was especially insightful on the nature and value of Gramsci's 'absolute historicism', maintaining 'that although a theory is certainly linked to the social relations of a particular epoch, some problems are perennial because underlying thoughts about a range of concrete particulars do recur … Ideas may thus transcend their origins although this can only be established by empirical investigation'.[44] Urging some sensible methodological flexibility, Femia argues 'an insistence on historicity is one thing; an *a priori* determination to fossilize all past quite another'.[45]

This has remained a focus of academic controversy, and prompted further flurries about contemporary applications of Gramsci: is he too Italian? Is he too pre-war? Is Italy too 'peripheral'? This has led to what Morton calls an 'austere historicism', which fixes Gramsci firmly in time and space, and attempts to prohibit the application of his ideas 'to events and movements that he neither knew about nor could have anticipated'.[46] It requires, Bellamy argues in the fullest exposition of this 'austerity', 'detailed knowledge of Italian history and culture as well as Gramsci's pre-prison activity in order to appreciate the distinctively Italian dimension and political tradition of his thought'.[47] This is a salutary call for historical accuracy and specificity, but it goes against Gramsci's own conception of 'absolute historicism', which Morton pits against the more 'austere' version and, following Cox, describes as 'conscious of its own relativity but through this consciousness (it) aims to achieve a broader time perspective in order to become less relative'.[48] Ultimately, Morton endorses Hall's call for 'thinking in a Gramscian way', the spirit of the more applied if politically doomed British Gramscism, which returns us thankfully to the wider world.

But even in US academic Gramscism there has been some recognition that bourgeois hegemony has proved remarkably resilient, not to say rudely healthy. This has prompted the classification of at least three separate phases or types of hegemony – the emergent, the dominant and the residual – which reflects the historical dynamism and multifacetedness of the process, and harks back directly to the work of Raymond Williams on culture.[49] The notion of 'dominant' (ultra- or 'turbo'-) hegemony is used to explain the relative novelty and brazen simplicity of the operations and prerogatives of US capitalism, what Gramsci called 'its ultra-modern form of production and of working methods', as well as the failure of any kind of popular socialism to become anything more than 'emergent'. The notion of 'residual' hegemony, among groups which were previously 'dominant' or even 'emergent', also helps to identify and explain persistent cultural forms (e.g. many British 'styles of life' or 'ways of thinking' of all classes) which have outlived their time, place and purpose but linger on in popular mentalities.

Other American Gramscians, including T.J. Jackson Lears, have suggested 'hegemonic cultures placed anywhere on a continuum from "closed" to "open"', to reflect their comparative levels of reliance on coercion and consent.[50] This allows Gramscian insight into societies otherwise summarily disregarded as 'authoritarian' or 'totalitarian', for example Iraq, Toby Dodge's study of which clearly explains why 'winning the peace' in a society built around coercive *and* consensual *Ba'athist* hegemony has proved so much harder than winning the war.[51] Jackson Lears continued to apply Gramscian insights to American history and society – e.g. his analysis of religious bodies as 'mediating institutions which enable the individual to escape absorption by an all-encompassing system' – which illuminates the strength and function of popular 'folk' Christianity among Afro-American and poor white communities.

This latter-day US 'Gramscism' has also sought to challenge simplistic accounts of heroic resistance to class, cultural and racial oppression by stressing the consensual and subaltern elements of hegemony. For Jackson Lears: 'The idea that less powerful folk may be unwitting accomplices in the maintenance of existing inequalities runs counter to much of the social and cultural historiography of the last fifteen years, which has stressed the autonomy and vitality of subordinate cultures'. Oppression by a hegemonic order is no safeguard against collusion, and in fact imposes collusion upon individuals forced to live within it. Sennett and Cobb's *The Hidden Injuries of Class* is cited by Jackson Lears as a distinctly Gramscian take on class oppression – 'workers have internalised a class struggle in their own minds, punishing themselves for their failure to acquire the culture's badges of ability even as they recognise that those badges are often a sham'. These dilemmas are often resolved by 'historical grievances'. Hence, they regard their continuing subjugation as the consequence 'not of exploitation but of their forefathers' "ignorance" or "poor doings"' (we might also regard such local explanations as honest 'plain spoken' recognition of the historic political failure of the US labour movements to which Sennett and Cobb's worker-interviewees had belonged). [52] Novels like William Styron's *Nat Turner* have explored, amongst considerable controversy (not least because Styron was white), levels of black complicity in slave societies.[53]

Recent British applications

In the more historically encumbered societies of 'old' Europe, with older and more complex 'national systems' of bourgeois hegemony, the working class has been stronger, more established and better organised, with some level of independent political representation but always subordinate to the prevailing capitalist order. This kind of acquiescence by elite elements of supposedly oppositional forces is for Gramsci a primary mechanism of hegemony, an essential element in the construction of a successful historic bloc, which itself consists in a seamless and barely visible alignment of 'the structures and superstructures' of capitalism such as now prevails across much of the world.[54] In other words, a ruling group gathers around itself an array of subordinate groups in support of the way it wants things run; in the process its own aims and actions become less vulnerable to scrutiny, hidden behind 'popular choice'.

Acceptance of this epochal 'common sense' is largely engineered by the 'transformist' incorporation of opposition elites. The British 'labour aristocracy' – the skilled craftsmen who founded the modern trade union movement – is an obvious historical example.[55] The Blair/Brown-hegemonized Parliamentary Labour Party in government – more consciously and proudly detached from the wider party and 'movement' than ever before in its 100-plus year history – is a more recent example. After the necessary turbulence of the Thatcher years, with their several moments of near-civil war or 'war of manoeuvre', New Labour Britain was 'settled down'. As Genovese observed of American class and race relations, the most successful hegemony is 'a process by which a given ruling class successfully avoids such confrontations'.[56] The violence of early Thatcherism – regular inner-city riots, the miners' strike and its brutal suppression, the constant low rumble of the 'troubles' in Northern Ireland – now seems scarcely credible; and that very incredibility is a testament to the success (and for capitalism necessity) of New Labour transformism.

As a transformist manoeuvre within Thatcherism, New Labour enabled the prevailing ethos of neo-liberalism to absorb new energies and impulses, including those of the 'new social movements' Laclau and Mouffe made much of as the basis for their new 'radical democracy'. In its shift from 'productivism' to 'consumerism', western capitalism has been feminised, multi-cultured, and (rather more problematically) gay-friendly-fied. This is a contemporary variant of a process Raymond Williams first highlighted in a more traditionally 'cultural' setting, to describe how emergent movements are assimilated into the dominant social order.[57] We can now take it further; as Jackson Lears put it with reference to regular raids on Afro-American culture by white liberals: 'Dominant groups can revitalise a hegemonic culture by incorporating what they imagine to be the instinctual vitality of the lower orders'.[58] In our own time and society, 1970s liberation movements have been transformed into twenty-first-century niche-markets. Or as Stuart Hall put it in his own inimitable way, capitalism has devised new means for 'the insertion of the masses in subordinate positionalities within dominant cultural practices'.[59] Thatcherism served 'within its project of regressive modernisation, to appropriate them to a reactionary political agenda and to harness to them the interests and fortunes of specific and limited social interests'.[60] This is where the Gramscian concept of 'subalternity' comes fully into play, to explain the masses' apparent connivance in their own manipulation and exploitation: they are simply expressing their own fundamental lack of power, 'making the best of a bad job', living with 'what is' rather than 'what might be'.

The use here of the term 'masses' is possibly archaic and certainly quaint in the age of 'individualism'. Raymond Williams observed in the mid-1960s that 'the mass is a category intellectuals reserve contemptuously for other people'; twenty-five years later, Dick Hebdige identified as a central component of postmodernism 'the disengagement of the intelligentsia from the masses … abandoning the struggle to construct majorities'. (Hebdige was a key figure in the early days of cultural studies, and took a prominent role in the Birmingham Centre for Contemporary Cultural Studies.)[61] By the 1980s the terms 'mass' and 'masses' were looking decidedly dog-eared.

From here, it was a fairly short step to Charlie Leadbeater's contribution to *Marxism Today*'s 'New Times' debate of 'alternative progressive individualism', not to mention Stuart Hall's late-1980s 'revolution of the subject'. Hall had earlier unequivocally opined that 'identity' is largely imposed by the hegemonic power, but by 'New Times' he was arguing that political change was increasingly a matter of personal choice.[62] By then – the era of 'the linguistic turn' – the unselfconscious, non-apostrophised use of the term 'the masses', like so much other traditional left-wing terminology, was virtually impossible in polite company. We can see here again the political left's leaching of certainty, the retreat from Gramsci's grandiose 'struggle for objectivity', which (in rather less inhibited times) was no less than 'the struggle for the cultural unification of the human race'.[63]

Grandiosity notwithstanding, Gramsci's 'struggle for objectivity' reminds us of the necessity of generalisation, the establishment of objective fact, even if only – and this is where his 'absolute historicism' comes into play again – as an instrument of hegemony. Conversely, the reduction of social reality to 'mere' subjective opinion, however 'revolutionary', is a classically subordinating, hegemonic manoeuvre. Social groups and movements are maintained in a 'subaltern' or subordinate, hence 'subjective' position by a hegemonic power – this is how hierarchical societies are run – even if some of their own elites are admitted into the ruling group's 'historical bloc' as junior allies and functionaries and 'organisers' (the true meaning of the much-misused Gramscian term 'organic intellectuals') of 'common sense': i.e. 'the practical way of creating a collective will' in all its 'ambiguous, contradictory and multiform' character.[64]

An entirely honourable purpose of Hall's 'revolution of the subject' was to establish the value of subjective experience in the historical account, but at a time when the relative power, wealth and status of whole societies of 'subjects' was being radically redistributed, having their personal stories (very much the dominant or 'hegemonic' form in contemporary literature, in the form of memoir and biography) listened to and retold was limited compensation, especially when they could by definition be derided as 'subjective' hence unrepresentative (this is a clear and recognised problem in oral history – which has also boomed in these 'new times' – with its tendency towards what Samuel and Thompson called 'naive realism').[65] In the meantime, as Stuart Hall was amongst the first to establish, Thatcherism was reconstituting 'the masses' in a radically different form, closer in some ways to a mediaeval 'mob' than a disciplined 'proletariat'.

The importance of 'subalternity'

So how does the concept of 'subalternity' help us through this morass of 'subjectivity' and 'decentring'? For a start, it explains how people can seem to choose, 'internalise' and on occasions celebrate their own oppression. As Jackson Lears put it, while the subaltern 'masses' are maintained in 'a condition of moral and political passivity … a contradictory consciousness mixing approbation and apathy, resistance and resignation … they can share a kind of half-conscious complicity in their own victimization'.[66] It is built into the process of everyday social interaction, a condition of existence. For Gramsci, within capitalism – a social system primarily defined by its economic arrangements, and as such profoundly 'economistic' – 'subaltern … activity cannot but be prevalently economic'. In other words, everything has its price, and every social encounter includes some element of financial transaction even if it's not wholly 'polite' to spell it out. This explains the peculiarly 'economic-corporate' character of Labourism – the central binding element (still) of modern British 'subalternity'[67] – and further, the emphasis within the 'new social movements' on the language of individual rights and 'equal opportunities' in the workplace. 'What's in it for me?' or, in its collective, 'socialised' variant, 'What's in it for us?' remains its rallying cry; and is also the principal, 'sectionalist' obstacle to Labour or working class, or even 'new social movement', unity and eventually hegemony.

But these are never simple or unilinear transactions, and they always require some level of give and take. Even (or especially) in Britain, hegemony is a complex process 'which may require selective accommodation to the desires of subordinate groups'.[68] Hegemony requires constant renegotiation, which (for Adamson) 'is bound to be uneven in the degree of legitimacy it commands and to leave some room for antagonistic cultural expressions to develop'.[69] These 'antagonistic cultural expressions' are what passes for much of the 'public discourse' in newspapers and other media, in the popular culture, political and moral affairs of capitalist societies. However 'accommodated' or 'antagonistic', the key Gramscian point about subaltern groups is that without fundamental, organised and purposeful change in the nature of their society and economy they remain subordinate.

Working with Gramsci's central concepts of hegemony and subalternity, and the insights which emerge from their interconnection, we can begin to see how the 'new social movements' – the female, gay, black and minority ethnic portions of 'the masses' – of 1980s and 1990s Britain might find themselves within a process (in Hall's earlier terms) simultaneously 'modernising/progressive' and 'regressive/conservative'. Gramsci had understood well enough and early on the processes of 'individuation' and 'self-actualisation' – key concepts within the new 'identity politics' – but had taken great care to set them in a concrete historical context; in his case, the 1920s communist worker who 'collaborates to "discover", to "invent" original modes of life', at a moment when the very foundations of capitalism were visibly trembling.[70] The process of revolution was for Gramsci always as creative as destructive, and as much about transforming oneself as one's society. In the case of the 1980s/1990s British 'new social movements', individuals were 'discovering' and 'inventing' themselves and their 'original modes of life' ('lifestyles' might be a more apposite translation for this later application) in the context of rampant, unbridled 'high' Thatcherism.

In that broader historical and social context, we can identify what one of the first proponents of postmodernism called 'the new cultural logic of capital ... a prodigious expansion into hitherto un-commodified areas'.[71] If the postmodern era began with the 'market utopianism' of Hayek, Friedman, Sherman and Joseph, what we ended up with is truly shameless market totalitarianism, where everything is for sale at the right price. No part of our lives remains beyond the reach of twenty-first century turbo-capitalism, including our genders, ethnicities, sexualities and pretty much every other aspect of our 'identities'. We are left with very few 'hiding places', and those we have are 'residual' elements of earlier or even pre-capitalist hegemonies: romantic love, family life, religious congregations, 'in kind' economies of favour-trading and commodity-swapping, self-securing neighbourhoods, even 'national' identities and cultures, all under mounting pressure from the new global consumer capitalism. Where once we were exploited for what we produced, we are now manipulated for what we can consume *and* assume by way of personal characteristics or 'personality'. Who we are has replaced what we do as measure and symbol of our social worth, especially as traditional forms of employment disappear. At an even deeper (or, in the peculiar twists of postmodernism, more superficial) level, what we look like to others has replaced what we think and feel in ourselves. We are, in our inescapably social context (there is still 'society'; albeit constantly reconstituted from new relationships and experiences), how we seem. This is a thoroughly postmodern development of 'personal identity', a brutal synthesis of

Arthur Rimbaud's '*je est un autre*' and Sartre's 'Hell is other people', at once terrifying and trivialising.

Work has been replaced by play as the focus of our existence, orchestrated by what André Gorz calls the 'oblivion merchants', as capitalism – the relentless pursuit and exploitation of economic potential – encroaches ever deeper into our personal, private spheres: 'The industrialisation, through home computers, of physical and psychical care and hygiene, children's education or sexual technique is precisely designed to generate capitalist profits from activities still left to individual fantasy. It is leading towards that social *trivialisation* of the most intimate areas of individual behaviour which Jacques Attali has described as the "society of self-supervision".' On the back of this has emerged an entire industry of 'professions of the self', counselling, analysing and 'reflecting back' bruised personalities.[72] In this society of image, of Lacan's constant and wary 'gaze', appearance is everything, which explains the centrality of 'cultural signifiers' like label and brand, and of 'methods of governance' like public relations and 'spin'.[73]

The Gramscian critique of 'post-Marxism' and 'postmodernism'

Stuart Hall's critique of Laclau and Mouffe's 'post-Marxism', and the broader currents of postmodernism within which it located itself, is all the more powerful because of his evident sympathy with elements of its 'discourse'; in particular his 'revolution of the subject'. He understands that 'the personal is political', celebrates the 'superstructures' of culture, politics, ideology and social relations, and recognises the strategic and popular bases of 'the new social movements'. He would support much of the post-Marxists' call for new forms of 'radical democracy'. However, he points out that it is not all quite so new or 'post' as they might claim – they 'continue to stand on the shoulders of the very theories they have just definitively destroyed'.[74] The Marxism they claim to be transcending is of the closed, dogmatic and deterministic form which Marx famously declared made him not want to be a Marxist at all, and which Gramsci branded 'economistic', whether in its Second or Third International guises. It had certainly not gone away by the 1980s, but outside the few remaining 'Marxist-Leninists' in the CPGB and the Labour 'hard left', where it retained a certain secondary nuisance value, it exercised very little real influence in modern Britain.

In Marx and Gramsci, 'the philosophy of praxis' is a much more dynamic, creative and multi-layered approach. For Hall:

> ... relative openness or relative indeterminacy is necessary to Marxism itself as a theory ... Understanding 'determinacy' in terms of setting of limits, the establishment of parameters, the defining of the space of operations, the concrete conditions of existence, the 'given-ness' of social practices, rather than in terms of the absolute predictability of particular outcomes, is the only basis [of a modern, creative, practically useful Marxism].

This, because of its stress on contingency and choice of action, is 'Marxism without guarantees', but like Gramsci it remains recognisably Marxist.[75] The central problem for 'post-Marxism' is that once it purports to tear itself up wholly from its roots, it has no clear place in the world: 'there is no reason why anything is or isn't potentially articulable with anything. The critique of reductionism has apparently resulted in the notion of society as a totally open discursive field'.[76] It ends up acknowledging only the 'super-structural' and detaching itself from any conception of the effects of the economy on society; it is

> reductionism upward, rather than a reductionism downward as economism was ... The discursive position is often in danger of losing its reference to material practice and historical conditions ... Their problem isn't politics but history. They have let slip the question of the historical forces which have produced the present.[77]

1980s post-Marxism turns out to be anti-historical, both a curious echo of Althusser's 1970s 'Marxism is not a historicism' and a precursor to Fukuyama's 1992 declaration of 'the end of history'; and apparently the final triumph of liberal democracy.[78] As such, it represents a protracted and abstruse sigh of resignation from the political left, in headlong retreat from its own introverted dogma and the more recent assault from the ideological right. Its distaste for history also explains the almost total lack of any historical examples in Laclau and Mouffe's work (or current ones for that matter), and its strong sense now of dated-ness (again like Althusser) – which also applies to much of the practice of New Labour and other 'Third Way' political projects, with their facile novelty, wilful superficiality, giddy rhetorical promiscuity and constant, wide-eyed self-reinvention. It also makes Jackson Lears' essay of the same year, 1985, which is packed with fascinating historical examples and covers ostensibly the same terrain of 'cultural hegemony', all the more remarkable.

So much for 'post-Marxism'. Hall's broader critique of the much more influential 'postmodernism' is that it has a decidedly and narrowly American flavour. It

> ... not only points to how things are going in modern culture, but it says first that there is nothing else of any significance – no contradictory forces and no counter-tendencies; and second that these changes are terrific and all we have to do is reconcile ourselves to them ... It's another version of that historical amnesia characteristic of American culture – the tyranny of the New ... There is only the present and all you can do is be with it, immersed in it.[79]

Hall recalls that Marx called this device, usually an ideological function on behalf of a currently dominant force, 'eternalising', and as such a contribution towards hegemony. At the same time, postmodernism represents a loss of faith in progress and modernity, and taps into deep wells of disillusionment and disappointment with much of modern life, thus establishing one of those dynamic contradictions – a 'double shuffle' simultaneously forward- and backward-looking – which elsewhere Hall described as characteristic of the era.[80]

Marshall Berman's *All That Is Solid Melts Into Air* received its first British publication in 1985, the same year as Laclau and Mouffe's *Hegemony and Socialist Strategy*.[81] Berman's work is an extraordinarily broad and fertile contemplation of modernity and the contrary impulses of modernism, which he defines as 'any attempt by modern men and women to become subjects as well as objects of modernisation, to get a grip on the modern world and make themselves at home in it'. Berman is scrupulous in his use of real historical examples and analysis of social relations, unlike Laclau and Mouffe, and in his pursuit of 'an alternative modernism that would assert the presence and the dignity of all the people who had been left out'. This is an alternative to earlier reactionary responses to modernity that were

based on 'the fear of freedom that modernity opens up for every individual, and the desire to escape from freedom by any means possible',
represented most obviously in fascism; and also to contemporary
responses to the supposed exhaustion of modernism.

For Berman, 'Postmodernist social thought pours scorn on all the
collective hopes for moral and social progress, for personal freedom
and public happiness that were bequeathed to us by the modernists of
the eighteenth century Enlightenment'.[82] One of postmodernism's
leading advocates, Jean-Francois Lyotard, went so far as to claim to
have 'lost even nostalgia for the lost narrative', and planted himself
squarely in the perpetual present, in what the sociologist Fred Bloch
called the 'great forgetting' of the late twentieth century.[83] For all its
talk of diversity and de-centring, postmodernism stands revealed as an
ideological softener for neoliberal expansionism. Does this matter?
Very much so, given that the demoralising, 'de-constructive' and
wilfully confusing impulses of postmodernism have done so much to
condition our contemporary 'de-centred' lives, our 'diverse' and
multi-vocal 'public discourses', and our 'multi-cultural', 'poly-valent',
atomised/individualised societies.

'Modernising' Britain

So how might this apply to the politics and ideologies of 'modern'
Britain? If Modernism was an intrinsically political movement,
'modernisation' is itself always a political and cultural act, perhaps the
most central and persistent in ancient, change-resistant societies like
our own. It is not simply a technical or managerial process, but
challenges and seeks to change people, perhaps above all those in
subordinate or 'subaltern' groups who do not have the power to resist
or shape change. It is profoundly political and democratic: is
'modernisation' done to or by people? It also raises questions about
the efficacy of 'change-agents' themselves, above all the state and the
political system. Much post-war British history can be read as a
generally failed attempt by the state to 'modernise' the British people
themselves, or in more technical terms to 're-engineer' the nation's
'human resources'. Reforms in education and training, health and
social services, punishment and incarceration, have all been directed
towards that end, especially under the post-war social-democratic
welfare-statist settlement. Industrial policy and state intervention in

the economy – Crosland's despair at 'wastage of talent' and Wilson's 'plans for everything' – persistently sought to transform from above the values, livelihoods and communities of the 'old' white, patriarchal working class which had provided the historical backbone of Labourism.[84]

This social-democratic form of modernisation was one among the many victims of Thatcherism, which literally gave up on the British working class, simply broke it into innumerable fragments. It offered the most respectable, compliant and conformist of those fragments a hand up into the 'property-owning democracy' and consigned the rest to the underclass drudgery of cheap clothes, fast food, sub-standard housing and alcohol and recreational drugs, which themselves became lucrative niche markets. These were alternative directions within a quite different, post-social democratic, wholly market-conditioned 'conformism' (another important concept in Gramscian hegemony: 'Conformism has always existed; what is involved today is a struggle between "two conformisms", i.e. a struggle for hegemony, a crisis of civil society').[85]

In the meantime, the brightest and best of the 'new social movements' leapfrogged the residual white underclass. We are told repeatedly now that 'modern' Britain consists of a much more 'diverse' population. What this basically means is that some black and minority ethnic individuals have been admitted to the middle classes; that middle class women lead more prosperous, independent and fulfilling lives than their mothers did; and that almost everybody in these exalted circles can now lay claim to at least one gay friend or even gay couple. This again represents real historical progress for the individuals involved – just as Labourism did for its securely proletarian beneficiaries – but for the remaining, indeterminate, 'identity-less' mass of the population it offers very little but resentment and envy, by definition largely 'negative' identity. Especially so when they experience more recent waves of immigration as direct competition for jobs, wages, homes, space, and the far less easily located but just as emotive 'our country'. In one among many curious historical twists of recent times, the indigenous white British masses have become 'counter-cultural'.

This is a quite different 'identity politics' to the optimistic visions of the left in the 1970s and 1980s; it's much more like those identified in the mid-1990s by Eric Hobsbawm and others in the seething, vicious communal wars of the former Yugoslavia.[86] Hobsbawm was by now quite scathing about 'outgroups, re-baptised for publicity purposes as new social movements', and flatly insisted that 'coalitions of minorities cannot be hegemonic' (so much for the CPGB's 'broad democratic alliance').[87] This reactive and negative 'identity politics' takes the form of a simmering backlash amongst the self-identified majority population against what they experience as elite attempts to 'modernise' them. For J.G. Ballard, writing some years later but articulating the same sense of 'progressive' disillusionment as Hobsbawm:

> What I think we're seeing is the white tribes of England reasserting their identity. This is not necessarily a racist thing, I don't think. But there have been so many waves of immigration into this country – Asians, blacks, Kosovans, Poles. And I can see that football is one of the ways in which the white working class can say 'remember us'. It's a rallying call to the old tribal instincts that multi-culturalism has buried under this tissue-paper eiderdown of correct behaviour.[88]

These are all primarily ideological and cultural issues, reflecting the 'lived experience' of the fragmenting working class and the break-up of Labourism, but they have political ramifications. The problem for the New Labour 'transformist' adaptation is that, unlike its parent Thatcherism (or its own 'older brother', the 1980s Social Democratic Party), it cannot wholly leave behind these old Labourist masses, not least because it still relies periodically on their 'core' votes. As Stuart Hall points out, 'it always has to address that part of its constituency which hasn't locked into the new message'.[89] This surely accounts for the continuing, largely sentimental popular attachment to the National Health Service, which occupies a near-mythical place in recent British history as the one undisputed 'legacy' of Labourism, especially for its generations of 'dependent' (and relatively unhealthy) working-class clients. The NHS is the one area of public service where New Labour massively increased government spending without prior marketising 'reform'. At the same time, it has tinkered with it and allowed its outlying fields to be farmed for commercial opportunity while its inherent conflicts and deep-seated faults – the continuing dominance of hospital consultants, for example, or the over-reliance on expensive drugs, or the emphasis on treating illness at the expense of promoting health – go unresolved. Much as they would like to, New Labour could not entirely leave 'Nye Bevan's finest moment' behind. Even the deficit-cutting Con-Lib coalition feels obliged to 'ring-fence' it.

If the NHS remained the ultimate Labourist sacred cow, we can view much of the other legislative programmes of New Labour government as an attempt to synthesise Labourism and its abiding preoccupation with the discipline of the poor, indigent and delinquent, with the authoritarian populism of Thatcherism, into a new 'modern' form of statism. It was harder, more unforgiving, less patient than ever before, and equipped for social rather than economic intervention; the politics of 'tough love', perhaps one last desperate attempt at 'modernising' the British people. The Brown government at its 2007 zenith proposed that 'teenagers will have to stay at school or college until 18 or take an on-the-job course. Those failing to attend will get an ASBO and those breaching these face a £50 penalty and possibly community sentence'.[90] This was the first attempt to raise the school-leaving age – another abiding Labour theme – under the aegis of the criminal justice system. Like so many New Labour initiatives, little more was heard of this once it had garnered a day or two's worth of headlines, but it had served its bigger purpose of orchestrating the nation's 'mood music'. Raphael Samuel was talking about the SDP, but he could as easily have been talking about its 'little brother' New Labour, when he described it as 'a political counterpart to the phenomenon of gentrification': the SDP/New Labour can be understood as 'the imaginative "modernisers", taking on the national equivalent of a run-down street'. [91] And in the process, expelling the established residents and making it impossible for their grumbling offspring to afford to live there. This takes us back to the central strategic question of all 'modernising' projects in capitalist societies: how to subjugate 'market economics' to the requirements of social cohesion and political democracy.

'Sociological marxism' – Gramsci meets Polanyi

One of the most significant recent developments in Gramscian study was the article 'For a Sociological Marxism: The Complementary Convergence of Antonio Gramsci and Karl Polanyi' by Michael Burawoy, which appeared in the journal *Politics and Society* in June

2003. Comparable in scope and ambition to T.J. Jackson Lears' 1985 'The Concept of Cultural Hegemony', or G.A. Williams' 1960 'Egemonia', Burawoy's article aims towards a new Marxism for 'a post-communist age' through a synthesis of Gramsci's concept of 'civil society' and Polanyi's notion of a 'socially regulated market':

> For Gramsci advanced capitalism is marked by the expansion of civil society, which with the state acts to stabilise class relations and provide a terrain for challenging capitalism. For Polanyi expansion of the market threatens society, which reacts by reconstituting itself as active society, thereby harbouring the embryo of a democratic socialism.[92]

Both Jackson Lears' and Burawoy's articles are of course American, and testify to the relative vigour of academic Gramscism in the US, but they have attracted sympathetic attention in the UK and elsewhere.

Karl Polanyi (1886-1964) was a Hungarian social-democratic intellectual, involved in radical politics in Budapest and Vienna in his young adulthood, and roughly contemporaneous with Gramsci. His best known work, *The Great Transformation*, was widely acclaimed at the time of publication in 1944 as the foundation for a distinctively historical sociology.[93] It was a closely detailed study of the land enclosures in England, which, Polanyi argued, brought to an end the paternalism of 'Speenhamland', and spawned the exchange mechanisms of contemporary capitalism, including an identifiable, defensively collectivist working class. Polanyi's historical account is somewhat questionable, as Burawoy and others have pointed out, but his understanding of the destructiveness of capitalism does help to explain the fundamental defensiveness of British working-class 'economic corporate' politics and culture, and in doing so connects with Gramscian 'subalternity' and its historical manifestation in Labourism.[94] Polanyi highlighted the cultural, political and moral defences that 'active society' generates in order to protect itself from the ravages of the unchecked market. This is what, for Burawoy, connects Polanyi to Gramsci's conception of civil society: 'Society occupies a specific institutional space within capitalism between economy and the state, but where "civil society" spills into the state, "active society" interpenetrates the market'.[95] Taken together,

Gramsci and Polanyi offer a means of both understanding and over-coming the complex nexus of economy, state and society which is characteristic of contemporary liberal-democratic capitalism. The primary political objective for the left becomes 'an order that subor-dinates both economy and state to a self-regulating community'.[96]

From quite different theoretical frameworks and political traditions, Gramsci and Polanyi mounted a complementary critique of 'positivism' – which, for Burawoy, was 'a social science removed from lived experience, removed from history, removed from the collective will of classes, removed from the indeterminism of politics, and removed from the search for a new intellectual and moral order'.[97] They also both reacted against the vulgarities of the 'orthodox German Marxism of their time ... imbibed Italian and German idealism [and] took their political inspiration from Russia – Polanyi from the Populists with their peasant base, Gramsci from the Bolsheviks with their proletarian support'. Polanyi in exile and Gramsci in prison embarked upon 'their second encounter with Marxism'.[98] This was informed by their common recent experiences of fascism, whose primary effect was to close down free, voluntary, civil or active society, and thus the terrain upon which capitalism could be challenged. This was its fundamental difference from both liberal and social democracy, with their 'political parties, print media, mass education and all sorts of voluntary associations', which may have been subject to hegemony but at least allowed for challenge.

For both Gramsci and Polanyi, every 'national society' required detailed historical analysis, to establish its distinctive 'balance of class forces' and 'the capacity of some dominant class to represent the general or universal interest' as a popular 'common sense'.[99] It was then up to 'populist' (for Polanyi) or 'organic' (for Gramsci) intellectuals to identify the kernel of 'good sense' in the experiences and ideologies of the masses, and turn them into a new, hegemonic 'popular consciousness' capable of a 'practical transformation of the world'.[100] Polanyi's most distinctive theoretical contribution was a development of Lukacs' concept of 'reification', which had attempted to explain the ebbing of proletarian revolution through capitalism's 'turning [of] relations into commodities', which had the effect of alienating and demoralising the working class. Burawoy, following Polanyi, argues that, however immediately profitable, this was a palpably destructive turn: 'The commodification of land threatens agriculture and the environment, the commodification of labour threatens to so degrade workers as to disable them, and the commodification of money threatens to create such uncertainty for capital as to make modern business impossible'.[101] Each of these processes is easily recognisable in the contemporary world, including the 2009 'credit crunch' recession brought on by the 'commodification of money' into ever more complex and 'toxic' bundles of debt. For our current purposes, we might usefully extend it to the 'commodification' of identity, the commercial exploitation of personal desire and experience, style and relationships.

Combined with Burawoy's account of the failure, in Gramscian terms, of proletarian revolution – 'Without an ideology to found a new order, without material concessions to attach its allies, and without a state to organise its domination through a combination of force and consent, how can the working class ever replace capitalist hegemony with its own?' – we can see the scale of the task in hand.[102] For Polanyi, the way out of the impasse lies in cultivating amongst the working class what Gramsci called a 'hegemonic attitude', in effect taking responsibility for the general well-being of society: 'Socialism is essentially the tendency inherent in an industrial civilisation to transcend the self-regulating market by consciously subordinating it to democratic society'.[103] If this relies rather too much on the notion of an 'inherent tendency', and understates the element of capitalist resistance, it does at least privilege a democratic class politics and a free society within which it can be conducted. Polanyi's focus on the market, and the process of exchange within it, also enables a very necessary concern with consumption and consumerism – now established as a political and ideological terrain in its own right – as well as the classically Marxist preoccupation with production and productivism.

Using Burawoy's 'sociological Marxism', we can also look again at the 'new social forces' in conditions of advanced capitalism and liberal democracy, and ask whether they are inevitably 'hegemonised' by the dominant power or 'historic bloc'? Are they fated to refresh and reinvigorate capitalism, or might they 'prefigure' a different society and economy? The simple, suitably Gramscian/Polanyian, answer is not necessarily – to anything. Any social phenomenon – even, in British circumstances, the stumbling behemoth of Labourism – contains at least some 'prefigurative' features or even elements of 'potential counter-hegemony'. It all depends on political action and broader strategy, on what you actually do; on contingency and circumstance and the politics with which you meet them. In particular, can a progressive political agency – not necessarily the archaic and much-derided 'party' form, but something capable of acting in a recognisably 'political' way – coordinate the actions and aims of new social forces, in such a way that they help to prefigure socialism rather than reinvigorate capitalism?

The 1980s and 1990s represent a whole series of object lessons in how not to conduct this kind of democratic left alliance politics in Britain, from the initial failure to understand the enormity of Thatcherism to the militant syndicalism of the miners' strike, from the crass posturing of 'municipal socialism' to the 'revolutionary subjectivism' of 'New Times' and the exclusive separatism of much black, gay and feminist politics. All had the effect of deepening the subalternity of particular groups and the social isolation of each one, not least by creating antagonisms between them and with the residual white working class. The global 'passive revolution' of neoliberalism, Burawoy's 'market utopianism as an arm of political domination', made their common task of liberation objectively that much harder.

The onslaught of Thatcherism, its distinctively British application, had a passive revolution's characteristic effect of seriously weakening the whole framework of the civil society within which these 'struggles' were conducted; shunting it aside to make way for a new configuration of economy and state, displacing the welfare state with the 'business state' as the primary instrument and terrain of hegemony, and further undermining networks of communal support and solidarity.[104] What had been subaltern defence mechanisms within the post-war Labourist dispensation – the welfare state and the NHS, municipalism and local government, liberationist resistance to racial and sexual oppression, all just possibly 'prefigurative' of democratic socialism – were turned on their heads and transformed into key ideological devices within Thatcherism: scroungers, the loony left, political correctness, the threat to 'the family', illegal immigrants, and even a whole decade ('the sixties') when things went wrong.

In the meantime the left's political agencies have atrophied. The CPGB ceased to exist in 1991, leaving behind a smattering of intransigent rumps and ghostly relics for each of its constituent parts.[105] The Labour left only just survives in the form of shrivelling campaign, coordination and lobby groups, and barely-read publications and policy statements.[106] Labour Party individual membership stood at 177,000 in May 2007, by far its lowest figure since records began. 10,000 joined or re-joined when Blair left the following month, but this recovery was not permanent. Individual membership has declined from 407,000 in 1997, 198,000 in 2005, and 182,000 in 2006.[107] If there is a 'Modern Prince' or even Princess coming to save us, it's hard to see where he or she is coming from.

Notes

1. T. Nairn, in *Approaches to Gramsci*, p179.
2. G. Nowell Smith, *Screen Education 22*, 1977.
3. A.D. Morton, 'Historicizing Gramsci: situating ideas in and beyond their context', *Review of International Political Economy* 10 (1), February 2003, p120.
4. G. A. Williams, *Proletarian Order*, p335.
5. A. Callinicos, *Althusser's Marxism*.
6. W. Thompson, *The Good Old Cause*, p171.
7. G. Andrews, *Endgames and New Times*, pp 140/178.
8. P. Anderson, *Considerations on Western Marxism* (London 1976).
9. M. Prior & D. Purdy, *Out of the Ghetto*, p72.
10. A. Gramsci, *SPN*, p384.
11. David Harris, *From Class Struggle to the Politics of Pleasure* (London, 1992).
12. G. A. Williams, *Proletarian Order*, p235.
13. I. Deutscher, *Stalin* (London, 1972); *The Prophet Unarmed: Trotsky 1921-1929* (London 1975).
14. A. Gramsci, *SPN*, p218.
15. A. Gramsci, *SPN* p381.
16. M. Burawoy, 'For a Sociological Marxism', *Politics and Society* vol. 31 no. 2, June 2003, p211.
17. A. Gramsci, *Further Selections from the Prison Notebooks*, ed. & trans. D. Boothman (London, 1995), p416. Hereafter referred to as *Further SPN*.
18. A. Gramsci, *SPN*, pp341, 395,417, 421, 431, 465.
19. A. D. Morton, 'Historicizing Gramsci', p131; A. Gramsci, *Further SPN*, pp331, 348, 406.
20. Nowell Smith, 'Gramsci and the National Popular', *Screen Education*, p15.
21. G. A. Williams, *Proletarian Order*, p306.
22. S. Hall, *Hard Road to Renewal*, p47; F.A. Hayek, *The Road to Serfdom* (London 2001) & *The Constitution of Liberty* (London 2006); R. Cockett, *Thinking the Unthinkable* (London 1994), p203.
23. A. Bennett & K. Kahn-Harris, *After Subculture* (Basingstoke 2004), p1.
24. P. Willis, *Learning to Labour* (London 1978).

25. J. Clarke, in S. Hall (ed.), *Resistance Through Ritual*, pp47/8.
26. D. Hebdige, *Subculture: The Meaning of Style* (London 1979).
27. A. McRobbie & J. Garber, in *Resistance through Ritual*, p220.
28. A. Bennett & K. Kahn-Harris, *After Subculture*, p7.
29. S. Frith, *Sound Effects* (London 1983), pp219-220.
30. E. Laclau & C. Mouffe, *Hegemony and Socialist Strategy* (London, 1985)
31. T.J. Jackson Lears, 'The Concept of Cultural Hegemony', p592.
32. G. Fiori, *Antonio Gramsci Life of a Revolutionary*, p13.
33. M. Burawoy, 'For a Sociological Marxism; The Complementary Convergence of Antonio Gramsci and Karl Polanyi', *Politics and Society*, Vol. 31 no. 2, June 2003, p225.
34. N. Geras, 'Post-Marxism?, *New Left Review* 163, 1987.
35. P. Ives, *Language and Hegemony in Gramsci* (London, 2004).
36. Hay, *The Political Economy of New Labour*, pp60, 99.
37. *Guardian*, 23 September 2006.
38. Hay, *Political Economy of New Labour*, pp99/100.
39. A.D. Morton, 'The Grimly Comic Riddle of Hegemony', *Politics*, *2006* Vol. 26 (1), pp62-72.
40. M. Burawoy, 'For a Sociological Marxism', citing P. Chatterjee, *Nationalist Thought and the Colonial World* (London, 1986); and I. Grewen & C. Kaplan, *Scattered Hegemonies* (Minneapolis, 1994).
41. A.D. Morton, 'Structural Change and Neo-Liberalism in Mexico: "Passive Revolution" in the Global Political Economy', *Third World Quarterly* 24(4), 2003; R. Shilliam, 'Hegemony and the Unfashionable Problematic of 'Primitive Accumulation', *Millennium: Journal of International Studies* 33(1), 2004; A. Bieler & A.D. Morton, 'The Gordian Knot of Agency-Structure in International Relations: A neo-Gramscian Perspective', *European Journal of International Relations* 7(1), 2001; R.W. Cox, 'Gramsci, Hegemony and International Relations', *Millennium: Journal of International Studies* 12 (2), 1983.
42. F. Fanon, *Black Skin White Masks* (London, 1986).
43. J. Femia, *Gramsci's Political Thought: Hegemony, Consciousness and the Revolutionary Process* (Oxford, 1981).
44. A. D. Morton, 'Historicizing Gramsci', *Review of International Political Economy* vol. 10 (1) pp131/132.
45. J. Femia, *Gramsci's Political Thought*, p17.
46. R. Bellamy, 'Gramsci for the Italians', *Times Literary Supplement*, 14 August 1992, p5.
47. A.D. Morton, 'Historicizing Gramsci', p127.
48. A.D. Morton, 'Historicizing Gramsci', p133.
49. T. J. Jackson Lears, 'The Concept of Cultural Hegemony', only recently anthologised in Britain (J. Martin ed., *Critical Assessments of Leading Philosophers* (London, 2002)); *SPN* p280/1; R. Williams, *The Long Revolution*.

50. T. J. Jackson Lears, 'The Concept of Cultural Hegemony', p573; T.J. Jackson Lears, 'A Matter of Taste: Corporate Cultural Hegemony in a Mass Consumption Society', in L. May (ed.), *Recasting America: Culture and Politics in the Age of Cold War* (Chicago 1989), pp38-57.
51. T. Dodge, paper presented to UEA *Gramsci and History* conference, 2006.
52. T.J. Jackson Lears, 'The Concept of Cultural Hegemony', p573; R. Sennett & J. Cobb, *The Hidden Injuries of Class*, p55.
53. W. Styron, *Nat Turner* (London 1989).
54. A. Gramsci, *SPN*, p366.
55. F. Engels, in E. Hobsbawm, *The Forward March of Labour Halted?*, p7.
56. E. Genovese, *Red and Black* (New York 1971), p369.
57. R. Williams, *Culture and Society* (London, 1958).
58. T.J. Jackson Lears, 'The Concept of Cultural Hegemony', p596.
59. S. Hall, *Stuart Hall: Critical Dialogues in Cultural Studies*, p139.
60. S. Hall, *Stuart Hall: Critical Dialogues in Cultural Studies*, p232.
61. R. Williams, *The Long Revolution*; D. Hebdige, in S. Hall & M. Jacques (eds.), *New Times*, p80.
62. C. Leadbeater, in *New Times*, p137; S. Hall in *New Times*, p119; in *Silver Linings*, ed. Bridges & Brunt (London 1981).
63. A. Gramsci, *SPN*, p445.
64. A. Gramsci, *SPN* pp438, 423.
65. R. Samuel & P. Thompson, Introduction to *The Myths We Live By* (London 1990), p2.
66. T.J. Jackson Lears, pp570 & 573.
67. A. Gramsci, *SPN*, p455.
68. T.J. Jackson Lears, p571.
69. W. L. Adamson, *Hegemony and Revolution* (Los Angeles 1980), p174.
70. A. Gramsci, 'The Communist Party', in *Ordine* Nuovo, 4 September 1920, cited in G.A. Williams, *Proletarian Order*, p228.
71. F. Jameson, 'The Cultural Logic of Capital', *New Left Review* 146, 1984, p78.
72. A. Gorz, *Farewell to the Working Class* (London 1982), pp84/7.
73. J. Lacan, *Ecrits: a Selection* (New York 1977).
74. S. Hall, *Critical Dialogues in Cultural Studies*, p25.
75. S. Hall, *Critical Dialogues in Cultural Studies*, p45.
76. S. Hall, *Critical Dialogues in Cultural Studies*, p146.
77. S. Hall, *Critical Dialogues in Cultural Studies*, pp146, 147, 148.
78. F. Fukuyama, *The End of History and the Last Man* (New York 1992).
79. S. Hall, *Critical Dialogues in Cultural Studies*, pp133, 134, 137.
80. S. Hall, 'New Labour's Double Shuffle', in *Soundings* 25.
81. M. Berman, *All That Is Solid Melts Into Air* (London 1985).
82. M. Berman, *All That Is Solid Melts Into Air*, pp5, 8, 9, 10, 'Preface to Penguin Edition' (1988),

83. J.F. Lyotard, *The Post-Modern Condition* (Minnesota 1984), p31.
84. D. Marsden, 'School, Class and the Parents' Dilemma', in *Class*, ed. R. Mabey (London 1967), p36.
85. A. Gramsci, *SPN*, p242, ft. 42.
86. E. Hobsbawm, *Politics for a Rational Left*.
87. *Politics for a Rational Left*, p156.
88. J. G. Ballard, *Daily Telegraph*, 2 September 2006. A. Pearmain, 'England, the English and the National-Popular', *Soundings 38*.
89. S. Hall, personal interview, 12 January 2004.
90. *The Times*, 3 November 2007.
91. R. Samuel, 'The SDP and the New Middle Class', in *Island Stories* (London 1998), p264.
92. M. Burawoy, 'For a Sociological Marxism', *Politics and Society* 2006, p193.
93. K. Polanyi, *The Great Transformation*, London 1944.
94. M. Burawoy, 'For a Sociological Marxism', p221.
95. M. Burawoy, 'For a Sociological Marxism', p198.
96. M. Burawoy, 'For a Sociological Marxism', p199.
97. M. Burawoy, 'For a Sociological Marxism', pp200/1. *SPN* editor Geoffrey Nowell Smith puts it thus: 'Gramsci was in general hostile to all forms of positivism, and saw sociology as one such form, mainly because it did not see the world as something to be transformed': 'Gramsci and the National Popular', *Screen Education 22*, 1977, p12. Gramsci's suspicion of sociology, 'the philosophy of non-philosophers', was one of the bases for his ferocious attack on Bukharin in 'Problems of Marxism', *SPN* pp425, 430.
98. M. Burawoy, 'For a Sociological Marxism', p205.
99. M. Burawoy, 'For a Sociological Marxism', p206.
100. A. Gramsci, *SPN*, p333.
101. M. Burawoy, 'For a Sociological Marxism', p212.
102. M. Burawoy, 'For a Sociological Marxism', p227.
103. K. Polanyi, *The Great Transformation*, p234.
104. M. Burawoy, 'For a Sociological Marxism', p240.
105. A. Pearmain, 'Twenty Years On: Whatever Happened to the Communist Party?', *Socialist History* (Spring 2011).
106. A. Pearmain, 'Labour's Critical Friends: Compass, the Labour Left and the CPGB', *What's Left?* ed. M. Prior (2010).
107. *The Guardian*, reporting a speech by deputy leadership candidate Jon Cruddas MP, 12 June 2007.

5. The 'Euro-communist' Roots of New Labour: Marxism Today

New Labour did not usher in a new era but more properly belongs to the end of the previous one.

Martin Jacques, editor of *Marxism Today*, 1998[1]

Marxism Today was founded in 1957, as the 'theoretical and discussion journal of the Communist Party of Great Britain', in order to provide doctrinal guidance for the party's new strategy of a distinctively *British Road to Socialism*, itself first adopted in 1951, allegedly at Stalin's direct instigation'.[2] By the later 1950s the CPGB was making strenuous efforts at political reorientation after the convulsions of the Soviet invasion of Hungary, Krushchev's revelations at the 1956 congress of the CPSU of Stalinist repression, and the subsequent departure of many British party members. At least part of *Marxism Today*'s founding intentions, according to Kenny and others, was to provide a point of contact with those departing intellectuals, many of whom were getting involved in 'the first New Left'.[3] For its first twenty years, the journal was broadly orthodox, under the editorship of James Klugman and the general supervision of the CPGB's leadership and officialdom. The bulk of its articles were concerned with elaborating the Marxist classics and applying them to British and international conditions. At several significant moments, links were made with the concerns of 'the wider movement': the development of 'socialist humanism' by E.P. Thompson and the New Left in the later 1950s, for example; the 'Marxist-Christian dialogue' initiated by Vatican II; or *The May Day Manifesto* of 1967/8, whose committee meetings Klugman attended and which was favourably reviewed in the party press.[4]

The *Marxism Today* of the mid-1970s was a dry, generally dull publication, small print packed into dense columns. It was reluctant to look too deeply at the issues and themes that preoccupied the ebbing wave of post-1968 recruits to the CPGB, especially those drawn by the promise of what became known as 'Euro-communism'. Many of that generation were just as deeply touched by feminism and other forms of identity politics and sexual liberation, pop and youth culture as by communism, but these themes found little echo in Klugman's *Marxism Today*. Neither did most of the 'new thinking' within Marxism, which was helping make sense of the peculiar atmosphere of western, social-democratic, affluent/consumerist advanced capitalism, with its growing social tensions amid material comforts; especially the 'Frankfurt School', with its stress on alienation and reification, concepts drawn from the younger, more 'idealist' Hegelian Marx.[5] The Frankfurt School tended towards an all-encompassing, heavily fatalistic Marxism, but its emphasis on culture and ideology (with several appreciative nods towards Gramsci) began to loosen the grip of 'economism' and 'reductionism' on orthodox Marxism. The work of Lukacs, Benjamin, Adorno, Arendt et al connected directly with the contemporary, neo-Freudian psycho-social insights of Herbert Marcuse, Frantz Fanon and Juliet Mitchell, and the existentialism of Sartre and Camus.[6] These were elements of the 'counter-culture' which sat comfortably with the new more open-minded and democratic communism.

Above all, 'Euro-communism' aimed at a clean break with the repressive, anti-democratic politics of the Soviet Union and Eastern Europe, especially after the invasion of Czechoslovakia in 1968. But Klugman's *Marxism Today* reflected the ambivalence of the party's traditionalist leadership, which was at that stage still ideologically and – it would emerge after the party's dissolution in the 1990s – financially dependent on the CPSU.[7] Even the growth of Euro-communism in Europe was initially cast in defensive terms. The 'journal' carried PCI general secretary Enrico Berlinguer's article in 1973 on the military overthrow of the Allende government in Chile, which argued that the Popular Unity alliance had been too narrow and exclusive, its majorities too small and weak to forestall the armed reaction of the right, and its reforms too rapid and provocative. If the Marxist left was to come anywhere near government power in the west, Berlinguer warned, it had to broaden its strategic base and popular appeal, and deepen its commitment to democracy. This was a challenging and innovative intervention in the general atmosphere of outrage at the Pinochet coup. But *Marxism Today* gave very little coverage to the more positive, constructive efforts of the Italian Communists at their own local and regional levels, or their continuing attempts to form a new national government. That was left to other publications and organizations, such as the publishing house Writers and Readers, which published *Red Bologna* in 1977, an account of the communist-run city's social provision and civic culture of participation.[8]

There was not much mention of Gramsci either; just four introductory and review articles between 1967 and 1977, a small proportion of the burgeoning 'literature of Gramsciana' or 'Gramsciology' of those momentous ten years.[9] According to Cozens there were, published in English over that ten year period, eight book-length collections of Gramsci's own writings, eleven books about Gramsci, ten introductory and review articles, fifty-four theoretical articles and at least four PhD theses.[10] Almost all of these appeared in non-communist publications; the most sustained and intensive 'middle-period' explorations of Gramsci were conducted well outside the CPGB. But *Marxism Today* did carry articles and debates in the earlier 1970s that were imbued with the new Gramscian approaches emerging within the CPGB following the publication of *Selections from Prison Notebooks*.

'Nothing to do with the CP': Martin Jacques takes over

Martin Jacques took over the editorship of *Marxism Today* in 1977. He now acknowledges that, as a student at Manchester and Cambridge, he had 'started off as a pretty conventional Communist, always on the liberal side, but broadly part of the orthodoxy'.[11] The turning point for him was the May 1968 *evenements* in France, which excited him and much of his political generation but were not supported by the French CP. This was followed soon after by the Soviet invasion of Czechoslovakia: 'By the end of 1968, I wondered what I was still doing in the CP.' He says he stayed because for the first time the CPGB openly criticised the Soviet Union, and the party leadership supported him in struggles with the Stalinists in the student movement: 'I suppose what really kept me in was that I stayed within the Marxist tradition. Gramsci and the Italian tradition appealed to me, being of an intellectual frame of mind, more than the

Labour tradition, which didn't really attract me because it didn't seem to me to be very thoughtful'; a typically anti-Labourist basis for the recruitment to the CP of a number of post-1968 intellectuals.

Martin had been elected to the Executive Committee of the CPGB as early as November 1967, as a prominent student activist, 'but I was patronized and ... hardly anybody agreed with what I secretly felt'. Mike Prior was also a CP student activist at the time (he was involved in the famous occupation at Essex University in 1968/9, and the only student expelled for it; he was reinstated with the help of 'a hot-shot lawyer paid for by the CP', who terrified the university authorities into submission). Prior remembers Jacques as 'a slightly odd figure in the 1970s, rather peripheral ... you always thought he was sympathetic (to the dissident, anti-Stalinist current gathered around the 'Smith group' of which Prior was a member[12]) but you could never quite put your finger on him'.[13] Jacques' own account is that he worked hard through the late 1960s and earlier 1970s in student and university politics:

> It was a very convulsive period, you had the two elections in 1974, the miners' strike. Then in 1975 I gave a speech to the Executive Committee and for the first time I had something distinctive to say, which addressed the heartland of left, Labour movement politics. It was about the inadequacies of industrial militancy of the 1970s and the decline of the left.

Jacques was closely involved in the revision of the *British Road to Socialism*, the CPGB programme, which was approved at the party's 1977 Congress. He was asked to become editor of *Marxism Today* that year, when Klugman retired:

> But I didn't want to do it. It had never appealed to me. I didn't think the journal was any good beyond the odd piece. I drove a bargain – as long as I didn't have to leave the Executive Committee and I could be on the Political Committee (the supposedly decisive inner core of the party leadership), then I'd do it. I was in a very powerful position, but as soon as I got on the inside it was a terrible experience ... Here was an organisation that was kind of empty. There was nothing there. Here was this committee that spent ages and ages and ages talking and just got nowhere. The discussions were

not interesting, the people were not interesting ... It was like a tree that had died, but it takes quite a long time for the tree to fall over.

Mike Prior was at the time involved in trying to force the pace of political and organisational change in a more consciously Euro-communist direction. He now feels that Martin Jacques 'saw his chance to set up an independent editorial position': 'It was the point where the party had lost control. They were terrified of being accused of anti-democratic practice and so on, even though they had always practised it inside the party. In fact, by this stage you could be as dissident as you liked.' Mike co-authored *Out of the Ghetto*, ostensibly a contribution to the pre-Congress *BRS* debate, but rejected on the grounds of length.[14] When he and his co-author David Purdy distributed Xeroxed copies at the 1977 Communist University of London and elsewhere, they were called before their respective CP district secretaries and very lightly admonished.[15]

The 1977 Congress, the only such event ever recorded for television in a fascinating Granada TV documentary, proved to be the highpoint of British Euro-communism.[16] Over the following two years, the party leadership reasserted control, and in tacit alliance with the Stalinists defeated the Euro-communist push for inner-party democratic reform at the 1979 Congress. 'It was really a kind of counter-attack,' says Jacques:

> I was dropped from the Political Committee in 1979. During that period of disappointment and defeat, I began to take *Marxism Today* seriously, because I could effect change. On everything else I was impotent, but I could do something with *Marxism Today*. As early as September '78 we had 'Forward March of Labour Halted?', Eric Hobsbawm's article, and in January '79, we had 'The Great Moving Right Show', Stuart Hall's piece on Thatcherism. Very quickly the position began to develop. In October '79 we redesigned it, with photographs and everything. It started quickly to become talked about, and by autumn 1980 we had a trial in W.H. Smith. In October '81 we were on general, national sale in newsagents. Our circulation went up from three thousand to nine or ten thousand. Before then it had served two functions, on the classic Stalinist model of the intellectual: one, for discussing obscure theoretical questions; and two, for legitimizing the line of the CP. It then

became the centre of the most important intellectual argument on the left, which was nothing to do with the CP, but with what was happening in British society, the decline of the left and the rise of Thatcherism. Both of these were utterly distinctive to *Marxism Today*. Neither of them were what CUL (Communist University of London) was about, but of course they spoke to a much larger audience when we went public. In one step, *Marxism Today* moved right outside the CP world. In '81, I went back on the Political Committee, because the wind wasn't so cold and *Marxism Today* was so successful.

The magazine's status within the party, and the autonomy that accrued from that, was strengthened by the controversy in 1982 over an article written by Tony Lane about the trade union shop stewards' movement.[17] Lane argued, in terms not too dissimilar from Hobsbawm four years earlier, that the trade unions' elected and appointed officialdoms were growing detached from their mass memberships. Further, there were signs of a 'new working class elite' in some areas and unions, which was sustained by 'the expense account syndrome' and 'the franchise of perks and fiddles', and driven by 'careerist motivations'. It was a mildly populist critique of the trade union bureaucracy, which would not have seemed out of place in *The Sunday Times* or *Socialist Worker*, but the CP Stalinists seized upon it. The party's Industrial Organiser Mick Costello responded with an article in the *Morning Star*, still notionally the party's daily newspaper but in reality controlled by the 'militant labourists', describing Lane's article as a 'gross slander on the labour movement'.[18] Various other CP members or supporters in the trade unions weighed in, criticising the 'elitism' of *Marxism Today* and calling for Martin Jacques to be sacked as editor of what they still pointedly called 'the journal'.[19]

Martin Jacques, at this point still a member of the CP's executive and political committees, responded by demanding that the party support him and dissociate itself from the attacks on *Marxism Today*. They represented 'a gross distortion of what the article actually is and says'; but, he pointed out, they had also broken the bounds of 'democratic centralism', the procedure whereby internal disputes were kept and settled within the party, and which had been a target for repeated criticism by the earlier Euro-communists.[20] When the issue came to a vote at the CP political committee, Jacques' critics were defeated by 8 votes to 6. As Andrews notes, 'from this point on, the party was split in two; the leadership and Gramscian Euro-communists were in control of the party and the Costello/Chater group controlled the *Morning Star*'.[21] The remaining nine years of the Communist Party's history were largely consumed by the internal conflict between these contending factions.[22] (The *Morning Star*, 'the daily paper of the left', doggedly continues publication without its substantial Soviet subsidy.) *Marxism Today's* status within the party was enhanced, not least by its continuing commercial success and favourable publicity, which enabled Martin Jacques to develop its independent editorial policy pretty much as he wished, 'right outside the CP world'.

Marxism Today's move away from the CP was not universally approved even amongst its Euro-communist supporters. Pat Devine remembers 'having quite a lot of discussions with Martin about his distancing from the party, which I could see from his point of view, because he hated having to go to all these committees. But the fact was without the party, *Marxism Today* couldn't survive. It was materially dependent on the CP in financial and personnel terms'.[23] Alan Lawrie argues that there were further forms of dependency: '*MT* also needed the identity of the party, because a lot of what it did was kind of shock/horror "man bites dog" stuff. It needed the credibility of being part of the party, in order to be shocking. On the other hand, Martin could always play the party if he needed to'.[24] Alan also remembers 'in the early 1980s talking to people involved in it, who were saying the party's finished, and I was surprised by that. I always felt there was another project in there, in *Marxism Today*, but I never knew what it was.'

Mike Prior had by then left the Communist Party, but:

along with a number of other people in the party, I was actually rather appalled by what Martin Jacques did with *Marxism Today*. I thought it was hypocritical, that he gradually moved it into a position of implicit hostility towards the Communist Party, particularly its history, whilst at the same time being subsidised by the party. Many members of the CP hated *Marxism Today*. Martin took to getting people who weren't Communists to write for it. Some were good, some weren't. I didn't like Martin's aversion to history, which he wrote out of the equation, and substituted for it a kind of ... popular culture thing. It never seemed to go anywhere, which always seemed to me the problem with *Marxism Today*. In the end, the fact that it was removing itself so ostentatiously from the CP, but also from the trade unions, from the organs of popular politics in Britain, meant that it ended up with no process for actually doing things.[25]

David Purdy now argues that what *Marxism Today* created was 'vigorous debate amongst intellectuals about various ideas that didn't have much purchase on policy or social movements … There wasn't enough attention to policy … One thing we learned in the 1970s was that good analysis was necessary but not sufficient. You have to have an interventionist politics, and *Marxism Today* was never very good at that'.[26] Pat Devine puts it in explicitly Gramscian terms: 'The problem with *Marxism Today* was that to create a radical left agenda, you would need policies that appealed to real forces in society and had some chance of helping those forces coalesce into some sort of bloc … Having gone through this process of boldly criticising many of the shibboleths of the conservative left, it didn't really address the need for a strategic way forward.'[27]

Instead, and in keeping with the commercial realities and cultural trends of the period, *Marxism Today* offered a kind of 'super-journalism', with a nearly closed roster of star contributors marshalled by a small core of staffers around Martin Jacques, many of whom (both contributors and staffers) would find celebrity amongst the emerging 'commentariat' of the 'media age'. Martin Jacques himself has become a notable commentator since the demise of *Marxism Today*, with sporadic columns in *The Guardian* and elsewhere, and, after spending some years in Hong Kong, has acquired an expertise in China. He now accepts that 'if I was doing it again, there are some things I would do differently, but basically it was great and I look back on it proudly. It broke through to a much wider discussion, beyond just the left, and even engaged sections of the right'.

He argues that 'as the CP rotted, *Marxism Today* became its only success-story: 'By 1982 I only saw the CP as a means of sustaining *Marxism Today*, which was a complete change from 1977 when I took the job.' As the 1980s wore on, and the Communist Party and the broader left wilted under the impact of Thatcherism, *Marxism Today* widened its readership and further elaborated its two basic signature themes: the onset of Thatcherism and the decline of the left. Nobody did more than Stuart Hall to shape and elaborate those themes, especially the 'regressive modernisation' of Thatcherism. Stuart had been deeply involved in the British left since the mid-1950s, as a contributor to *Universities and Left Review*, founder member of the New Left and first editor of *New Left Review*. He was an early activist and advocate of CND, a contributor to the *May Day Manifesto* in 1967 and from the mid-1970s a regular contributor to the Communist University of London. Martin Jacques invited him to join the editorial board of *MT* in the late 1970s, Stuart told me, 'as one of two non-Communists, with David Edgar, and we never joined the party. About then, I think we regarded *Marxism Today* as having floated free! Still committed to furthering democratic change within the party, but looking more outwards to the political scene as a whole...'.[28]

People involved in the production, distribution and promotion of *Marxism Today* recall Martin Jacques' distinctive editorial style. 'Nobody was ever paid for writing for *Marxism Today*,' says Pat Devine, 'and Martin was a most draconian taskmaster, making people rewrite time and time again, but he turned it into an extremely influential journal, and then in a conscious change of name, magazine. Martin was just not interested in an in-house party journal.' Other staff members from that period recall the intense pressure of working on *MT* at that time – everyone was expected to work just as hard as Martin, who worked all the time.[29]

Mark Perryman set up a *Marxism Today* reading group in Dudley, a small town in the West Midlands, and recalls that '*MT* was very proud of this, that one of the few *Marxism Today* discussion groups was in this place called Dudley ... I was approached by Martin Jacques. Would I come and work for *MT*, but there wasn't really a job'.[30] Mark was invited onto the editorial board; then, when 'the circulation manager was desperate to leave, I took over, without having had any marketing background'. He gives a wholly positive account of his experience, including the period of 'producing *Marxism Today* filofaxes and *Marxism Today* wine ... in retrospect it did get a bit silly! The *Daily Mail* ran a full page profiling a Yummie, which was a young, upwardly mobile Marxist!'

Alan Lawrie observes that *Marxism Today*'s 'style of politics was very centralist, almost Leninist in the way it was organised':

> I was involved in organising a couple of 'Moving Left' shows [the CP's mid-1980s festivals of 'popular politics'], and afterwards I was

told I could come to the 'collective'. You always felt you were being moved onto another platform. There was always a process of talent spotting or a league table. There was a formal structure, an editorial board, then a collective of people who organised it, but it had no correlation at all to party organisation. The Party appointed the editorial board, but there must have been a decision made at some stage to give Martin a free hand. *Marxism Today* felt like a bit of an elitist organisation. There was a core, an inner core, and then there was Martin …

On the other hand, there is almost universal recognition of *Marxism Today*'s appeal and impact, way beyond the Communist Party or even the ten thousand people who at its peak subscribed to or bought the magazine. Alan Lawrie again: 'I remember picking up *Marxism Today* in the early 1980s and realizing it actually felt like something of the early 1980s, not twenty years before. It was really lively, there were some really good debates and articles in it.' Martin Jacques himself looks back on it proudly:

> This was the best conversation on the left, and it was streets ahead of anything else. All the rest of it, the CULs and so on, was about intellectuals. This broke through to a much wider discussion. It wasn't a CP discussion, though it did involve the CP. It was a novel cultural project … it didn't belong to the left, but it came from the left.

A rather less positive account is provided by Francis Beckett's generally unsympathetic CPGB history, *Enemy Within*, in which 'Martin Jacques may be the only person in seventy-one years for whom joining the CP turned out to be a smart career move'.[31]

Communists and Labourists

If *MT*'s link to the Communist Party was increasingly tenuous, its broader relationship with the Labour Party was never straightforward either. Martin Jacques recalls that the magazine's political perspective 'wouldn't keep still, so Labour people would attack us on something – like "Forward March of Labour Halted" – then two years later agree with us.' A trawl through pamphlets produced at the time by the

Labour Co-ordinating Committee – the most receptive to *MT* of all Labour's 1980s factions and groups – confirms this time-lag (though it's usually longer than two years). *Labour and Mass Politics – Rethinking our Strategy,* written in 1982 by Charles Clarke and David Griffiths, accepts Hobsbawm's analysis from four years previously of 'the Labour Party's narrowing electoral base', and extends its critique to 'tenuous links with other progressive forces, over-identification with bureaucratic state structures and uninspiring inner-Party routines'.[32] Two years later, John Denham's *How the Labour Party – and the Left – Can Win* further endorsed Hobsbawm's judgement in observing that 'the social and economic conditions which enabled right wing social democracy to achieve some success have passed'.[33] In 1990, in an LCC collection *New Maps for the Nineties – A Third Road Socialist Reader,* Trevor Fisher contributed a long and appreciative account of Gramsci and his conception of 'socialism as a process of change' and 'the importance of pre-figurative activity'.[34] Finally, according to Paul Thompson and Ben Lucas' introduction to *The Forward March of Modernisation,* published on the occasion of the LCC's 1998 disbandment, 'the history of the LCC has been about getting Labour to come to terms with [Hobsbawm's 1978 'Forward March' *MT*] analysis, and to modernise its ideology, politics, style, structure and message'. [35]

On the other hand, Stuart Hall observes that people in and around the Communist Party have never really understood the Labour Party, and perhaps the temporal disjuncture between *MT* and Labour's inner discourse illustrates this. It also helps to explain a certain gullibility with which *Marxism Today* responded to Labour overtures in the 1980s, such as Neil Kinnock's famous (and apocryphal) flattery of his 'favourite Marxist' Eric Hobsbawm, which arguably blunted Hobsbawm's later analysis of New Labour, or Peter Mandelson's 1989 remark to Jacques, 'We'd never have done what we did without you …'.[36] Tony Blair himself contributed two pieces to *Marxism Today* in 1990/91, in themselves fairly unremarkable, which suggests that this most carefully image-conscious of politicians saw some advantage in it for himself and his career. The first was a 'Back Page' interview of the sort which would become a staple of magazine features over the years to come ('When was the last time you prayed? Yesterday; What is the most common colour in your wardrobe? Dark blue').[37] The second was a standard piece of Third Way rhetoric, with many of the 'not only but also' syntactical devices and 'beyond left and right' rhetorical flourishes which would become equally familiar in the New Labour years to come. [38]

For much of its history, the Communist Party had been politically quarantined, primarily by the Labour Party's own apparatus, which was uniquely attuned and resistant to 'communist infiltration' (especially under General Secretary Morgan Phillips, 1944/61).[39] Recently disclosed evidence from the 1970s indicates just how far Labour was prepared to take its anti-communism. When the Italian Communist Party was on the verge of election to government in 1976, a paper was produced in the British Foreign Office entitled 'Action in Support of a Coup d'Etat or other Subversive Action': 'By its nature a coup is likely to be an unexpected development, but theoretically a coup could be promoted … it would presumably come from the right wing drawing in the army and the police'.[40] The involvement of the CIA in far right anti-communist activity in Italy is well known, in particular 'Operation Gladio', and by extension the involvement of British secret services is not surprising. What is novel is the involvement of high level officials in the Foreign Office, under the Labour government of James Callaghan, contemplating among other options 'direct intervention in support of a coup encouraged from outside' (which is pretty much what happened in the *anni piombi*, or 'years of lead' to come).[41]

Of course, the British Communist Party rarely came anywhere near government or for that matter outright suppression (though it was heavily monitored and infiltrated by the secret services; and many of its early leaders experienced periods of imprisonment), but Labour in government and opposition found other ways of keeping the CP at a distance, most notably the 'bans and proscriptions' of the 1940s and 1950s aimed at communists in the trade unions, education, the media and the civil service.[42] The effects of ostracism were reflected in the CP's own internal culture, which was self-sufficient to the point of insularity, and more than a little suspicious and resentful towards the outside world.[43] For all its commitment to 'mass politics', and occasional upsurges in membership and political impact, it had the functional characteristics of a sect.[44] As a result, individual communists had very little to do with the Labour Party, especially (and this may seem odd) if they were party officers and functionaries rather than activists and officials in the 'wider labour movement'.

This held true for the CP's journal/magazine as much as its organisers and secretaries. Most if not all the people in and around *Marxism Today* in the late 1970s and 1980s (apart from its 'celebrity' contributors) were party employees and officials (albeit with a critical, 'renegade' streak) like Jacques, venerated party intellectuals like Eric Hobsbawm who had sat out the several waves of disgusted resignations, or people whose main experience of 'mass politics' had been in peripheral movements like the National Union of Students and who volunteered their time and youthful enthusiasm on a pretty much expenses-only basis. Stuart Hall was highly unusual in not being any of these things, an established academic and independent intellectual, which may explain the consistent and durable quality of his contributions.

On the Labour side, there has always been a tendency to use intellectuals for the party's own doctrinal or electoral purposes, and unceremoniously cast them aside when they've served those purposes. Desai endorses the historical judgment implicit in J.M. Keynes' explanation for never joining: 'the intellectual elements in the Labour Party will never exercise adequate control'.[45] Marquand observes that 'the relationship between the Labour Party and the progressive intelligentsia, on which it depended for ideas and which alone could validate its claim to be a potential party of government rather than the vehicle for a social interest, had always been tense, uneasy and ambiguous'.[46] Drucker draws a sharp distinction between the 'doctrine' of the Labour Party, which allows 'middle class intellectuals (of both right and left) to give voice to its ideas', and the party's broader 'ethos', which derives from the working class 'experience of exploitation' and subsequent grudging 'deference'.[47] This helps explain why, even at the highpoint of Labour intellectuals' influence in the 1950s, their impact on the broader party was limited; as Coates notes, 'the victory of revisionism was a victory without deep roots in the party'.[48] And when, several years later, the Labour left fought back and defeated party leader Hugh Gaitskell over Clause IV, it was 'a shadow fight' resulting in 'a victory without substance for the left'.[49] Most of the party just got on with the endless round of subscription-collecting and electioneering, and left the intellectuals to fight it out amongst themselves.[50]

Of course, by the 1980s this uneasy relationship between Labour intellectuals and workers was showing signs of breaking down altogether, especially with the fractious departure of most of what was left of the 1950s Gaitskell/Crosland generation of revisionist intellectuals (including David Marquand) into the short-lived Social Democratic Party. For Cronin, *Marxism Today* – and its late-1980s debate about 'New Times' in particular – served a specific historic purpose for the Labour Party:

> Public intellectuals of the left moved the political discourse surrounding Labour's future away from the foci of the late 1970s and early 1980s – on alternative economic strategies, on the failures of the party's leadership, on the bitter feuding between left and right – and towards a perhaps grudging recognition that the battles of the past should not determine the politics of the future. The claims about New Times might well have been overstated, but they had the great virtue of shifting the terms of the discussion.[51]

The question is: how far and in what direction? Neal Lawson began work in the labour movement in the mid-1980s, initially as a trade union official then as a researcher for Gordon Brown. He 'personally found *Marxism Today* very useful, but I don't think it had that much impact in the Labour Party. Labour by and large is a very inward-looking organisation, and doesn't have much dialogue with other organisations. *Marxism Today* was pretty marginal to most Labour thinking in that period, sadly'.[52] The Labour-aligned magazine *New Socialist* was a conscious, not wholly successful attempt to emulate *MT*'s 'awareness raising' function for Labour, which survived for only a few years in the mid-1980s.[53] It was a worthy publication, relatively outward-looking for the Labour Party, and as such another example of the most useful historical function of the CPGB on the British left: the largely inadvertent, detached and usually delayed provocation of intelligent thought and discussion within Labour.

Publishing politics: from journal to magazine

Pat Devine notes the conscious change in format and style from 'journal' to 'magazine', and Martin Jacques talks of *MT* as a 'novel cultural project'. During the 1980s there was a massive increase in the number, circulation and influence of magazines in Britain, such that commentators have talked about the beginnings of a distinctively 'magazine culture of communication, information consumption and leisure reading'.[54] They usually mean fashion, style and music magazines like *The Face*, *ID* and *Q*; quite consciously devoted to celebrating the new cultural concerns of mass consumer capitalism associated with Thatcherism. But with the help of innovative journalistic, design and production techniques – including breaking the stranglehold of the print unions in the *Today* and *Times*/Wapping disputes of 1986/7 – virtually every area of specialist interest could be catered to.

In the five years between 1982 and 1987, Jerome reports, weekly and monthly titles registered with the Publishers Association increased from 573 to 4,834, and combined monthly sales from an estimated three to over eight million. It wasn't just that there were more magazines; the new technologies and industrial relations of publishing made it economical to provide for smaller, more specialised readerships. Jerome's new, expanded 'magazine culture' undoubtedly provided an arena within which Jacques' *MT* could flourish, especially when it negotiated its distribution deal with W.H. Smith and carved out a new 'niche market' among the fashionably political. Martin Jacques is now wholly unapologetic about this process of commercialisation and marketing. In his introduction to the online collection of *Marxism Today* from 1980 to 1991, he describes how 'people expected a magazine of this title to be leaden, boring and predictable. It most certainly was not ... The tomb-line design, reminiscent of academic journals, had by 1986 transmuted into a magazine characterized by memorable design panache ... Here was *Marxism Today* at its brilliant best: big picture analysis, hugely relevant, mining the deeper changes which were to transform the whole character of the world in which we lived'.[55]

If *Marxism Today* carried a constant 'element of surprise', it was in part because of the crisis within Marxism itself. As Mike Prior puts it:

> ... the economics of Marxism had been laid waste by people like Hindess and Hirst, and the Cambridge economists who destroyed the labour theory of value. The various sociologists, coming at it from various psychoanalytical positions, destroyed the concept of class. By the early 1980s, there was a multiplicity of Marxisms to choose from, so *Marxism Today* had this odd position of being called *Marxism Today* in a period when Marxism was at an extremely low point, which the magazine sought to reinforce. It made no attempt

to revive Marxism. If anything it made clear that it favoured further destruction of this thing called Marxism. By 1982 Marxism had gone, well before the fall of communism.[56]

Martin Jacques told me 'If you really pushed me, I'd call myself a Gramscian.' He would also describe the whole *Marxism Today* project as Gramscian, in the sense that it was an ambitious attempt to reach out beyond the traditional concerns, styles and constituencies of the left and construct new coalitions of discussion and interest: a new 'historic bloc'. We might question whether a magazine, Jerome's vehicle of 'information consumption and leisure reading', is a suitable vehicle for such a hegemonic project. But what is most striking about *Marxism Today* under Jacques' editorship, from a Gramscian perspective, is just how little mention of Gramsci there is. In its whole eleven-year heyday, from 1980 to 1991, there are only three articles whose primary focus is on Gramsci, and two of those are reviews of books by other people who make substantial use of Gramsci.[57] The only full article is Stuart Hall's magisterial 'Gramsci and Us', which started out as a speech at the Marx Memorial Library to mark the fiftieth anniversary of Gramsci's death, and was included in the June 1987 edition of *MT*.

Notes

1. M. Jacques, 'Wrong!' *Marxism Today* special issue 1998.
2. At the 1991 'Special' CPGB Congress, Nina Temple would disclose 'Stalin's role in writing the first edition of the British Road to Socialism in 1950' alongside 'the secret, massive funding of our Party by the CPSU'. N. Temple, 1991 Congress, Opening Speech to the draft new constitution.
3. M. Kenny, *The First New Left*, pp6/7; G. Andrews, *Endgames and New Times*, p12; W. Thompson, *The Good Old Cause*.
4. G. Andrews, *Endgames and New Times*, p81.
5. P. Anderson, *Considerations on Western Marxism* (London 1976).
6. H. Marcuse, *One Dimensional Man* (London 1972); F. Fanon, *Black Skin, White Masks* (London, 1986); Juliet Mitchell, *Psychoanalysis and Feminism* (London 1975).
7. F. Beckett, *The Enemy Within*, pp216, 221.
8. M. Jaggi, R. Muller, S. Schmid, *Red Bologna* (London 1977).
9. These were J. Harvey, 'Antonio Gramsci', *MT* vol. 11 no. 4, April 1967, pp114-120; J. Harvey, 'The Prison Notebooks of Antonio Gramsci', *MT* vol. 15 no. 12, December 1971, pp360-366; M. Jacques, 'Notes on the

Concept of Intellectuals', *MT* vol. 15 no. 10, October 1971, pp307-317; R. Simon, 'Gramsci's Concept of Hegemony', *MT* vol. 21 no. 3, March 1977, pp78-86.

10. P. Cozens, *Twenty Years of Antonio Gramsci: A Bibliography of Gramsci and Gramsci studies published in English, 1957-1977* (London 1977).
11. M. Jacques, personal interview, 24 November 2003.
12. G. Andrews, *Endgames and New Times*, p63.
13. M. Prior, personal interview, 18 June 2004.
14. *Out of the Ghetto* was eventually published in book form by Spokesman in 1979.
15. M. Prior, personal interview, 18 June 2004.
16. 'Decision British Communism', Granada TV, 1977.
17. T. Lane, 'The Unions; Caught on the ebb tide', *Marxism Today*, September 1982.
18. *Morning Star*, 26 August 1982.
19. G. Andrews, *Endgames and New Times*, p203.
20. G. Andrews, *Endgames and New Times*, p206.
21. G. Andrews, *Endgames and New Times*, p207.
22. A. Pearmain, 'Twenty Years On: Whatever Happened to the CPGB?', *Socialist History* (Spring 2011).
23. P. Devine, personal interview, 6 January 2004.
24. A. Lawrie, personal interview, 17 June 2004.
25. M. Prior, personal interview, 6 April 2004.
26. D. Purdy, personal interview, 6 January 2004.
27. P. Devine, personal interview, 6 January 2004.
28. S. Hall, personal interview, 12 January 2004.
29. S. Davison, personal interview, 13 October 2004.
30. M. Perryman, personal interview, 9 March 2004.
31. F. Beckett, *Enemy Within: The Rise and Fall of the British Communist Party* (London 1995), p228.
32. C. Clarke and D. Griffiths, *Labour and Mass Politics – Rethinking our Strategy*, Labour Co-ordinating Committee 1982, p1.
33. J. Denham, *How the Labour Party – and the Left – Can Win*, Labour Co-ordinating Committee 1984, p2.
34. T. Fisher, 'The Crisis of the British Left', in *New Maps for the Nineties – A Third Road Socialist Reader*, described as 'A Clause 4 Chartist Publication' but later claimed by the LCC in its 1998 history (see below).
35. P. Thompson & B. Lucas, *The Forward March of Modernisation*, Labour Co-ordinating Committee 1998, p1.
36. M. Jacques, personal interview, 12 December 2003; Kinnock's remark is not recorded anywhere.
37. T. Blair, Back Page interview, *Marxism Today*, July 1990, p48.
38. T. Blair, 'Forging a New Agenda', *Marxism Today*, October 1991 (the penultimate issue).

39. K. Morgan, *Harry Pollitt* (Manchester 1993).
40. *The Times*, 14 January 2008; *La Repubblica*, 13 January 2007.
41. T. Jones, *The Dark Heart of Italy*; P. Ginsborg, *Italy and its Discontents*.
42. F. Beckett, *Enemy Within*, p115; S. Parsons, in *Labour's Promised Land?*, ed. J. Fyrth (London 1995).
43. R. Samuel, *The Lost World of British Communism* (London 2006).
44. J. Callaghan, *The Far Left in British Politics* (Oxford, 1987).
45. R. Desai, *Intellectuals and Socialism*, p5.
46. D. Marquand, *The Progressive Dilemma*, pix.
47. H. Drucker, *Doctrine and Ethos in the Labour Party*, p10.
48. D. Coates, *The Labour Party*, p88.
49. D. Coates, *The Labour Party*, p93.
50. H. Drucker, *Doctrine and Ethos*, p82.
51. J. E. Cronin, *New Labour's Pasts*, p309.
52. N. Lawson, personal interview, 28 January 2004.
53. J. Curran (ed.), *The Future of the Left* (London 1984) is a collection of New Socialist's most insightful articles.
54. B. Jerome, *The New Media* (London, 1993), p37.
55. http://www.amielandmelburn.org.uk/collections/mt/index_frame_r.htm.
56. M. Prior, personal interview. For Barry Hindess and Paul Hirst see *Pre-capitalist Modes of Production* (London, 1975), their best-known work.
57. G. Robinson, review of P. Togliatti, *On Gramsci and Other Writings*, *Marxism Today* (May 1980); B. Jessop, 'The Gramsci Debate', *Marxism Today* (February 1980).

6. The 'Euro-communist' Roots of New Labour: 'New Times'

In his introduction to the online *Marxism Today* collection, Martin Jacques cites 'three debates that for me define the historic importance of *Marxism Today*'.[1] The first ensued from Hobsbawm's September 1978 'Forward March of Labour Halted?' and the second from Hall's 'The Great Moving Right Show' published four months later. Together they helped create a new 'common sense' that the Tory radical right was in swift ascendancy and that the old labour and communist left was in rapid decline. Arguably, in establishing these nostrums across the 'broad left' – analysing and codifying its historic defeat – *MT* inadvertently helped to consolidate the new hegemony. These debates would preoccupy the left and much of the wider political arena for most of the 1980s, as everyone struggled to adjust to the new order.

Martin Jacques' third favourite debate, prompted by the 'New Times' edition of *MT* in October 1988, was a determined attempt to cheer up and move on. There was more than a hint that the magazine was bored with its two defining themes, which were now widely accepted and, with Thatcher's third and most crushing general election victory in 1987, starkly evident in the changing political landscape. 'New Times' was above all an attempt to find some new basis for left-wing politics. If manufacturing industry, the fully employed manual working class, the public services, the welfare state and the rest of the post-war social democratic consensus and of the legacy of Labourism were now abandoned and dispersed, were there new sites of progressive action, or of Gramscian-style 'pre-figurative struggle' (though such terminology would not now be common around *Marxism Today*), for the much-reduced and chastened left?

The primary focus of 'New Times' was the supposed shift from the

'Fordist' methods of mass production analysed in Gramsci's essay 'Americanism and Fordism' (the only substantial commentary in the prison notebooks on contemporary society) to the newer, more retail-oriented 'post-Fordist' models of business and industry pioneered in the 1970s and 1980s in Germany, the US and above all Japan. This fundamental change transferred power from producers to consumers; from big, established, hierarchical corporations to smaller, innovative, 'flatter' and 'leaner', more adaptable and more egalitarian enterprises; from the production of objects to the processing of information; from fixed, geographical communities of place and class to communities of interest and identity and affect. Were there opportunities within these deep economic, cultural and social shifts for new kinds of political intervention? The old ways of doing politics were now useless. For Cronin: 'New Times betokened a post-industrial, post-modern world that bore scant resemblance to the familiar and traditional world of the labour movement and the Labour Party'.[2]

Up to now, the new right had been able to make the running and remake this new post-Fordist world in its own image, mainly because of the political ineptitude of the old left. But it didn't have to be that way: according to Stuart Hall and Martin Jacques' introduction to the *New Times* book collection: 'New Times is a project to prise Thatcherism and that world apart'.[3] There were hazards along the way: 'a temptation to exaggerate the new' and play down 'the lines of continuity' in settled capitalist societies like Britain; and 'a danger the left will produce a slightly cleaned-up, humanized version of the radical right'. These were 'new times for capitalism' as well as for everyone else, offering opportunities to create and exploit 'new social divisions, new forms of inequality'.[4] What was needed was 'a unified counter-hegemonic force as the agency of progressive change'. At this point, it was not possible to specify quite what form that might take, but it was clear that 'The Leninist model of society ... is historically exhausted.'

The technical, less plainly political case for 'New Times' was made in Robin Murray's 'Fordism and Post-Fordism', which has a similarly definitive feel to Hobsbawm and Hall's 1978/79 articles, and alongside them helps to identify the epochal features of Thatcherism.[5] However, there is in Murray, ten years on from Hobsbawm and Hall, an even clearer sense of distancing from the traditional concerns and audiences of British socialism. Murray's focus is on what an earlier article of his called 'the introduction of a quite new stage of capitalist production. In the USA it is referred to as "flexible specialisation", in France as "neo-Fordism".'[6] In particular, it is concerned with the introduction of the new Information Technology (IT) into the conception, design, production, distribution, marketing and retail of goods and services. As such, it represents a quite distinctive take on the common 1980s sense of awe at the possibilities of computerisation.

In contrast to Fordism, with its 'inflexibility' and 'vulnerability to sudden falls in demand', its unresponsiveness to the individual consumer and its deskilling and demoralisation of the mass producer, post-Fordism ensures a closer, more efficient and profitable fit between demand and supply – 'Market niching has become the slogan of the high street'. This poses major challenges for industry and services. The most successful firms have introduced post-Fordism into the production process itself: 'The line has become flexible. Instead of using purpose-built machines to make standard products, flexible automation uses general-purpose machines to produce a variety of products'. Additionally it involves and entrusts its workforce in 'Quality circles … each breakdown is seen as a chance for improvement'. In return, workers receive 'jobs for life and corporate welfare' in a new industrial settlement.

These developments are not necessarily reactionary: 'some are rooted in the popular opposition to Fordism … which flowered after 1968 in the community movements and the new craft trade unionism of alternative plans'.[7] And there were clear connections to the new politics of personal identity and individual choice, which were not intrinsically oriented to the left. This 'open-endedness' or 'contingency' of New Times means that 'things can go either way'. The left can refuse to ride the tiger, and fastidiously maintain its customary first response of disdain towards innovation within the bounds of capitalism. Or it can climb on board and attempt to influence the course the tiger takes through the jungle; this would be, broadly speaking, the strategic orientation of New Labour.

Further contributions to the New Times debate ranged widely over the preoccupations of the splintering left. Fred Steward offered a sympathetic critique of the emergent politics of environmentalism but concluded that 'the successful combination of "greening" and "modernization" is a formidable challenge'.[8] Dick Hebdige attempted a parallel reconciliation, between the socialist tradition and the postmodernism of Baudrillard and Lyotard.[9] Goran Therborn's 'The Two-thirds One-third society' surveyed the political ramifications of mass unemployment, which were not necessarily progressive.[10] Charlie Leadbeater's contributions to 'New Times', 'Power to the Person' and 'Thatcherism and Progress', clearly foreshadowed his influential books of the late 1990s and many of the preoccupations of New Labour, most obviously the 'personalisation agenda' which continues to flavour the rhetoric of 'public sector reform'.[11]

From a more critical perspective, Mike Rustin acknowledged the basic 'New Times' argument as 'the nearest thing we have to a paradigm which can link widespread changes in forms of production to changes in class relations, state forms and individual identities'.[12] But there was a real danger that changes in the productive process can be made to seem much more simple, consistent and uniform than they actually are. Across an increasingly interconnected world, post-Fordism could easily co-exist with Fordism or even pre-Fordism; it all depended on the local 'balance of forces' and 'stage of development'. Further, coming to terms with the present hard realities of Thatcherism might lead 'New Times contributors to make unfortunate concessions to values that are probably better simply regarded as those of the other side'. Paul Hirst argued that *Marxism Today* 'is good at challenging dogmatic and old-style socialism, but in coming close to celebrating Conservative economic success it offers the Left few weapons to challenge economic liberalism'. [13]

Finally Stuart Hall considered 'The Meaning of New Times', and attempted to summarise the preceding debate.[14] This is one of the fullest accounts of Hall's take on 'modernity' and 'post-modernism' but reflects some of his own late-1980s disorientation and dismay at just how profoundly correct his original characterisation of Thatcherism was turning out to be, and more than a hint of frustration with the left's response to it. Hall had begun the decade with doubts of his own about the durability of Thatcherism – whose 'new doctrines' were wilting under the impact of 'harsh economic realities'. [15] Now he offered the consoling thought that 'Thatcherism was itself, in part, produced by new times'. It might not be quite so dominant, historically determinant or 'epochal' after all. The left must seek out opportunities for the 'democratisation of culture' within the upheavals of 'commodified consumption'. However, denied its customary 'totalising logic', it must do this without any preconditions or guarantees – 'One, so to speak, plans for contingency'.[16]

There is very little about how or by what these interventions might be made, or what political agency might give them permanent effect. What we are seeing here is in fact a clearing of old terrain, and tentative new connections being made which would lead eventually to the political practice of New Labour. Transposed onto an unreformed electoral system – not to mention a resurgent global capitalism – the free-ranging New Times 'positional politics' leads directly to the politics of careful and constant 'positioning' within the parliamentary marketplace. When Hall goes on to talk about 'politics as a war of position', it is a slightly desperate Gramscian reminder of his original intentions and preferred responses to the 'contingencies' of New Times, but by now it is too late. Within the left's much diminished field of political operations in the 1980s, the impulses of modernisation were too weak and the forces of tradition (not to say reaction) too strong. One of the deep ironies of 'New Times' is that it would fall prey to precisely those 'contingencies' it attempted to lay bare, and contribute directly to the formation of a political project Hall et al would eventually declare 'Wrong!' At around the same time Hall (unlike most other 'New Times' contributors) would honourably own up to a 'certain responsibility' for New Labour.

'New Times' was characteristic of the late-1980s moment of cultural, ideological and political disorientation felt especially deeply on the left. It was very good at focusing long overdue attention on underlying changes in the economy and society in Britain and elsewhere, stimulating widespread discussion about what those changes meant and would come to mean, and separating out deeper economic and industrial processes from the ideologically derived and driven and the politically contingent. But was it really that new? 'Affluence' and 'consumerism' were first identified as significant social trends in the 1950s, following the global post-war boom driven by American prosperity and expansionism. Their applicability to Britain and Europe were far less self-evident (though the stratifications they reflected within the working class, based on differentials of 'aspiration' and 'respectability', can be identified in 1930s 'popular Toryism' or even late nineteenth-century radical Liberalism and Labourism), not least because post-war economic recovery was much more patchy and protracted here. But even if only on the level of public rhetoric, they provided the justification for a new kind of left-wing politics; especially on the revisionist, Crosland-ite and still consciously social democratic wing of the Labour Party.[17]

They were then a major sub-theme within the public discourse of the 1960s and beyond, usually expressed in commentary on widening materialism, social mobility and economic growth. The specific policy initiatives of Thatcherism, the basis for its refreshed hegemony among the subaltern classes, can be seen as the extension of those consumerist principles of individual rights, desires and prerogatives into previously (and briefly) collectivised provisions like housing, health and education and the ownership of utilities. Was 'New Times' merely a semi-conscious and somewhat delayed accommodation to this newly reinstated capitalist reality, at least in the British context; and as such yet another symptom of the left's historic decline, rather than the bold and determinedly optimistic renewal it set out to be?

There is a relatively short piece towards the end of the *New Times* collection, 'The Decline of the Party' by Sarah Benton, who was at the time political editor of *New Statesman and Society*. Benton had been the editor of the CP's weekly journal *Comment* for some years in the late 1970s and early 1980s, and is currently an associate editor of the quarterly magazine *Soundings*, part of the CP's legacy and as such a successor of sorts to *Marxism Today*. Modern parties evolved, she argued in her 1989 'New Times' article, to represent the interests of social classes within the nation-state, to claim a share of national wealth and prestige and to make demands of the state which purported to govern national societies. In these 'New Times', none of these entities and categories held true. Social classes had fractured and dispersed; the nation had been superseded by supranational institutions above and regional loyalties below; the role of the nation state in society had been challenged and undermined by Thatcherism. These changes posed particular challenges to the Labour Party, whose historic purpose had been to gain the maximum possible material benefit for the working class from the British nation state. As we now know, New Labour would in large part be the answer to those challenges. But strangely, an article on 'The Decline of the Party', written for its 'magazine' and as part of a debate leading towards its penultimate congress, makes absolutely no mention of the Communist Party.

'New Times' and the Communist Party

By the late 1980s, the relationship between the magazine-format *Marxism Today* and the CPGB was much more close and collaborative again, after the various earlier conflicts and standoffs. But as the party's 'only real recent success' and the 'only tool left in the box' (to quote people involved on either 'side'), it was very much conducted on *Marxism Today*'s terms. The 'New Times' debate was partly conceived as preparatory to the 1989 CPGB Congress, to which *MT* editor Martin Jacques was asked to give the main political speech: a noteworthy 'decision to break with precedent', as Andrews puts it mildly.[18] The speech would normally have been given by the party's General Secretary, but Nina Temple had only just replaced Gordon McLennan. The introduction to the later *New Times* collection, written by editors Martin Jacques and Stuart Hall and published after the 1989 Congress, makes clear the new balance of power between party and magazine when it talks about the need 'to develop the magazine's political project beyond the analysis of Thatcherism and the crisis of the left'. The collection was published by CPGB publisher Lawrence and Wishart, '*in association with Marxism Today*'; even small publishing details reflect *MT*'s new status.[19]

It's as if the magazine is itself now a political party, capable of shaping the political and ideological terrain it operates upon, at a time when its CPGB sponsor was nearing an all-time low in membership, support and influence, and its own final demise. Mark Perryman, then *MT* circulation manager, recalls arguing: 'Look, *MT*'s developed as a model for something new. Can we somehow develop something organisationally out of that ... which would have been part-party and part-non-party?'[20] The commercial success of *Marxism Today* in the new media age contrasted sharply with the 'post-political' decline of the party that had established, sponsored and continued to subsidise it. While the CPGB (uniquely among Communist Parties across the world) was embarking on the process of disbanding itself, its former journal – now magazine – was hubristically pursuing a grand 'project ... to make better sense of the world, and on that basis to realign the Left with that new world'.[21]

For Gramsci the function of topical literature is to enable the reconstitution of ruling historic and subaltern 'blocs' around certain ideas and themes, the molecular, day-to-day changes that refresh the 'common sense' of hegemony. Elsewhere, he conceives of 'party' as more or less any agency capable of political intervention.[22] He cites '*The Times* in England', the self-styled 'newspaper of record', as his primary example of this phenomenon, as well as more obvious Italian examples which were consciously established in the process of setting up new parties, such as the socialist *Avanti!* or the PCI's own *Unita*. Perhaps he would not have been too surprised to find the 'New Times'-era *Marxism Today* operating not just as a faction within the British sister-party of the PCI, as it had been doing for close on ten years, but as a 'political party' in its own right. Mark Perryman now argues that some part of the motivation for 'New Times' was commercial:

> After the Tories won in 1987, it was very obvious that sales of *MT* were beginning to decline. We felt we had to try to create a debate, which is your most cost-effective marketing tool. It took about a year to put together, that New Times issue, and it sold sensationally, on the basis of the ideas that it itself was creating. Previously *MT* could ride the fact that there was a miners' strike on, or Thatcher winning in 1979, so it was completely reactive. This was different, this was proactive.

As Cronin points out, the real political object and potential agent of 'New Times' was not the Communist Party but the Labour Party of Neil Kinnock. Labour had just suffered its third successive general election defeat and now largely accepted that there was something epochal, or at least historically distinctive, about the 'hegemonic project' of Thatcherism. 'New Times' 'made evident and reinforced the loss of faith in both the old corporatist policies of Wilson and Callaghan and in the more left-wing policies associated with Benn and the so-called hard left', and offered at least a glimpse of a new more promising approach.[23]

'New Times' was the CPGB's last major survey of the outside world before it finally turned in on itself. With the evident redundancy of traditional 'class struggle', the CP went looking for a radicalism beyond class, in the stew of 'identity politics', the wilful irreverence of postmodernism and even 'post-Marxism'. These were always slippery concepts, and as with much of modern life the CP was late in coming to them. One 'Euro-communist', who chose to leave at this point, observes that by the late 1980s: 'New social forces weren't that new any more, they were all around you. The party paid lip-service, by saying we must have more women or whatever, but really its hearts and minds were back in the industrial militancy of the seventies.'[24] 'New Times' was also hailed as a determined effort 'to begin the difficult but vital transformation', as the CP Executive Committee (EC) report to the 1989 Congress put it, 'from the era of critique to the era of reconstruction'.[25]

The focus of the debate at the 1989 CPGB Congress was 'The Manifesto for New Times', drafted over the course of the previous two years by a working party including Beatrix Campbell, Martin Jacques, Charlie Leadbeater and Nina Temple, and drawing upon the parallel *MT* debate. The Manifesto makes very little mention of the CPGB itself; the section headed 'Communist Party' provides a thumbnail sketch of the communist past based on mounting rejection of Stalinism, and a communist future based on an ill-defined 'realignment of the left', with hardly a word about the party's demoralising present.[26] By the same token, there is no sustained critique of Labourism, beyond a lament that 'the reforming zeal of the immediate post-war period slowly gave way to the miserable pragmatism of the Callaghan era'.[27] Instead, 'The Manifesto for New Times' invests whatever faith and confidence it retains for political agency in 'broad social movements, for instance anti-nuclear campaigns'.

In the meantime, the CP's self-effacement continued. The three extracts from the 'Manifesto for New Times' in the book collection make no mention of the CP; the second extract 'Paths to Renewal' even goes so far as to call for 'some form of federation or strategic alliance between the opposition parties: Labour, the SLD, the nationalists and the Greens' that weirdly does not include the CP itself! The Communist Party of 1989, having on several occasions in its 69 year existence written individuals or whole groups out of its own history, is now busily obliterating itself, though this time in a spirit of embarrassment rather than ruthless revisionism. CP National Secretary Ian McKay wrote on behalf of the Executive Committee to party members and bodies on 17 May 1989, in a covering letter to 'The Manifesto for New Times', that 'We want to make it clear at the outset that what is being published is not a draft of a new edition of the *British Road to Socialism*. While principles outlined in the *BRS* are still valid, some features of the strategy it proposes are no longer appropriate.'[28]

Debate at the 1989 Congress itself added little of substance to the 'New Times' debate. Mark Perryman recalls 'a sort of grudging acceptance of the Manifesto. Every line was looked at and it was "Oh yeah, we'll just about accept that". It scraped through, but we (*MT*) were just giving up the ghost on the organisation.' This atmosphere of reluctant compromise made for some jarring contradictions. While the public substance of CP debate was all about the excitement of 'New Times' and the 'era of reconstruction', the report to Congress of its Executive Committee observed (in its very first sentence) that 'the Thatcher government has intensified its attacks on working people' and purported to detect 'the beginnings of a fightback expressed in many important struggles', primarily old-fashioned industrial disputes. Much was made of the anti-poll tax campaign, but apart from having 'issued hundreds of thousands of leaflets' there is little evidence of local or national CP involvement, let alone its customary 'strategic leadership'. The campaign was in fact far too anarchic and occasionally violent for the always staid and orderly Party to be centrally or comfortably involved in.

Newly appointed Secretary (she had dropped the 'General' because of its historical connotations) Nina Temple's 'reply to the discussion' was similarly conflicted, with a number of attempts to reconcile 'New Times' with rather older ones. 'New Times means co-existence' she declared, carefully deploying the term advanced by the Soviet Union to maintain the 'peaceful' equilibrium of the Cold War. On the issue of the party's name, which would become crucial over the next two years, 'Personally, until there is a political realignment of substance, I favour reclaiming the word Communist rather than changing our name, as whatever we called ourselves, we'd still be known as "the former Communist Party".'[29] There was other evidence of political disorientation: while a recruitment leaflet finished with a tick-box against the statement 'Yes I would like to join a party of organised Marxism, the Communist Party', the party's constitution still maintained that 'the Communist Party is guided by the theory and practice of Marxism-Leninism'.[30]

In the meantime, party membership and finances recorded inexorable decline: the EC reported that: 'The party membership at July 1987 was 10,350. At 7 September 1988 it was 8,546. The membership figure reported to the July 1989 meeting of the EC was 7,615'.[31] The largest part of these losses was accounted for by the departure of *Morning Star* supporters to form the 'Communist Party of Britain'. People were still joining the CPGB in some numbers – 285 between November 1988 and November 1989, spread proportionately across the country, with plenty of them contributing enthusiastically to Congress debates – but nowhere near enough to offset deaths and departures.[32] The accounts reveal 'Excess expenditure over income (of) £52,211' for the period 1987-9, and large losses on publications, including (over those two years of 'New Times') £68,562 on *Marxism Today*.[33]

The end of *Marxism Today*

Marxism Today folded in late 1991, a few months after the Communist Party of Great Britain. For all the talk of free-spirited independence, 'the only tool left in the box' could not survive the destruction of the toolbox. Without the party subsidy, the magazine was no longer financially viable. A number of options for keeping going were explored, including incorporation into *The Guardian* newspaper as a supplement, but they came to nothing, not least because the CP subsidy was no longer available. According to Mark Perryman, the magazine's circulation manager until 1990, many of its personnel were in any case ready to move on, with 'commercial ambitions' of their own. Curiously, the demise of the Soviet Union had provided new openings in *MT*'s final years:

> There was great interest in the Soviet Union, in terms of Gorbachev and so on. *Marxism Today* wasn't the originator of 'Bolshevik chic' but it was able to ride that wave. We set up something called Central Committee Outfitters, and suddenly the magazine was producing T-shirts, which would sell in tens of thousands and become a valuable source of income.[34]

'We also had a very ambitious advertising manager,' Mark recalls, 'who's now a TV producer, a guy called Malcolm Clark who was completely different to any advertising manager we'd had before':

> He really wanted to go out and get corporate advertising. He said we can't just be dependent on the GLC and the trade unions. He started bringing in advertising, high fashion advertising basically, which

created quite a backlash amongst the readers. He also developed a personal ads site in the magazine; it was quite racy, too much for some of the readers. This kind of thing became a big part of the magazine's image. It wasn't really part of the political agenda, but it coincided with some of the material, for instance Frank Mort and Angela McRobbie, who were much more permissive to consumerism than anyone on the left before. Suddenly, we were producing Bolshevik chic T-shirts, carrying adverts from Paul Smith and articles about the glories of shopping at Marks and Spencer.

Mark would take his T-shirt selling expertise into the enterprise Philosophy Football. Its trademark product is T-shirts with portraits and quotes of famous leftists, including Gramsci. It also continues to capitalise on 'Bolshevik chic'; one of its recent ventures was a set of 'original Russian Revolution plate designs to give to friends and family suffering from false consciousness'. [35]

Stuart Hall now feels that in these later stages of *Marxism Today* there was a real tendency towards 'hero-ising consumption and designer capitalism, in an attempt to get in with the new forms'.[36] For him, it coincided with the magazine's 'strategic mistake' of declaring that the left, and pretty much any politics of collectivism, was dead. The challenge of Thatcherism required the left, battered but still breathing, to take a wider reach – 'to encapsulate individualism within a politics that is inclined to the left'. Instead, *MT* effectively celebrated Thatcherism and declared the left beyond salvage. Hall was 'never part of the Demos strategy', the New Labour-inclined think tank co-founded by Martin Jacques and Geoff Mulgan, who subsequently became Head of Policy in Prime Minister Blair's office. By 1997, Hall was confessing 'a peculiar responsibility for the Blair phenomenon ... for launching some of these new ideas which have then been appropriated cosmetically and installed in a different kind of project'.[37] There is here a subtle but clear and significant parting of the ways between central elements involved in *Marxism Today*.

In the magazine's final regular issue, in December 1991, Martin Jacques wrote a farewell editorial and an article surveying his fourteen years as editor.[38] The tone of both pieces is breathless and confessional, superficially striking, with bunches of short, punchy sentences, such as we have become used to in the proliferation of magazine writing: '*Marxism Today* was a free spirit. We may have come from the CP, but we were never of it. We may have been on the left, but we were never imprisoned by it. We were dissidents, living on the edge, occupying an intellectual diaspora.' The magazine's legacy, he goes on in rather more traditional style, 'might be twofold: that it has helped to make ideas central to the way we think about politics, and it has put a nail in the coffin of blinkered partisanship, otherwise known as pig ignorance.' When Jacques took over, '*MT*' was extremely low in the CP's priorities, a journal for party intellectuals selling around 3,500.' He turned it into the voice of 'the dissenting academy which had grown up in and around the Communist Party – imbibing Gramsci, going euro-communist, breaking with Stalinism, taking feminism seriously... It was open-minded, restless, heretical and promiscuous'. In October 1981, the distribution deal with W.H. Smith increased sales threefold, and soon the magazine was embroiled in the debate on the left about how (or whether) to respond to Thatcherism: 'Put crudely, the Bennites, CP Stalinists, the Trotskyist groups and conservative forces were on one side and MT, the euro-communists, the soft Left and the Kinnockites were on the other.'

Towards the end of the editorial, Jacques says 'I don't want to explain here why we are closing. I have done that elsewhere in the issue.' Presumably he means the article 'The Last Word', but in fact this later piece is oddly coy about the reasons for the magazine's closure. There are general references to the 'events in Eastern Europe' in 1989, which 'made it abundantly clear that our title was now an albatross'. Jacques writes that he had decided in 1987 that 'I was tired, I was fed up with being broke and I wanted a new challenge.' During that period, he says, he began to see 'the relationship with the CP as a busted flush'. Beyond that, there is no clear explanation, though there is a curious parenthesis at the end of the very first paragraph – '(If only we had known about the Moscow gold ...)' – referring to then-recent revelations that the CPGB had been receiving clandestine funding as late as 1979, in some years as much as £100,000 per annum, and quite possibly into the 1980s.

Oddly, Geoff Andrews' chronicle of the CPGB's 'endgames' also only mentions the revelations in passing, as the ostensible reason for Jacques and others to resign from the CPGB (Francis Beckett's *Enemy Within* rather goes to town over them). They do help make sense of something those of us with experience of running other organisations and of managing budgets used to wonder about at the time: how did the CPGB, with plainly dwindling membership and disclosed income, maintain its levels of activity, staffing and accommodation? The rumoured regular legacies from aristocratic and wealthy old communists (including a number of East End 'sweatshop' proprietors), and the rental income from some very valuable central London properties (grouped into a portfolio identified as 'Rodell', and still generating a substantial income for 'Unlock Democracy', the Lib Dem-fronted successor organisation – after several other incarnations – to the CPGB), would only go so far. Beckett's is the fullest account of 'Moscow gold' and the 'bag-carrier' role of the CP functionary Reuben Falber, but even this never quite gets to the bottom of it, not least because Falber (now dead) stuck by 'the Bolshevik instinct not to give any information that he does not have to give'.[39]

Towards New Labour

There were notable common features between the working methods of 'New Times'-era *Marxism Today* and New Labour; the experience of the former may have helped to form the political approach and outlook of some of the key people also involved in the latter, most obviously Charlie Leadbeater and Geoff Mulgan. One of those common features is a strong, often dominant, older male figure at the heart of things. In the case of New Labour, it was what Chadwick and Heffernan call 'the Blair-Brown duumvirate ... the party's public presence since 1994 has been very much the product of Tony Blair and Gordon Brown'.[40] There are a number of possible explanations – the determination of particular individuals, the media preference for clear 'leaders', the development of 'celebrity politics', even the decline under Thatcherism of collective or cooperative styles – but it helps to explain why so many of the commentaries on New Labour have reduced 'the project' to the ups and downs of Brown and Blair's tense but symbiotic personal relationship and 'alpha-male' struggle for sole supremacy.

Likewise, it is impossible to examine the record and influence of the latter-day *Marxism Today* without considering its dominant personality, Martin Jacques. He was undoubtedly fortunate (for all his stated reluctance in taking on the post) in the timing of his editorship of *Marxism Today*; just when the modern 'magazine culture' was taking off, and the left was casting around for new topics and explanations (if not necessarily practical suggestions of what might be done about it, which would have shaken the dominant 1980s' mood of resigned passivity). At the same time, the CP was desperate to be associated with any kind of success, and ready and able to continue its substantial subsidy. Jacques' personality and CP sponsorship certainly achieved results. *Marxism Today* was a model of topical political and cultural commentary, unparalleled on the British left. Even now, its pioneering influence can be felt: *Gay Times* recently re-branded itself '*GT*', with new layouts and typefaces, just as *MT* did twenty-odd years ago, and saw its distribution outlets and readership figures shoot up. Its editor describes the re-branding exercise as a consciously 'post-gay, post-queer politics' move. Twenty years on, in these ever newer times, it seems that 'gay' has become the liability Marxism was in the 1980s.[41]

It is also noticeable that certain character types were attracted to work for *Marxism Today*, especially the ones Geoff Andrews refers to as 'Martin's boys': all variously competent and intelligent, ambitious and irreverent, heavily committed and enthusiastic. They were also available and reliable; not to say compliant and biddable. Again, the parallels with New Labour are startling, especially in its latter-day Brownite manifestation. And like Brown's inner cabal, these were mostly boys; *Marxism Today* in its heyday did not involve many women. Those few who were involved are especially scathing about its atmosphere and ethos: one talks tactfully about her 'problematic working relationship' with Martin, while another who worked closely with him for several years refers to 'interesting challenges'. The journalist Beatrix Campbell would simply refuse to follow Martin's requests to constantly re-write her contributions. Instead, she would reportedly wait till the very last deadline before re-submitting her unaltered copy.[42]

For the record, I found Martin Jacques pleasant enough at our single meeting in 2003, but I was struck by his own highly selective account of his past (as well as a sense that he was haunted by it). There was no mention for example of the CP subsidy to *Marxism Today*, or even more extraordinarily of his own part in setting up (with Geoff Mulgan) the highly influential New Labour-aligned think tank Demos in 1993. Certain communist habits of history-telling persist; perhaps Martin did not entirely shrug off 'the classic Stalinist model of the intellectual' he says *Marxism Today* was based on before he took over. When I looked up 'Demos' on Wikipedia, the entry did not mention Martin Jacques by name, but simply said the think tank was 'set up by journalists from Marxism Today'. For its part, the Demos website does not give any account at all of the organisation's history; the organisation apparently re-invents itself, New Labour-style, every bright new morning.

As for the 'legacy' of *Marxism Today*: what did it leave behind apart from fond memories and a certain sense of retrospective shock that the British left could produce a publication which people found worth reading and good to look at? Clearly, the contributions of Stuart Hall stand up well, and constitute an enormously suggestive and insightful body of work; but they would more than likely have found other outlets in his chosen professional field of cultural studies, alongside his more academic work. *Marxism Today*'s signature themes, the decline of the left and the hegemony of Thatcherism, were a model of 'applied Gramscism'; but their delineation did as much to demoralise as to disillusion the remnants of the political left. In doing so, they created a political, moral and emotional vacuum which New Labour – following the soft left, Kinnock and 'New Times' – was ready and willing to fill. The magazine succeeded in drawing some new and bright young people briefly into the Communist Party, but if this was ever a conscious part of the party's strategy for renewal or even survival, it clearly failed.

In 1991, the Communist Party was disbanded and replaced by the Democratic Left.[43] It was just as acrimonious a process as any of the party's debates of the 1970s and 1980s. Pat Devine, a lifelong party member and prominent Euro-communist from the current's earliest 'first phase' formation thought 'the atmosphere at the final party congress was poisonous':

> I've often thought about it, because it's not easy to explain. It turned into a sort of anticommunist witch-hunt, as if the new leadership carrying through this transition wanted to totally erase the past and start again. Within the *Marxism Today*/Euro-communist group, there were a number of different strands. The people around Nina Temple [the party's final General Secretary, and previously a party official her whole adult life] were not fully-fledged or committed Euro-communists, and they hadn't really thought through the posi-

tions like we had. For example, what happened in Eastern Europe and the Soviet Union came as much more of a shock to them than us.[44]

Andrews reports that '7000 … remained in the CPGB at the time of dissolution … [Democratic Left] membership declined from an initial figure of 1,500 to under 700 by the time it folded'.[45] The Democratic Left was itself superseded in 2000 by the 'New Politics Network', which after various legal disputations inherited the CPGB's financial legacy (estimated by Beckett in 1997 as 'money and assets worth more than £2 million') and used it mainly to promote cross-party electoral reform. More recently it amalgamated with the constitutional reform group Charter 88 to form 'Unlock Democracy', whose members are mostly Liberal Democrats.

The Communist Party of Great Britain was the only communist party in the world to disband itself voluntarily. Even the apparently discredited and historically redundant CPs of Eastern Europe hung on, changed their names and programmes and in a number of cases have been returned to national government, perhaps indicating that their own previous hegemony had not been solely based on coercion. In reunified Germany, the most slavishly pro-Soviet CP of all has managed to reinvent itself as a component of *Die Linke*, working alongside left-wing Social Democrats and in informal alliance with the Greens, and gaining a percentage share of the popular vote (just) in double figures. Meanwhile, the notably 'grown-up' German political culture continues to expose and come to terms with the horrors of partition and the *Stasi*-state.

Even in Russia the CP survives, primarily as a repository for nostalgic yearning for simpler, more stable times, but still a real political force within a primitive democracy. The Italian Communist Party split into two primary successor organisations: the respectable, mainstream Party of the Democratic Left (recently re-modelled as the Democratic Party) and the Re-founded (and generally unapologetic) Communist Party. The two forces were re-united in the wide and rather fractious parliamentary coalition supporting the Prodi government which fell in April 2008; both have struggled to cope with the consequences, but at least they exist.[46] In China and Vietnam, powerful CPs govern with little challenge, within a newly globalised model of 'state capitalism' that seems to offer promising routes to

orthodox economic development. Communist Parties in other countries as different as Japan, Sweden and India have managed to survive
and renew themselves, attracting new types and generations of recruits
to their practical critique of global capitalism, to the extent that they
now exercise serious political influence and in some cases, usually in
some kind of 'progressive alliance', government power.[47]

Without the negative association with the 'real existing socialism'
of the Soviet Union and Eastern Europe – its bureaucratic and inefficient economies, its repressed civil societies, and its debased,
manipulated politics – it has proved possible for CPs to 'renew' themselves more thoroughly than many other non-communist political
organisations forged in the various revolutions and wars of the twentieth century, Hobsbawm's tumultuous 'age of extremes'. So why did
the CPGB alone wind itself up? Plainly the party was a historic failure
in broader political terms, but it had managed to survive far harder
times than the late 1980s: the bewildering turn to 'class against class'
and 'social fascism' in the Comintern third period, for example, or the
early Second World War period of the Nazi-Soviet pact ('Uncle Joe
says Stand on your head'[48]), or the worst of the Cold War in the
1950s. It's hard to avoid the conclusion, from the written and spoken
accounts available, that it was mainly a matter of the personal exhaustion and in some cases personal ambition of the few hundred people
still actively involved by the early 1990s. In that sense, 'New Times'
served notice that 'the party is over'.

Notes

1. *Marxism Today* online collection, www.amielandmelburn.org.uk.
2. J. Cronin, *New Labour's Pasts*, p304.
3. S. Hall & M. Jacques, *New Times*, pp11/12.
4. S. Hall & M. Jacques, *New Times*, pp16/17.
5. R. Murray, 'Fordism and Post-Fordism', in S. Hall & M. Jacques, *New Times*, p38, first published as 'Life After Henry' in *Marxism Today* October 1988.
6. R. Murray, 'Benetton Britain: The New Economic Order', in S. Hall & M. Jacques, *New Times*, p56, first published in *Marxism Today* November 1985.
7. R. Murray, in S. Hall & M. Jacques, *New Times*, pp43, 45, 47.
8. F. Steward, 'Green Times', in S. Hall & M. Jacques, *New Times*, p72, first published in *Marxism Today* March 1989.

9. D. Hebdige, 'After the Masses', in S. Hall & M. Jacques, *New Times*, p88, first published in *Marxism Today* January 1989.
10. G. Therborn, 'The Two-thirds One-third Society', in S. Hall & M. Jacques, *New Times*, pp111/112, first published as 'West on the Dole' in *Marxism Today* June 1985.
11. C. Leadbeater, 'Power to the Person' and 'Thatcherism and Progress', in S. Hall & M. Jacques, *New Times*, pp137/149.
12. M. Rustin, in S. Hall & M. Jacques, *New Times*, p303; first published in *New Left Review*.
13. P. Hirst, in S. Hall & M. Jacques, *New Times*, p327/328; first published in *New Statesman and Society*.
14. S. Hall, 'The Meaning of New Times', in S. Hall & M. Jacques, *New Times*, p116. This article does not seem to have appeared in *Marxism Today*.
15. *The Hard Road to Renewal*, p59.
16. Hall, in S. Hall & M. Jacques, *New Times*, p129.
17. A. Crosland, *Can Labour Win?* Fabian Tract 325 (London, 1960); R. Crossman, *Labour and the Affluent Society*, Fabian Tract 324 (London, 1959); M. Abrams, *Must Labour Lose?* (London, 1960).
18. G. Andrews, *Endgames and New Times*, p219.
19. M. Jacques and S. Hall (eds.), *New Times* (London, 1989), p11.
20. M. Perryman, personal interview, 9 March 2004.
21. S. Hall & M. Jacques, *New Times*, p11.
22. A. Gramsci, *Letters from Prison*, ed. L. Lawner, pp50/51.
23. Cronin, *New Labour's Pasts*, p308.
24. A. Lawrie, personal interview.
25. *EC Report*, 1989 CPGB Congress, p18.
26. *Manifesto for New Times*, p20.
27. S. Hall & M. Jacques, *New Times*, p28.
28. I. McKay, letter from EC, 17 May 1989, People's History Museum CP archive.
29. 1989 Congress materials.
30. Recruitment leaflet (written by *MT's* Mark Perryman) and 1987 Aims and Constitution included in 1989 Congress materials, CPGB archive.
31. *EC Report*, 1989 CP Congress, p8.
32. 1989 Congress Preparatory Circulars.
33. *EC Report*, 1989 CP Congress, p22.
34. M. Perryman, personal interview 9 March 2004.
35. Advert in *London Review of Books*, 29 November 2007.
36. S. Hall, personal interview, 12 January 2004.
37. L. Terry, 'Travelling the Hard Road to Renewal: A Continuing Conversation with Stuart Hall', *Arena Journal 8*, p55.
38. M. Jacques, *Marxism Today*, December 1991, pp3 & 28/29.
39. F. Beckett, *Enemy Within*, pp218/220; G. Andrews, *Endgames and New*

Times, p220; see also A. Pearmain, 'Twenty Years On: Whatever Happened to the Communist Party?'.
40. L. Chadwick and R. Heffernan, *New Labour Reader*, pp3, 4.
41. J. Galliano, *GT* editor, personal conversation, 28 November 2007.
42. P. Devine, personal interview, 6 January 2004.
43. G. Andrews, *Endgames and New Times*, p245; F. Beckett, *Enemy Within*, p233.
44. P. Devine, personal interview, 6 January 2004.
45. G. Andrews, *Endgames and New Times*, p245.
46. P. Anderson, *London Review of Books*, 25 March 2009.
47. *The Guardian*, 24 April 2009.
48. F. Beckett, *Enemy Within*, pp90/101.

PART II: CRITIQUE OF NEW LABOUR

7. The Makings of New Labour

If there is any individual who links *Marxism Today*, 'New Times' and New Labour it is Charlie Leadbeater, the most ambitious and successful of 'Martin's boys', serial contributor to the 'New Times' debate, *Financial Times* journalist and author of two best-selling New Labour-era books, *Living on Thin Air* and *Up the Down Escalator* – which earned him the accolade of 'fascinating thinker' from none other than Tony Blair.[1] Taking a slightly different route to New Labour 'guru'-status was Phillip (now Lord) Gould, who, from an advertising background, provided key polling data and ideas for Neil Kinnock's reorientation of the Labour Party and then for the Blair/Brown 'project'. Leadbeater and Gould came from neighbouring and similar places, Basingstoke and Woking in Surrey, adjacent stops on the train from Waterloo. Both made much of their home towns as formative influences on their politics.

There is a section in Leadbeater's 1988 'New Times' article 'Thatcherism and Progress', barely a page long, called 'Progress in Basingstoke', which is remarkably similar to the opening sections of Phillip Gould's 1998 *The Unfinished Revolution*, the *Ur*-text of New Labour.[2] Leadbeater's take is rather more negative, but both adopt a tone of rueful yearning. Gould refers to his home town of Woking as 'the land that Labour forgot', and argues that Labour needs to reconnect with the people he grew up amongst if it's to stand any chance of re-election. Leadbeater blames 'the development office ... planners, producers and experts of rational, scientific, instrumental, unrelenting, ordered and disciplined progress' for 'the collective nightmare that Basingstoke became', where there was nothing to do but shopping, 'individual consumption, buying and selling'. For

Leadbeater, the basis for 'acquisitive Thatcherism' was 'the failure of the modernisation of the 1960s'.

Gould grew up a little earlier, and has rather fonder memories of 'a twilight suburbia where most people were neither privileged nor deprived, but nearly everybody was struggling to get by – which was not pretty and grew uglier – where people lived in unassuming council estates or in tiny semi-detached houses'.[3] These were 'ordinary people with suburban dreams who worked hard to improve their homes and their lives; to get gradually better cars, washing machines and televisions; to go on holiday in Spain rather than Bournemouth. These people wanted sensible, moderate policies which conformed to their understanding and their daily lives'. This is what – directly echoing the earlier 'revisionist' vocabulary of affluence and aspiration, right down to the references to household appliances and foreign holidays – the suburban dreamers were supposedly looking to Labour for; and these are the people Gould understands as the 'target' constituency for the New Labour project.

The problem for Gould's account of Labour's 'ordinary working-class supporters' is that, since its formation as a parliamentary constituency in 1950, Woking has always returned Conservative MPs, with generally somewhere between 46 and 67 per cent of the vote. Even in the year of Gould's master-minded New Labour landslide, 1997, the Conservative MP Humphrey Malins was returned with 38.4 per cent; the Labour candidate came a fairly distant third. Likewise, Leadbeater's Basingstoke has elected Tory MPs since its formation as a constituency in 1885, with a solitary Liberal in 1923/24. Both of these places were hotbeds firstly of Baldwinite 'popular Toryism' and then of 'vengeful' Thatcherism, overwhelmingly 'middle-class' constituencies, electorally and ideologically shaped by 'their visceral hostility towards manual workers and their institutions, especially trade unions' – and the Labour Party.[4] They contained hardly any industry, but served as dormitories for clerical and managerial commuters into London. Labour didn't 'forget' Woking and Basingstoke, because it never really knew them in the first place.

But these hard psephological and socio-economic realities have little purchase in the reminiscences of Gould and Leadbeater. These are New Labour's 'psycho-geographical' roots, in the alternately fond and embittered memories of growing up in the lower social reaches of the Home Counties. There is in this mentality an ambivalence that is similar – oscillating as it does between achievers' contempt and escapees' class guilt – to the mood among the 1950s and 1960s 'scholarship boys' (and some girls) who formed the backbone of revisionism and then the SDP. Gould and Leadbeater's separate accounts of their personal origins illustrate where New Labour thought it was coming from, the people it thought it was appealing to, and the growing friction between social reality and electoral politics.

The central theme of Leadbeater's 'New Times' contributions was that the left should cultivate an 'alternative progressive individualism', to counter the aggressive anti-socialism of Thatcherism, while conceding greater personal choice over consumption and lifestyle. By 1998 his range had widened considerably. The basic thesis of *Living on Thin Air* is that 'globalisation is good', proceeding from the post-war American realisation that 'there's a great big world out there … and gee, they're just like us!'.[5] Leadbeater decries 'defensive, inward-looking, nationalistic economic policies' such as most European countries have traditionally favoured, and advocates 'a more integrated global financial system', which is in any case taking shape, so we'd better get used to it. The mood throughout is one of enthusiastic resignation.

According to Leadbeater, Britain is peculiarly ill equipped to participate in this 'globalised' future, 'competing in the knowledge era' fatally handicapped by its 'long-standing weaknesses': 'too many children leave school without a good grounding in basic literacy and numeracy … our investment in training, skills and lifelong learning is still too feeble'.[6] In other words – the refrain which featured in so many declarations of New Labour policy in government, and which can be traced back into the moralistic roots of Labourism and its sense of improving mission – the British people are not fit for market and need 'modernisation'. Meanwhile, every other developed country – from social-democratic Europe to free-trade North America (all, in reality, and through boom and bust, warily protective against the effects upon their own people of globalisation) – is supposedly throwing itself into the global party.

Consumption and Information Technology are the new motors of this entirely progressive 'consensual capitalism'.[7] The 'entrepreneur' strides this stage alone, a new mythic hero (a Gramscian 'modern prince'?) for a new age of never-faltering, 24/7 'business', constantly embracing the 'future' and manipulating the 'intangible', negotiating his or her way through an 'ecology of institutions', with 'computers (always 'sophisticated') … threaded through our clothes', 'cannibalising' other people's ideas and creations, 'unlearning' the unhelpful habits and preconceptions of the past.[8]

A 'suburban populism' of the 'progressive middle class'

> Tough and tender; strong but fair. Already I was becoming a New Labour child … All I have wanted since I was a small boy was the chance to have a campaigning role in electing a Labour government.
>
> Phillip Gould's account of his 1950s childhood [9]

New Labour's account of its own 'project' has always been fairly straightforward.[10] To begin with, it was about restoring Labour's credibility and electability after years of fruitless opposition, sectarian in-fighting and policy confusion. More grandly, it aimed for a 'progressive' future in which Labour would reassemble the 'radical Liberal-Labour' coalition of the late nineteenth century under its own new management, become 'the natural party of government' Harold Wilson had prematurely proclaimed in the 1960s, and fulfil Labour's historic mission to banish the Conservatives to permanent opposition. It would be open, confident and optimistic; comfortable in its own sense of destiny; modern and modernising. It could dispense with the tawdry business of deals and pacts and manoeuvres that had sustained the Labour governments of the 1970s. It would finally quell the background noise of industrial 'strife' and the outmoded politics of class conflict by itself absorbing whatever 'progressive' impulses remained in the Liberal tradition and its more recent Social Democratic accretion.

As Tony Blair put it in 1998, echoing his mentor and regular dinner party companion Roy Jenkins (the originator of the term 'radical centre' during preparations for the SDP), New Labour 'draws vitality from uniting the two great streams of left-of-centre thought – democratic socialism and liberalism – whose divorce this century did so much to weaken progressive politics across the West'.[11] Three years earlier, just after becoming Labour's leader (and while some electoral accommodation with the Liberal Democrats still seemed necessary and desirable), Blair had paid glowing tribute to New Labour's 'progressive liberal cousin ... a credo of social reform and state action to emancipate individuals from the vagaries and oppression of personal circumstance'.[12] For Phillip Gould, always the most evocative and revealing of New Labour's strategists, the 'project' was both 'the last line of defence against people's fears and memories (and) alone ... the broad progressive church of British politics'; it represented a 'new suburban populism ... beyond the left-right divide and excessive political correctness'.[13] New Labour was consciously pitched (at least by ad-man Gould) at the emboldened, ambitious, materialistic, mainly southern English middle class that had been reconstituted by the social and economic liberalism of the 1970s and 1980s, leaving 'cloth cap' Labourism behind but still put off by traditional 'stuffy' Conservatism. Until 1997 and for some time after, the product proved popular.

There then followed a struggle with the hard 'realities' of government office; its possibilities and frustrations in roughly equal measure. New Labour was torn several ways between its high political ambitions and inspirational rhetoric, the cumbersome 'turning supertanker' nature of the modern state, the commitment to maintain tight Tory public spending plans, and desperation not to upset anybody except – purposely and productively – the left. When New Labour did seem to upset other people – as with Robin Cook's 'ethical foreign policy' – it backed down sharply. The 'sure touch' of the government's first year – best exemplified by Blair's inspired handling of the death of 'people's princess' Diana, and Brown's granting of 'independence for the Bank of England' – gave way to the rather less assured handling of the Ecclestone Formula 1/tobacco advertising affair, Peter Mandelson's mortgage, and the ill-fated Millennium Dome.[14]

A steadily booming economy, based domestically on rising house prices and limitless credit and globally on Chinese growth and American sub-prime mortgages, underwrote a decade of easy living, and covered over the widening social and political cracks. The continuing travails of the Conservatives – specifically their own failure to find a new post-Thatcher sense of purpose or an appealing leader – ensured New Labour re-election in 2001 and 2005, but the positive sense of historic mission had faded. Blair's evident obsession with 'legacy' as his premiership unravelled suggested he was more concerned with the past and his own future than with the country's present. The euphoria of May 1997 steadily evaporated into bitter reminiscence and longing for what might have been, with more than a hint of embarrassment over getting so carried away with it all. Did 'things ... get better'? Apparently not. New Labour's briefly re-unified 'progressive social alliance' stood exposed as an expedient electoral gloss over deeper fractures in a society increasingly ill at ease with itself. Blair's 'young country' was still profoundly divided by the old stratifications of class status and demeanour, not to mention the new conflicts of identity and culture. Beneath the buzz and bang of credit-fuelled consumption and construction, its 'binge and bling', Britain remained resolutely un-transformed. Political ennui set in; the electoral landslide settled into scattered heaps at the bottom of the hill.

During its most recent period, the New Labour 'story' has been of a quickening loss of confidence, personnel, support and momentum. There was a palpable sense of disappointment amongst Labour's members, activists and supporters; and widespread casting around for explanations, turning points and scapegoats. Brown's premiership bore all the signs and symptoms of a weary endgame, with the onset of the kind of deep cyclical capitalist 'bust' he claimed as Chancellor to have banished forever. Commentators were generally impressed by the Prime Minister's 'assured' handling of the credit crunch and the recession (or at least his capacity for following 'expert' advice), but voters were not. The electoral debacle of 2010 was widely anticipated; the only question was its scale and distribution. Some comfort was derived from the avoidance of 'meltdown', and denying the Conservatives a parliamentary majority, but among the multiple mixed messages delivered by the British people on 6 May 2010 was the death of New Labour.

The Guardian, the project's house-magazine (though in this election carried away on 'Cleggmania' and urging support for the Lib Dems), reported an ICM poll finding: 'Asked whether the Labour Party has improved Britain or not since 1997, 28 per cent say yes and 44 per cent no, with 24 per cent saying it made no difference'.[15] With a roughly corresponding actual vote of 29 per cent (itself a historic low), Labour had managed to hold on to its loyal 'core', mainly through lavish deployment of boom-years tax revenues and its thoroughly traditional state patronage of the post-industrial northern conurbations, where public spending now accounts for over half the local economies. This was allied to similarly traditional fear-mongering about how quickly and brutally the Tories would cut off the largesse. The *Guardian* on polling day again: '(Gordon) Brown pleaded with voters to return home to Labour, again warning that their tax credits were under threat.' The 'core-vote' was duly shored-up, but the New Labour 'social coalition' of 1997 had evaporated; Phillip Gould's 'suburban populism' was gone, seemingly forever. In electoral defeat, Labour looks set to retreat to its emotional and geographical heartlands, to 'our people' who supposedly felt ignored by New Labour, especially the 'bigoted kind' of people described off-camera (but on-microphone) by Gordon Brown in Rochdale, and routinely evoked by post-Brown leadership candidates. Neil Kinnock declared that a trade unionist friend had greeted Ed Miliband's election as Labour leader with 'We've got our party back, Neil!'[16]

There is undoubtedly disenchantment in the heartlands, but, if they still bother to vote, they support Labour out of loyalty, habit, visceral anti-Toryism and the lack of any viable alternative. The Labourist allegiance of the 'progressive middle class' has always been much more conditional, and had begun to wane – as Tony Blair ruefully noted when he talked in 1998 about 'getting the betrayal in early' – almost as soon as New Labour took office.[17] But it fell away almost altogether when he took the country into an ill-justified and arguably illegal war in Iraq. Blair had attempted to justify earlier military adventures as 'liberal interventionism', a pre-emptive strike for freedom and democracy, which had some tenuous link to Cook's 'ethical foreign policy'. The right-wing Howard government in Australia, which was roughly contemporary and in *de facto* alliance with Blair and Bush, coined the term 'military humanitarianism' for the same approach.[18] By the time of the Iraq war, the high moral tone had given way to the *realpolitik* of junior, supposedly restraining, partnership with the world's only remaining superpower.

There were flurries of controversy stoked by 'left-wing hawks' in the media, who attempted to justify the occupation of Iraq as the overthrow of a fascist dictatorship, and of Afghanistan as some kind of feminist crusade. They were few in number but noisy in the print media, especially its 'quality titles': Nick Cohen in the *Observer*; Johan Hari in the *Independent*; David Aaronovitch in *The Guardian* and *The Times* (Aaronovitch had been given his first newspaper job by then deputy-editor of *The Independent* Martin Jacques in the mid-1990s; Jacques now describes him as 'a clever buffoon');[19] and Christopher Hitchens apparently everywhere. There was also some element of coordination by the academics and 'public intellectuals' of the *Euston Manifesto* group, which included several of the above as well as left-wing notables like Will Hutton and Norman Geras. Together, they helped embolden Blair to withstand the much deeper and more widespread opposition to the war, but once the war was won (and the 'peace' clearly lost) most moved on to other hobbyhorses. Little more was heard of the creed of 'liberal interventionism' as swift military victory turned into protracted, bloody occupation, security and 'counter-insurgency'. Its advocates and tenets occasionally resurfaced, in fearful contemplation of the consequences of abrupt withdrawal from the messes which ill advised intervention had created, but this was about holding the fort rather than building 'new democracies'. Attempts to square the circle continued – memorably in US General Stanley McChrystal's description of his mission in Iraq as 'armed social work' – but nobody was taken in.[20]

Of political failure and expediency

If the public face of New Labour was always one of 'bright-eyed, neophyte enthusiasm, most graphically represented by Blair's perma-grin', behind the scenes it was rather more downcast, Gordon Brown on a bad day; a kind of 'Dorian Gray' in reverse.[21] To find out why, we need to look – as New Labour usually refuses to do, at least in public – at the prior experience of the project's elite and at some of its historical precursors in the Labour Party. This goes against New Labour's avowed distaste for history – as in Blair's declaration to a startled European Assembly in 1995 that 'Everything is new, new, new!', the 2001 election slogan 'Forward not Back', and its leaders' routine pleas to look to the future and not squabble over the past. Having said that, even if only in what Ross McKibbin has called their 'compulsory and generally dreadful' memoirs, the project's leaders have tried to give some account of their 'journey'.[22]

The simple weariness of eighteen long years in opposition, from 1979 to (eventually) 1997, supposedly took a heavy cumulative toll on a whole political generation of Labour MPs, advisers and officials. The Labour Party itself remained in fairly vigorous health throughout this period, with membership at around 300,000 and – as important to its local membership and organisational capacities as the number of MPs – with more councillors and councils than ever. This was a defensive, classically 'subaltern' strength, especially as Thatcherism centralised state power, grievously weakened local government and deepened its own 'authoritarian populist' appeal, but it did supply Labour with a steady source of motivational grievances for its still substantial ranks of activists. By 1997, party membership had reached a modern peak of over 400,000 (over half have since lapsed), with busy local parties and a fearsome machine for mobilising its electorate. But Labour's parliamentary leaders regard the 1980s as a lost decade of debilitating frustration and bickering.

This fatigue factor is most apparent in accounts by 'strategists' Peter Mandelson and Phillip Gould and the memoirs of ex-ministers like David Blunkett, Mo Mowlam and Robin Cook.[23] For Gould, the 1983 election defeat delivered 'a shiver of fear in the night', and the subsequent nine years of Kinnock's leadership (1983-92) were a 'terrible failure'.[24] For the others, in their self-styled political prime, the sheer grind of opposing a determined, apparently popular government enforced personal accommodation and political adjustment. Thatcherism did induce a kind of weary despair amongst its opponents, but the Kinnock years were as much about the organisational reconstitution as the political destruction of Labour. In that process, the defeat of the 'conservative left' was as important as the onslaught of the 'radical right', to deploy the 'four-cornered' political topography in common use in and around *Marxism Today* in the later 1980s.

By the time New Labour took shape, all the varieties of 1980s Labour leftism had been vanquished or exhausted. Tony Benn records in his diaries the steady restoration of right-wing control over the party's committees and policies; from the inside, Fabian Society Secretary Diane Hayter charts the concerted 'fightback' of the Labour right 'stayers' after the SDP schism.[25] Labour's internal centre of political gravity drifted inexorably rightwards from the Bennite hard left to the soft left, the Kinnockite 'centre left' and finally the 'modernisers' who would form the core of New Labour. For Heffernan, 'Labour's 1997 Manifesto echoed the economic priorities outlined in the 1979 Conservative Manifesto' which had brought Margaret Thatcher to power.[26] The fearful adjustment to

Thatcherism, obscured by all the talk of a 'new future' for a 'young country', was complete. Even the policies of the 'Limehouse Declaration', the basis for the 1981 secession of the Social Democratic Party from the briefly Bennite-inclined Labour Party, were considerably more 'socialist' than New Labour's.[27]

Looking even further back, the exhaustion of the 'old' Labour right in the 1970s had laid the basis for the early 1980s ascendancy of the left inside the Labour Party and, on this account, at least two of those epochal general election defeats (1983 and 1987). The Labour left had always been there, in various forms and sizes and degrees of influence, but was normally kept to the margins by the imperatives of electoral politics and trade union corporatism. What emboldened it in the 1980s were the manifest failures of the Wilson (1964-70, 1974-76) and Callaghan (1976-79) governments, the decline of the trade unions, and the subsequent fragmentation of the previously dominant and unified Labour right. Seyd points out that 'old' Labour had been an active partner in the destruction of the social-democratic consensus, with the general drift of policy to the right represented by 'In Place of Strife' in 1969, and the acceptance of IMF-imposed public spending cuts in 1976.[28] This served to rally the left in opposition, as much against its old party leadership as the new Tory government, aided to some degree by the post-1968 influx of activists and ideas.

The strategy of the late-1970s/early-1980s Labour left was tightly focused on transforming the party's constitution, through mandatory reselection of MPs, an 'electoral college' for the leadership, and wider determination of the party manifesto. Though advanced through the rhetoric of greater democracy, the political aim was to forestall future 'betrayal' of a sort that had historically hampered the struggle for socialism; Seyd and Whiteley's analyses of Labour Party membership in 1992 suggest that this inner-party strategy was broadly successful.[29] Even if their resistance to Thatcherism was misguided and ineffectual in the broader political arena, the Labour left pretty much banished the 'old right' from the party apparatus.[30] Part of the right defected to the SDP, but by no means all; a surprising proportion of MPs, estimated by Crewe and King at around three-quarters, initially went with the prevailing leftist wind or sheltered among the huddled 'stayers' who eventually and crucially aligned themselves with Neil Kinnock.[31]

The broader 'labour movement' turned in on itself under the onslaught of Thatcherism and the rubric of 'new realism'; and the intellectual currents of Labour revisionism dried up altogether. This meant that non-socialist or anti-left currents within the Labour Party had to find some 'new' guise for the 1990s and beyond, suitably adjusted for the 'new times' of Thatcherism and consumer capitalism. The old 'machine politics' of the traditional Labour right – the left, for all its shortcomings, was at least rhetorically committed to more open styles – would not fit the re-constituted, 'modernised' party, or for that matter the new populist democracy of the media age.[32] New Labour has on occasions paid obeisance to Croslandite 'revisionism' and the current of social democracy within Labourism. The Miliband/Saville critique of 'parliamentary socialism', which was one of the first and most expansive analyses of Labourism, posited just such historical continuity on Labour's right, guaranteed above all by the imperatives of institutional parliamentarism.[33] But on closer inspection New Labour's politics are a long way from Anthony Crosland or even Shirley Williams. This has been the cause of the often wistful, latter-day disaffection of Roy Hattersley and other veteran Labour right-wingers.

There was some recognition within New Labour, most evident in the connection with 'New Times' and the *Marxism Today* critique of the traditional left, that social democracy had been as thoroughly vanquished by Thatcherism as every other existing current of socialism. For Phillip Gould, they all represented a 'failure of modernisation'.[34] New Labour's reverence for Crosland and revisionism is generally skin-deep; an example of the semi-religious, ritualistic, almost reflex use of personages and trends in Labour history to which various currents within the party turn in order to establish their own supremacy. It is a mode of legitimisation in the anthropology of Labourism, Marquand's 'romanticized past' deployed as a 'weapon in battles about the present and future'.[35] New Labour's politics displays little familiarity or empathy with Crosland's *Future of Socialism*, and even less with the leftward turn he took just before his death in 1977. So, a simple revival of Crosland and revisionism wouldn't do either, not least because it would have required a programmatic radicalism Blair and Brown et al would not countenance.

New Labour's attitude towards the 1980s Social Democratic Party – which genuinely if briefly did lay claim to the revisionist legacy, and even to the radical reformism of R.H. Tawney, whose surname was appropriated for the SDP's own short-lived think tank – is even more ambivalent. On the one hand, it does not openly acknowledge any positive relationship or political debt, largely out of grudging respect to the Labourist tribal tradition which mythologises its traitors as much as its heroes. Labourism was deeply and permanently offended by the SDP 'defection'; far more so than by the substance of the SDP's politics, which had generally sat comfortably within Labour's 'broad church'. Blair could openly espouse central SDP themes, but he could not openly acknowledge their source of inspiration in 'turncoats' like Roy Jenkins. On the other hand, many SDP 'defectors' from Labour gravitated back to the party under the aegis of Blair and New Labour. Roger Liddell, who worked closely with Mandelson to flesh out the project, and Andrew Adonis, who (now ennobled) helped to shape New Labour's policies in government (and most recently was delegated to the ill-fated negotiations over a 'Lab-Lib pact'), were both prominent members of the SDP.

Other ex-members of the SDP, like my interviewee Sue Slipman, have pursued careers within the 'civil society' and state administrative infrastructure the New Labour government has constructed around itself. From that vantage point, she says, she has set about 'confronting New Labour with the question of are they part of the modernising agenda or do they still hold with Labourist values', and 'opening up the entrepreneurial approach to social justice and equal opportunity'. This strand of SDP thinking seems to be thriving in the 'third sector' of 'social enterprise' and community action (though, in the form of the 'Big Society' and the 'personalisation agenda', it remains to be seen how it stands up to the rigours of recession); but New Labour was careful to keep it at arm's length from the state. Sue currently criticises New Labour for not having gone far enough in sloughing off its Labourist roots, and failing to 'engage hearts and minds in a transformative project', which she feels that at its best the SDP represented.[36] This refrain of disappointment in New Labour is most consistently and plaintively articulated by another ex-founder member of the SDP, the *Guardian* columnist Polly Toynbee, alongside an ever more desperate struggle to 'keep the faith'.

The defeat of both traditional right and left wings of the Labour Party and the broader labour movement within a relatively short period of time – that momentous decade either side of 1980 – left the way clear for a supposedly 'new' political approach: a 'Third Way' between left and right, and more broadly beyond the traditional, class politics of capitalism and socialism.[37] More to the point, the defeat of large parts of the Labour Party's traditional political wings – whether by external forces like Thatcherism, by each other or (arguably in the case of the hard left) by themselves – left the whole party politically disorientated and demoralised. It was therefore deeply vulnerable to New Labour's selective attacks on Labourism and Blair's repeated and purposeful attacks on the party itself – which advertised both his personal determination and Labour's political renewal – and to its seductive offer of renewed 'electability'.

How serious a political project New Labour ever was is debatable. There has always been, at its heart, a kind of determined flippancy, a repertoire of in-jokes and plays on words, a barely suppressed smirk on key players' faces. The overriding priority was always getting re-elected, and 'principle' was secondary and adaptable. As so often, Phillip Gould rather gives the game away on New Labour's 'populism of the centre' when he describes it as designed both to acknowledge that 'everyone wants to be middle class these days' and to 'reconnect Labour to its heartland values'.[38] Thatcherism thrived on such internal contradiction, the politics of facing backwards and forwards at the same time, which fuelled its forward 'reforming' momentum but kept it securely rooted in reactionary popular mentalities; as a much smaller, narrower and shallower project, without the right's truly populist reach, New Labour founders upon it.

Gould is of course primarily an ad-man, and New Labour always was in large part a public relations exercise to convince the general public that 'Labour really has changed' and that the party activists – no matter how apparently enraged – no longer (if they ever truly had) posed a threat to the established order. But there is a sense in which New Labour was quite genuinely and honestly anti-Labourist. In this lay the project's most thorough-going 'modernising' impulse, even if only on the level of style and rhetoric. They understood that the secretive, manipulative, anti-democratic, 'machine politics' of the 1970s and 1980s labour movement made for repeated public relations disasters (and still does when occasionally exposed during industrial disputes), even if in practice and largely in private New Labour was quite prepared to deploy just such 'machine politics' in dealing with resistance or doubt.[39] New Labour represented a stylistic and rhetorical break with Labourism, but without fundamental political and cultural change in the Labour Party – which was tamed rather than transformed, acquiescent rather than enthusiastic – the break had no organisational or social base. The project merely exploited the historic weaknesses of Labourism. In publicly defining itself against the party, while steadfastly refusing political engagement with its membership and traditions (New Labour did remarkably little to change members' minds), it failed to overcome those weaknesses. The task became one of managing the public perception of Labour, rather than the political and organisational renewal of the party.

The New Labour way

New Labour acknowledged very early on the overwhelming realities of the 'media age', and took steps to court journalists, broadcasters and proprietors, or at least to neutralise their traditional hostility. Tony Blair famously flew halfway round the world in 1995 to offer Rupert Murdoch and his assembled News International executives an undertaking 'to reconstruct our ideology and organisation'.[40] The editors and executives of Murdoch's burgeoning newspaper and TV empire were treated to 'a wide-ranging speech in which Blair declared his enthusiasm for market forces and the family'.[41] Several notable figures had careers in the media before working for the Labour Party: Jones reports that 'Alastair Campbell, a committed Labour supporter, was formerly political editor of the *Daily Mirror* and a gifted tabloid journalist; and Peter Mandelson, despite having worked only briefly as a television producer on the ground-breaking political programme *Weekend World*, had built up unrivalled connections in the broadcasting and the entertainment industries'.[42]

The leaders of the project relentlessly deployed their experience and prior contacts to promote the New Labour 'message', and, according to Franklin, to intimidate and exclude journalists who were not 'on message'.[43] They were, it should be said, extremely good at it; it should also be acknowledged that the media were at least an equal partner in the curious *pas de deux* between politicians and journalists which has become known and widely derided as 'spin'. The dialectic of spin supplies the media with a reliable supply of interesting 'story', pre-digested and shaped 'copy' to fill the acres and hours of available space and time – what Nick Davies calls 'churnalism' – as well as an arena for politicians to transmit favourable and effective messages and images.[44] But it offers diminishing returns, especially on the politicians' side. As self-styled spin doctor Lance Price notes on New Labour's latter days, 'Whenever we complained that we were more spinned against than spinning, and we did it a lot, they rejected our arguments as just more spin'.[45] Even Alistair Campbell was reduced by 2004 to observing bluntly of journalists: 'They write drivel. They write rubbish. They tell lies.'[46] The dialectic of spin has produced a synthesis of public cynicism towards both politicians and the media and, brought to a head by the ongoing 'expenses scandal', the disgrace of an entire 'political class'.[47]

The use of focus group research on party policy – crucial to the shift away from Labour 'socialism' under Kinnock and the 'Shadow Communications Agency' in the 1980s – continued under New Labour as a source of new policy directions and initiatives and of public reaction to rather less easily defined matters of image and message.[48] This system was in part borrowed from the world of commercial marketing, advertising and public relations, where the project's self-styled mastermind Phillip Gould had pursued a pre-Labour career of sorts. But its use by New Labour was truly pioneering, and changed the practice of modern party politics fundamentally, away from 'street-level activism' (rather more accurately and less glamorously, the mechanics of canvassing, telling and 'getting out the vote' during election season) and towards focused, tactical electioneering through 'telemarketing' (telephone canvassing by party volunteers and increasingly by paid operatives) and the general media, which New Labour insiders have seriously hailed as the approach of a new-style, activist-free and even member-less 'virtual party'.[49]

Gould's own extraordinary account, *The Unfinished Revolution*, has become required reading for modern political activists, most notably Cameron's new Tories, who were reportedly instructed to read it by their newly elected leader.[50] But, as Gould makes clear, focus groups were simply one of the borrowings from the 'New Democrats' in the USA.[51] The Clinton presidential campaign of 1992, itself largely shaped by the experience of 'soft left' Democrat Presidential candidate Michael Dukakis' defeat in 1988, was applied almost wholesale in the run-up towards the 1997 British election. In particular, the techniques of 'rapid rebuttal', tactical 'leaking', negative briefing against opponents (including those supposedly on your own side if there is advantage in it) and related media management were used to neutralise unfavourable coverage, overcome criticism and to shout down opposition. 'Clintonian triangulation' – the blatant adoption of your opponents' more palatable policy proposals and careful 'positioning' and 'repositioning' within any particular policy debate in order to dominate the 'centre ground' has been a central element of the New Labour *modus operandi*; for Finlayson it was 'a "new progressivism" moving on from the "top-down" government of the New Deal or Great Society'.[52] Another less remarked upon and perhaps more surprising international connection was with Australia, whose Labour Party embarked on a similar project of 'modernisation' in the wake of 'radical' Prime Minister Gough Whitlam's dismissal and defeat in the mid-1970s. When eventually returned to power under Bob Hawke, Australian Labour was considerably more 'centrist', and has generally remained so.

There is now general agreement, especially on the extant left and (perhaps surprisingly) right of British politics, that New Labour represented an accommodation of some sort with Thatcherism, predicated on the defeat of Labourism.[53] Simply put, New Labour accepted as irreversible the political, cultural and social shifts of Thatcher's 1980s heyday. Heffernan describes this as a process of more or less passive acquiescence:

> The period 1983-97 is one in which explanations of the changing Labour Party are to be found and understood; taken in the round Labour did not so much change or modernise itself as it was changed by the impact of events. In short, where Thatcherism has led, the Labour Party of Kinnock, Smith and Blair followed.[54]

New Labour itself accepts – sometimes grudgingly, but pretty consistently – that the 'neo-liberal revolution' and the 'globalisation of capitalism' provide the context in which it has had to attempt to govern Britain. Geoff Mulgan, Blair's policy director for the first seven years of New Labour government (and another of 'Martin's boys' on *Marxism Today*), had written as early as 1989 of 'the irreversibility' of market reforms and consumer individualism.[55] Blair himself promised business 'less labour market regulation than in the USA'.[56]

So New Labour's deepest historical continuities lay not so much with the 'parliamentary socialism' of the 'old' Labour right, as with the 'market utopia' of radical Conservativism. Hay points out that 'insofar as globalisation exists, its origins can be traced to a series of highly political (and hence contingent) decisions to deregulate the financial market and to liberalise capital flows' in the 1970s and 1980s.[57] For Jenkins, 'The economic ideas underpinning Thatcherism can be found in embryo in debates in the 1950s and 1960s' on the Conservative right.[58] For Cockett, neo-liberalism had been actively constructed and promoted by lobby and campaign groups within and around the Conservative Party in the 1950s and 1960s: these groups were 'symptomatic of the realignment that took place in favour of economic liberalism during the mid-1970s. Their activities represented the end of the post war consensus'.[59]

It is a further measure of their success that by the 1990s 'irreversible' globalisation had become established as the prevailing wisdom, the 'common sense' of triumphalist, hegemonic capitalism. It had assumed the force of nature and, at its furthest US reaches, where business merges with religion to form that country's very particular 'historic bloc', 'culture war' or national-popular ideology, the evangelical fervour of 'free enterprise'. This sense of globalisation's inevitability has been a central element in the Brownite current within New Labour, and driven much of its approach to economic, employment, education and training policies, and to what it regards as its central preoccupations of welfare reform, urban regeneration and 'community cohesion'. This is what Neal Lawson refers to as 'making the people fit for market', and has a clearly moral as well as political or economic dimension.[60]

This is also where Brown drew most openly on the traditional rhetoric of Labourism – 'bringing out the best in people by policies that ensure opportunities for all' – and its moral purpose of improvement, as in Herbert Morrison's 'one of our purposes is to make men and women better than they are'.[61] There has always been a top-down, profoundly anti-democratic and authoritarian edge to Labour's 'social engineering'. But this 'new' Labourism, in a context of wilful and wholesale exposure to globalisation, has the effect of driving neo-liberalism deeper into our personal lives and communities.[62] It constitutes a new 'social interventionism' on its softer side, a 'new statism' on its more bureaucratic side, and, in its more punitive guises, a rather chilling 'social authoritarianism'. And now, with the recession and the much-touted 'death of New Labour', new variants are beginning to pop up in retrospective accounts of the project's failure. Contemplating the rise of the British National Party in one of the old Labour heartlands, against a backdrop of rising unemployment and the manifest limitations of urban 'regeneration', the leader of the Labour group on Liverpool City Council observed 'What we have failed to do is regenerate the people'.[63] There is here, as in so much left-wing politics in Britain, an undercurrent of profound disappointment in the working class.

The earliest acknowledged source of New Labour's social authoritarianism was Amitai Etzioni's 'communitarianism', 'a form of social control in which neighbourhoods regulate the conduct and morals of their members, demanding support for established norms and less individual assertiveness'; this was another US import that found a prominent place in New Labour rhetoric on its publication in 1995. The political basis of communitarianism is described by Paul Anderson and Nyta Mann as 'a response to the response [of] the ultra-Conservative Moral Majority movement to American disillusionment with mainstream liberalism and conservatism', a kind of counter-counter-counter cultural move, drawing the state into ever more local arenas.[64] Thatcher might have regularly railed against the 'excesses' of the 1960s, but she balked at direct state interference in personal conduct, not least because of the strong libertarian, anti-statist and market-individualist impulses within 'high' Thatcherism. New Labour – what Freeden calls 'this extraordinary blend of moderate American conservatism, elitist British Fabianism, and populism' – has no such qualms; it has been drawn relentlessly towards new forms of state intervention in society – Blair's 'social-ism' – just as it has felt forced to withdraw from old Labourist ones in the economy.[65]

This is the ideological fine detail, in Gramscian terms, of the 'transformist' adaptation by New Labour of the Thatcherite 'passive revolution', the sweeping changes imposed upon British society 'from above' during the 1980s and 1990s. Transformist political groups are by definition small, superficial, localised and 'conjunctural', generally confined to parliamentary institutions, and historically 'passive' rather than 'active'.[66] The formation of New Labour by what Heffernan refers to as 'the impact of events' is symptomatic of its ultimate passivity and timidity – of a non-hegemonic, 'subaltern' parliamentary political force – based as it is on the earlier loss of the quasi-hegemonic hold of the social-democratic consensus. Its only freedom of manoeuvre lies in extending the norms of Thatcherism into new arenas – such as personal and family life and local community institutions (and most obviously into health, housing and schools) – resulting in what Freeden calls 'a deficit of the liberal individuality New Labour wishes elsewhere to encourage'.[67] As such, New Labour has represented a kind of proxy hegemony, keeping Thatcherism's flame while more conventional Conservative forces regroup and refocus.

Etzioni has hardly been mentioned by New Labour for some years; his 'communitarianism' seems to have mutated, within the crucible of British social relations and traditions, into the busy-body, nosey-parkerdom of ASBOs and CCTV and moral panic about 'chavs'. The 'authoritarian populism' of Thatcherism, originally directed from afar against whole social groups, was localised – 'personalised' even – by New Labour to suit the newer times of individualised consumer capitalism. It was transformed into a 'social authoritarianism' focused on errant individuals and families, with little regard for their social circumstances, prior experience and inherited disadvantages (easily dismissed as 'excuses'). As moral philosopher Freeden concludes, New Labour's conception of welfare is a long way from earlier, expansive socialist conceptions of 'human flourishing and well-being … the ethical end of optimising human creativity and eliminating human alienation'. Rather, welfare has lost its universal reach and become 'targeted'; it is reduced to 'support services for the marginalised, the handicapped or the unlucky'; as such, it becomes a state-sponsored badge of stigma, both symptom and cause of 'the very social exclusion New Labour has loudly denounced'.[68] As the 'state' withdraws and 'society' intervenes, vulnerability is recast as 'dependency'; an entire culture and economy of shiftlessness is conjured up. On this reading the Con-Lib coalition government, with its 'double shuffle' of 'Big Society' and 'reduced state', simply has to take up the reins from its predecessor; a further, smoothly continuous 'transformist' adaptation within the Thatcherite 'passive revolution' that defines modern British history.

Notes

1. C. Leadbeater, *Living on Thin Air* (London 1998); *Up the Down Escalator* (London 2002).
2. P. Gould, *The Unfinished Revolution* (London 1998).
3. P. Gould, *The Unfinished Revolution*, p3.
4. R. Bell & S. Gunn, *Middle Classes*, p71.
5. C. Leadbeater, *Living on Thin Air*, p7.
6. C. Leadbeater, *Living on Thin Air*, p52.
7. A phrase I also came across on a guided tour of Ben and Jerry's ice cream factory in Vermont in 1996.
8. C. Leadbeater, *Living on Thin Air*, pp146, 45, 148, 41, 53, 79.
9. P. Gould, *Unfinished Revolution*, pp12 & 216.
10. P. Anderson & N. Mann, *Safety First: The Making of New Labour* (London 1997); C. Hay, *The Political Economy of New Labour* (Manchester 1999); S. Driver & L. Martell, *New Labour: Politics after Thatcherism* (Cambridge 1998); N. Jones, *Sultans of Spin: The Media and the New Labour Government* (London 1999); N. Fairclough, *New Labour, New Language?* (London 2000); A. Rawnsley, *Servants of the People: the inside story of New Labour* (Harmondsworth 2001); S. Ludlam & M. Smith (eds.), *New Labour in Government* (London 2001); A. Finlayson, *Making Sense of New Labour* (London 2003); A. Chadwick & R. Heffernan, *The New Labour Reader* (London 2003); J. Cronin, *New Labour's Pasts* (Harlow 2004).
11. T. Blair, *The Third Way: New Politics for the New Century* (London 1998); I. Crewe & A. King, *SDP: The Birth, Life and Death of the Social Democratic Party* (London 1995), p58.
12. T. Blair, *Let Us Face the Future* (London 1995) pp4, 11/12.
13. P. Gould, *Unfinished Revolution*, pp393, 398, 175, 178.
14. A. Rawnsley, *Servants of the People*.
15. *Guardian*, 6 May 2010.
16. BBC *Today at Conference*, 29 September 2010.
17. T. Blair, *speech to the Trades Union Congress*, September 1998.
18. T. Nairn, *London Review of Books*, 7 December 2007.
19. M. Jacques, personal interview.
20. S. McChrystal, *BBC News*, 30 September 2009.
21. S. Jenkins, *Thatcher and Sons*, p207.
22. R. McKibbin, *London Review of Books*, 12 March 2007.
23. P. Mandelson & R. Liddell, *The Blair Revolution* (London 1996); P. Gould, *The Unfinished Revolution*; D. Blunkett, *The Blunkett Tapes* (London 2006); R. Cook, *The Point of Departure* (London 2004); M. Mowlem, *Momentum* (London 2003).
24. P. Gould, *Unfinished Revolution*, pp21, 43.
25. T. Benn, *Diaries* (London 2003); D. Hayter, *Fightback* (Manchester

1996).

26. Heffernan, in *The New Labour Reader*, p49.
27. I. Crewe & A. King, *SDP*, p102.
28. P. Seyd, *The Rise and Fall of the Labour Left* (London 1987).
29. P. Seyd and P. Whiteley, *Labour's Grass Roots: The Politics of Party Membership* (Oxford 1992).
30. H. Pelling, *Short History of the Labour Party*, p172; D. & M. Kogan, *The Battle for the Labour Party* (London 1982); M. Crick, *Militant* (London 1984); P. Tatchell, *The Battle for Bermondsey* (London 1983).
31. I. Crewe & A. King, *SDP*, p105.
32. M. Westlake, *Kinnock the Biography*.
33. D. Coates, *The Labour Party and the Struggle for Socialism*, p85; R. Miliband, *Parliamentary Socialism* (London 1961).
34. P. Gould, *Unfinished Revolution*, p33.
35. D. Marquand, *The Progressive Dilemma*, p102.
36. S. Slipman, personal interview, 9 November 2005.
37. A. Giddens, *The Third Way: The Renewal of Social Democracy* Cambridge, 1998).
38. P. Gould, *Unfinished Revolution*, pp51, 178.
39. A. Rawnsley, *Servants of the People*; S. Jenkins, *Thatcher and Sons*; L. Price, *The Spin Doctor's Diary* (London 2005).
40. T. Blair, speech to News Corporation Leadership Conference, Perth W. Australia, July 1995.
41. P. Anderson & N. Mann, *Safety First*, p40.
42. N. Jones, *Sultans of Spin*, p311.
43. B. Franklin, in Ludlam and Smith (eds.), *New Labour in Government*.
44. N. Davies, *Flat Earth News* (London 2009), p59.
45. L. Price, *The Spin Doctor's Diary*, pxxvi.
46. N. Davies, *Flat Earth News*, p198.
47. P. Oborne, *The Political Class* (London 2009).
48. Frank Howard, personal interview, 12 October 2004. Frank worked for Phillip Gould in the Shadow Communications Agency, which was an informal publicity unit inside the Labour Party during the 1980s and pioneered much of the 'news management' techniques associated with New Labour.
49. *Guardian*, 12 October 2005.
50. *Daily Telegraph*, 17 October 2006.
51. P. Gould, *The Unfinished Revolution*, p135.
52. A. Finlayson, *Making Sense of New Labour*, p106.
53. S. Jenkins, *Thatcher and Sons*, p1.
54. R. Heffernan, in *The New Labour Reader*, p50.
55. G. Mulgan, *New Times*, p385.
56. T. Blair, *speech at launch of report of Commission on Public Policy and British Business*, 21 January 1997.

57. C. Hay, *Political Economy of New Labour*, p37.
58. S. Jenkins, *Thatcher and Sons*, pp3, 40.
59. R. Cockett, *Thinking the Unthinkable*, p232.
60. E. Balls, 'Open Macroeconomics in an Open Economy', in L. Chadwick and R. Heffernan, *New Labour Reader*, p106. N. Lawson, personal interview 28 January 2004.
61. J. Fyrth (ed.), *Labour's Promised Land?* (London 1995), p14.
62. Gordon Brown, *Mansion House Speech* 1998.
63. J. Anderson, reported in *Observer*, 3 May 2009.
64. A. Etzioni, *The Spirit of Community* (London 1993); P. Anderson & N. Mann, *Safety First*, pp247/8.
65. M. Freeden, in L. Chadwick & R. Heffernan, *The New Labour Reader*, pp45, 47; T. Blair, speech to Fabian Society 1994.
66. A. Gramsci, *SPN*, ft. 8 p58.
67. M. Freeden, in L. Chadwick & R. Heffernan, *The New Labour Reader*, p45.
68. M. Freeden, in L. Chadwick & R. Heffernan, *The New Labour Reader*, p46.

8. Neil Kinnock and the Labour Party Policy Review

The most immediate historical source of New Labour was Neil Kinnock's later leadership of the Labour Party and the 1987/89 Policy Review. This was a crucial transitional period in the party's modern history; for Heffernan it was plainly 'the precursor to New Labour, the flagship of the initial "New Model" party'.[1] While *Marxism Today* debated 'New Times', the Labour leadership was undertaking its own thorough overhaul of policy and approach, with surprising echoes of the rather grander exercise being conducted by *MT* and the magazine's nominal sponsor the CPGB. Both of these broad analyses, the Policy Review and 'New Times', took shape in the late-1980s, the moment of historical disorientation ensuing from the end of the cold war. They were absolutely central to New Labour's adaptation to Thatcherism and continued to exert substantial influence over the project's approach and fortunes over the following decade and beyond. As Freeden argues, 'current Labourism is, above all, ideologically eclectic; but it is emphatically not ideologically dormant'.[2]

The Kinnock leadership – which originated in the 'soft left' but became increasingly estranged from it as the Kinnockites strengthened their grip on the party and consciously moved towards the 'centre ground' of British politics – occupies a critical instrumental place in recent Labour history. As Heffernan argues, '1994 was not a "year zero" for the Labour Party, because Blair's reforms were built on the firm foundations established before he came to the leadership'.[3] Even Gould accepts that Kinnock played a role in changing the party's orientation, writing that, while 'Kinnock lost votes because he lacked voter appeal, [he] added them because of the changes he made to the party and its policies'.[4] For Kinnock's own biographer, though, it was mainly a negative 'deck-clearing' or 'clinical cleansing' exercise.[5] Kinnock himself is often seen as a figure of fun – the 'Welsh boyo' famously making a fool of himself at the Sheffield 'mega-rally' in 1992 – but this largely derives from the vicious press coverage he was subjected to, especially when he came anywhere near government.[6] He was a limited political leader, but his impact on the Labour Party over the course of his nine-year leadership was serious and wide-ranging.

Neil Kinnock's political background was impeccably left-wing in Labour terms. He was a product of the same cultural and moral mould as the other leading Welsh Labour politician and orator of the twentieth century Aneurin Bevan. Kinnock had been elected MP for the South Wales constituency of Bedwelty (later Islwyn) in 1970, and spent his early parliamentary career well away from government office, espousing causes associated with Labour socialism: the alternative economic strategy, unilateral nuclear disarmament, etc. The veteran Labour leftist MP Eric Heffer had gone so far as to call him 'an ultra-left posturer who would say anything to attract attention'.[7] But there is a clip in the BBC News coverage of his 1992 resignation, taken from around twenty years before – picturing him against a Welsh valley backdrop and still with most of his ginger hair waving in the wind – which perhaps indicates the potential for tempering his stance. He is asking in his characteristically roundabout and repetitive way, a pained expression on his freckled face, 'Can you have socialism in a capitalist economy? No, there are far too many paradoxes, too many confusions, too many arguments. It simply wouldn't work …'.[8]

The more politically experienced and less avowedly anti-capitalist Kinnock carefully maintained his independence from Labour's groups and factions, to the extent that in the later 1970s he operated as a 'lone voice' in a number of key debates in the party and parliament.[9] Similarly, he kept his distance from Tony Benn and the push for inner-party procedural reform and a more rigorously 'socialist' politics in the aftermath of the 1979 defeat.[10] Kinnock abstained in the final run-off between Benn and Denis Healey in the crucial 1981 deputy leadership election, when a handful of such abstentions by MPs was enough to give Healey victory.[11] When Michael Foot stood down after the 1983 defeat, Kinnock was deemed broadly acceptable to all the organisational sections and political wings of the party, and was elected leader with substantial trade union support. This included substantial elements of the left, somewhat chastened by their part in the internal schisms associated with Benn's deputy leadership campaign, the agitations of the 'hard left', and the worst general election performance in the party's history. One of Kinnock's first published articles as Labour leader, 'My Socialism' in the *New Statesman*, cited Gramsci twice (alongside Marx, Engels and Trotsky) as an inspiration.[12]

Kinnock could still be defined as being of the centre left of the party, but he shared a widespread view that Labour had made itself unelectable through being too left-wing. Instead of seeking to understand how the Labour Party might develop a politics that could challenge current hegemonic thinking, he retreated before it. Thus one of his first actions was to seek to reduce the powers of party activists in the constituencies and trades unions, on the grounds that they had alienated the wider Labour electorate.[13] In practice this meant a protracted battle inside the party to reduce and eventually expel the 'entryist' and 'workerist' Trotskyists of the Militant Tendency. Militant was never a particularly widespread or powerful force inside the Labour Party, beyond parts of London, Merseyside and Glasgow, but it was a noisy, disruptive, occasionally violent and deeply unpleasant nuisance. They deployed considerable energy, resources and personnel – not to mention the hard-bitten drive that sectarian Trotskyist organisations are able to apply to particular localised objectives – to taking over party organisations that had been hollowed out by decades of corruption, atrophy and in-fighting. These included constituencies and council Labour groups like Liverpool, Lambeth and Bradford, and the party's national youth section the Labour Party Young Socialists.

The rest of the Labour left disliked but tolerated Militant, on the basis of a certain 'socialist' solidarity and concern for democratic propriety. No doubt there was also concern among groups like Clause IV, Tribune and the Campaign for Labour Party Democracy that moves against this particular shadowy sect – known to themselves as 'The Revolutionary Socialist League' – might also expose their own quasi-factional activity to unfavourable scrutiny.[14] But the point of Kinnock's attack on Militant was only partly about clearing them out of the party. It also served to signal to the wider world that the whole Labour left, ascendant under Benn in the early 1980s, had now been brought to heel. As indeed it had; Panitch and Leys point out that by 1987 'Benn and the remaining new left activists had now been relegated to the party's margins, and no fresh generation succeeded them'.[15] At the 1986 Party Conference, where Militant was finally expelled, Kinnock gave a taste of what was to come when he espoused 'social ownership' as the primary economic aim of the labour movement, in place of the established Labourist shibboleth of nationalisation.[16] This was the first step towards what Smith sympathetically calls the 'post-Keynesian revisionism' that would characterise early New Labour economic thinking. Shaw – rather less sympathetic – calls it a return to 'pre-Keynesian orthodoxy'.[17]

Labour's third electoral defeat in a row in 1987 was commonly regarded as a model modern campaign, with groundbreaking poster and media campaigns overseen by Peter Mandelson and Phillip Gould, but the party was still well behind the Tories and, at just over 10 million, several million votes short of its historical high. While Labour was still suffering from the breakdown of traditional allegiances, the Tories continued to profit from it. According to Gould's post-election analysis, 'only 7 per cent voted Conservative because they always had done', which is not only a measure of Thatcherism's deepening hegemony and diverse electoral base, but also (following Hobsbawm) of the general breakdown of political tribalism.[18] Labour also had to contend with a relatively buoyant SDP/Lib Alliance vote, some months before the Alliance's own acrimonious merger (more accurately, a split between the Owenite 'social market' rump and everyone else in the SDP). Patricia Hewitt, then Kinnock's Press Officer, argued in an internal memorandum that at least the 1987 Labour campaign 'killed the Alliance'.[19] Ultimately of course, the SDP's failure to 'break the mould of British politics' and its effective absorption into the Liberal Party would do as much as anything to restore Labour's electability, and contribute a fresh wave of people and ideas to the formation of New Labour. Apart from earlier Trotskyist entryists and fellow-travellers, it was the first such 'new wave' of Labour recruits since the early 1970s, this time from the right.

But for now, Kinnock announced a thorough-going Policy Review, 'a process that would serve to reverse the recent domination of policy-making by the left and equip Labour with a conceptual framework, a rhetoric and a programme on which to base a renewed claim to the right to govern the nation'.[20] Kinnock's aides felt they had done as much as they could to repackage and re-present the established Labour 'brand' for the 1987 election campaign. According to Gould, the campaign's eventual failure had 'demonstrated the weakness of advertising and marketing':[21] the product itself needed a thorough revamp. Peter Mandelson, always more consciously 'social democratic', argued that the party needed 'an intellectually driven process of change', equivalent to the German SPD's 1959 reorientation towards the 'mixed economy' at Bad Godesburg, the key moment in the formation of modern European social democracy.[22] More parochially, Patricia Hewitt argued for a clean break with the concerns of the 'loony left': 'the gays and lesbians issue is costing us dear among the pensioners'.[23] Phillip Gould's account also rounds out the evident distaste within sections of revisionist Labour for the new 'identity politics' of the 1980s: 'The minority agenda of the emerging metropolitan left, of militant rights in welfare, race and gender, was completely divorced from what the British people want from a government'. (This did not stop him recounting with pride a poster which he instructed should 'use black hands, young hands, women's hands'.[24]) Even at its own metropolitan heart, emergent New Labour always was ambivalent towards these 'new times'.

Gould proposed to the National Executive Committee that 'working groups be established to prepare reports in all areas of policy', alongside focus group research into 'what are the real motivations influencing voting behaviour'. As Cronin notes, this new coupling of policy formation and market research implied that 'the party would go to where the voters were rather than expect voters to be moved towards the party by the strength of its arguments'; a fundamental reversal in the normal direction of political persuasion.[25] The planned review was endorsed by the party conference in September 1987, 'though without great enthusiasm'.[26] At this point – the high water mark of Thatcherism and the aftermath of its third general election victory in rapid, demoralising succession – there wasn't very much enthusiasm for anything in the Labour Party; a key historical precondition for its decisive shifts to the right.

The Policy Review was carried out by seven study groups on 'A Productive and Competitive Economy', 'People at Work', 'Economic Equality', 'Consumers and the Community', 'Democracy for the

Individual and Community', 'Britain in the World' and 'The Physical and Social Environment'. The lingering emphasis on Labour's traditional preoccupation with the economy is evident, with nods towards currently fashionable concerns over consumption, constitutional arrangements, and the environmental and international arenas. Study group membership was drawn from the Shadow Cabinet, the NEC and the trades unions – all the separate institutional wings of the labour movement, 'designed to produce consensus' – with the addition of selected outside 'experts'.[27] However, a tight timetable allowed for minimal consultation with the larger party and the outside world. What consultation there was, under the rubric 'Labour Listens', produced (for Cronin) 'inputs [that] were inconsistent and uneven, with correspondingly little impact, and the staged events served mainly as public relations'.[28] Colin Byrne, Mandelson's assistant, remembers this 'odd thing, which was basically about taking shadow ministers to town halls the length and breadth of the country to be shouted at by complete lunatics'.[29] From the left viewpoint, the consultation was organised with 'no concern for the representativeness of the meetings, which were mostly poorly attended ... nor were any mechanisms put in place to ensure that what people said was fed into the Policy Review'. The consultation exercise was designed to prove that 'people hate our policies', and to reinforce the message that they would need to be jettisoned to make the party electable again.[30] Kinnock himself later acknowledged that 'I saw to it that meetings were conducted in such a way as to make people remember the weaknesses [of Labour] far longer than they remembered the strengths'.[31] Sure enough, 'local party members ... did ultimately come to accept the need to win elections, but were still reluctant to remake the party's programme in order to do so'.[32]

At this point there was still enough resistance within the party to prevent a wholesale makeover, which meant that 'socialism' was not wholly jettisoned, but the overall effect of the Policy Review was to reduce, weaken and dilute the party's commitments across the broad range of policy. 'Social ownership', as trailed in Kinnock's earlier speech, displaced 'nationalisation', and 'regulation' displaced 'planning' and 'control'. By the time of the 1992 general election manifesto, this had been much further reduced; it called for public *control* (not ownership) of only a single industry/utility, Water –

which had not yet even been fully privatised by the Tory Government. As Shaw notes, 'Labour ceased to regard any modification to property relationships as a significant object of political endeavour'.[33] In the Policy Review there was rapid retreat from the commitment to take recently privatised industries back into public ownership, with only British Telecom and Water slated for 'social ownership' by a future Labour government.[34] While the review criticised the 'short-termism' of the City of London, it was 'coupled with a determination not to do anything very dramatic about it'.[35] The overall effect was to 'push the party's programme towards the centre, strike a note of moderation and fiscal responsibility, and stress, perhaps tendentiously, the identification of socialism with "social justice" and "freedom"'.[36]

The political aim was, according to Gould, 'to reach out to the new middle classes'.[37] The tax regime developed under Thatcher was to be largely retained, with careful avoidance of traditional Labour commitments to the redistribution of wealth. There was explicit acceptance of 'the market's role in spurring innovation and consumer choice'.[38] Interventionism – encapsulated in a 'Medium Term Industrial Strategy' – was to be confined to the 'supply-side' of the economy: incentives for research and development, favourable loans to small businesses, expanded training opportunities and a national minimum wage. The aim was to 'allow Britain to develop as a talent-based economy', under 'an enabling state' whose primary purpose was to equip workers for jobs in the fast-changing economy. This required a careful reorientation in the Labour Party's relationship with the trades unions, which had become increasingly troubled. Concern about trade unions having too much power – both within the country and within the Labour Party – had played a major part in the epochal electoral defeat of 1979 and Thatcher's subsequent political and ideological stranglehold over the country.

The regulation and limitation of trade union influence in the workplace and the broader economy had continued as a central theme of Thatcherism, expressed in successive phases of industrial relations legislation, with the evident approval of much of the British public, including (as Hobsbawm had noted) many trades unionists and Labour voters. Much ideological use was made by the Tories throughout this period of images and memories of the 1978/9 'winter of discontent', which had contributed to the defeat of the previous

Labour government under Callaghan. The Policy Review 'People at Work' study group, convened by former Bennite MP Michael Meacher, initially proposed a modest restoration of trades union rights and a 'charter for employment rights for individual workers largely modelled on the European Social Charter'.[39] But this section of the draft was rejected by the NEC in May 1989, and revised under the supervision of Derry (later Lord) Irvine to broadly accept the new Thatcherite status quo, in which form it was approved at that year's party conference.

For all its quibbles over such matters of detail – especially those which smacked of old-style European social democracy – Labour was embarking on a significant reorientation towards Europe and the European Commission, whose President Jacques Delors had famously addressed the 1988 TUC conference. As a result, 'the EC was embraced [by Labour] with more fervent passion than the rival (governing) party was doing at that point'.[40] This in itself represented a genuine historic shift in Labour's international orientation, away from an exclusive Atlanticist focus on the 'special relationship' with America, and prior to that the Empire and Commonwealth. But at the time it was simply interpreted in domestic political terms as a further turn to the right. However, there was a sense in which Thatcherite Britain was now much further to the right than continental Europe; 'progressives' could therefore glance across the Channel and find some solace for their political plight. Whereas previously 'Europe' had seemed an obstacle to 'socialism', it might now offer a way back to some form of it; this, as much as any token rightward shift, was the main point of Labour's new orientation towards the European Commission and related 'federalist' institutions.

Defence policy was another especially sensitive issue – given the use made by Thatcherism of the popular conception of Labour as 'soft on national security' – and it was a historic point of conflict between Labour left and right. Kinnock now used a shift on these issues for further contemporary symbolic purposes. Serious moves towards international détente, and the meeting between Gorbachev and Reagan in Reykjavik, gave Labour a chance to shift away from its electorally costly stance of unilateral nuclear disarmament, often derided as 'giving up something for nothing' and as such an affront to 'common sense'. After a period of some confusion and an apparent resurgence of unilateralism in and around the Labour Party, 'it was the Soviets who facilitated the turn on defence policy… (with) support for multilateral negotiations leading to multilateral reductions in nuclear weapons'.[41] This enabled Kinnock to retain his stated lifelong aim of 'renouncing nuclear weapons', but within a framework of serious and equitable international negotiations; and in immediate terms this got him off the inner-party hook.

The debate over the Policy Review at the 1989 Labour Party Conference produced 'a grudging consensus', primarily because of the decline of the Labour left. Tony Benn noted that the pre-conference NEC involved 'no hostility' – because the majority against the left was so enormous. For Benn the significance of the Policy Review was clear, within a broader lament for the state of the party: 'The NEC has abandoned socialist aspirations and any idea of transforming society; it has accepted the main principles not only of Thatcherism but of capitalism; and it thinks that now the party has a chance of winning office'.[42] Kinnock, however, ended up feeling that the Policy Review should have gone further, and that he had overestimated the strength of the left. In fact, during this period there was serious opposition to the Thatcher government, which in the 'poll-tax riots' of 1990 came close to outright civil revolt and helped bring about its political demise. But this opposition was largely expressed and organised well outside the Labour Party.

It is a measure of the political shifts already engineered within the party that this widespread anti-Tory extra-parliamentary political activism had little discernible effect on Labour, unlike what had happened in the early 1970s or even the 1950s. By the end of the 1980s the surviving impulses of modern left-wing activism in Britain, which had found a home of sorts in Labour in the aftermath of 1968, had moved back out of the party – and, arguably, the parliamentary arena altogether. With the continuing and deepening hegemony of Thatcherism, the collapse of 'communism' in the Soviet Union and satellite states, and the resurgence of the capitalist 'free-market' economy on a newly global scale, traditional socialist and left-wing politics were losing much of their purchase, drive and point. Within the Parliamentary Labour Party and the broader party organisation, the way was now open for a new approach, inserting its own distinctive policy substance into the political vacuum created by Kinnock's Policy Review.

The meaning of the Policy Review

Long after its conclusions were adopted by the party in 1989, debate continued over the Policy Review's wider historical significance for the labour movement. For Willie Thompson, 'it was not merely policy but the party's whole tradition and practice which was up for reconsideration'.[43] Smith argued, from a more centrist perspective (and without much supporting detail), that the Labour Party had 'to some extent returned to the revisionism of the 1950s and 1960s and to the social democratic traditions that had been important throughout its history'.[44] He also argued that: 'Tony Blair's successful bid in 1995 to rewrite Clause IV of the Labour Party constitution may with justification be regarded as the culmination of a revisionist project within the party – concerned both with demoting public ownership and endorsing the market economy – that was initiated in the 1950s'.

Roy Hattersley, a long-time admirer of Crosland, was one among many actively promoting the term 'democratic socialism' to represent this supposed theoretical thread. The 1988 party document *Democratic Socialist Aims and Values* was largely written by Hattersley, and looked towards 'the creation of a genuinely free society in which the fundamental objective of government is the protection and extension of individual liberty'.[45] This was to be achieved through revived and refinanced public services, and harked back to Crosland's central theme in *The Future of Socialism* that the primary purpose of social-democratic government was the funding and provision of public services to enable individual self-advancement. Similarly, revisionist-sympathiser Smith claimed that the Policy Review placed Labour firmly in 'the tradition of European Social Democracy … based on the commitment to welfare and state intervention as a means of creating a society with greater social equality'.[46]

Shaw argues that this interpretation misconstrues the logic underpinning the Policy Review and underplays the differences between revisionism and 'post-revisionist social democracy'.[47] The central aims of Croslandite revisionism, full employment and the pursuit of equality, had been rendered obsolete by the economic and political crises of the 1970s and 1980s, and particularly by mass unemployment, which had destroyed the power of the labour movement to impose a sense of social responsibility upon industry and the economy. This was crucial, because the labour movement was always revisionism's ultimate political instrument, both inside and outside the party. By the 1990s, the globalisation of capitalism had created an environment far less conducive to social democratic policies.[48] Crosland's idea of a strong social democratic state, with the backing of the labour movement's 'industrial wing' in the trade unions, able to dictate the terms of the capitalist economy within a 'sovereign' nation had proved wildly optimistic.[49] The reverses of the Thatcher era and its aftermath made it impossible to return to such a model.

According to Cronin, Crosland's earlier formulations of revisionism had gone so far as to argue that 'capitalism had already been replaced ... by statism', and with any traditional left-wing 'suspicion of the state forgotten', socialist government was largely a matter of administering the state in the interests of the majority.[50] But that prospect had been destroyed by Thatcherism – rhetorically and ideologically anti-statist, even as it persistently and ruthlessly used the state to enforce its political will – and by the wholesale reorientation of the economy under the rubric of neo-liberalism. Whether you described it as post-Keynesian revisionism' (with Smith), or 'pre-Keynesian orthodoxy' (with Shaw), Kinnock, and subsequently the core of New Labour, now held that 'it was only the private sector that could create the conditions for full employment, growth and therefore the wherewithal to finance improved public services'.[51] The social democratic state, directed by a powerful labour movement, had been conceptually neutralised. The conditions and tools of revisionist social democracy were no longer there; they exercised little substantial influence over the Policy Review, let alone the outside world.

In language and tone very close to *Marxism Today*'s long-standing critique of Labourism, Shaw characterises the social-democratic consensus, and its theoretical elaborations in revisionism, as a 'historic compromise with capitalism [which] abandoned any effort to radically redistribute power and wealth whilst conserving the aims of widening social opportunities and narrowing disparities in income, status and access to collective goods'. This meant that when business and industry withdrew from the historic compromise on the grounds that it was unaffordable, Labour was forced to renegotiate on terms much more favourable to capitalism. Citing a report by the National Institute of Economic and Social Research which had concluded that the economic policy differences between the two major parties were narrower than they had been for twenty years, Shaw concludes that:

> Given the extent to which the Conservative Party had moved to the right during this period, nothing attests more to the scale of the transformation Labour had undergone during the 1980s. Having abandoned full employment, a re-distributive fiscal policy and hence the pursuit of equality, revisionist expansive aspirations had contracted to post-revisionism's more modest aims of abating social distress, extending individual opportunity and incremental improvements to the public services. [52]

This was why Blair could declare, a few weeks before the 1997 election, that 'the post-war Keynesian dream is well and truly buried'.[53] And it is also why it is no surprise that one of the first murmurs of disenchantment with New Labour from within the Labourist tradition came from Roy Hattersley, one of Labour's most loyal advocates of Croslandite revisionist social democracy. Hattersley concluded quite early in the life of the New Labour government, well before the widespread disillusionment brought on by the war in Iraq, that New Labour owed far more to Thatcher than to his mentor Crosland.[54]

The most notable feature of the contemporary Labour Party is not so much the ascendancy of the 'right', whose base was always in the largely intact Parliamentary Party, as the demise of the 'left', traditionally located in the shrivelling constituencies. This has deprived the party of much of its internal dynamic and vitality; as if to confirm the point, the Labour left was not so much defeated by the Labour right as demoralised and dispersed by Thatcherism. If the Policy Review was a further chapter in the familiar Labour trope 'right revisionism/socialism betrayed', it was taking place in a distinctively late-1980s context, contemporaneously laid bare by 'New Times'. There are striking similarities between the tone, language and intent of 'New Times' and the strategic thinking that underpinned Labour's Policy Review, openly acknowledged at the time by Kinnock, Mandelson and others. For Cronin, the two 'debates' fit comfortably together, 'a first albeit critical chapter in the progressive whittling down of what the party promised to do in office, which was driven largely by the logic of electoral competition'.[55] For Hay, after the turmoil and in-fighting of the 1980s, the overall effect of the process was 'to re-establish political consensus on a Thatcherite basis'.[56]

Notes

1. R. Heffernan, in *The New Labour Reader*, p53.
2. M. Freeden, in *The New Labour Reader*, p43.
3. R. Heffernan, in *The New Labour Reader*, p57.
4. P. Gould, *Unfinished Revolution*, p142.
5. M. Westlake, *Kinnock the Biography*, p500.
6. A. Pearmain, 'When Politics Met Showbiz and Flinched: Neil Kinnock and the 1992 Sheffield Rally', available from andrew.pearmain@ntlworld.com.
7. R. Heffernan & M. Marqusee, *Defeat from the Jaws of Victory*, p22.
8. BBC 9 o'clock news, 13 April 1992.
9. M. Leapman, *Kinnock* (London 1986), pp18/19.
10. M. Leapman, *Kinnock*, p20.
11. R. Heffernan & M. Marqusee, *Defeat from the Jaws of Victory*, p24.
12. R. Heffernan & M. Marqusee, *Defeat from the Jaws of Victory*, p42.
13. P. Seyd & P. Whiteley, *Labour's Grass Roots*, p201.
14. M. Crick, *Militant* (London 1984).
15. L. Panitch & C. Leys, *The End of Parliamentary Socialism* (London 1997), p219.
16. H. Pelling & A. Reid, *A Short History*, p177.
17. M. Smith, *The Changing Labour Party* (London 1992), p27; E. Shaw, *The Labour Party since 1945*, p201.
18. P. Gould, *The Unfinished Revolution*, p87.
19. P. Gould, *The Unfinished Revolution*, p75.
20. J. Cronin, *New Labour's Pasts*, p291.
21. P. Gould, *The Unfinished Revolution*, p81.
22. D. McIntyre, *Mandelson and the Making of New Labour* (London 1999), p174.
23. P. Hewitt, memorandum February 1987, reported in P. Gould *The Unfinished Revolution*, p72.
24. P. Gould, *The Unfinished Revolution*, pp50, 64.
25. J. Cronin, *New Labour's Pasts*, p292.
26. M. Westlake, *Kinnock: the Biography* (London 2001), p424.
27. J. Cronin, *New Labour's Pasts*, p293.
28. J. Cronin, *New Labour's Pasts*, p293.
29. J. Cronin, *New Labour's Pasts*, pp293/4.
30. L. Panitch & C. Leys, *The End of Parliamentary Socialism*, p223.
31. L. Panitch & C. Leys, *The End of Parliamentary Socialism*, p340, footnote 18.
32. P. Seyd and P. Whiteley, *Labour's Grass Roots*.

33. E. Shaw, *The Labour Party since 1979*, p88.
34. H. Pelling & A. Reid, *Short History*, p180.
35. J. Cronin, *New Labour's Pasts*, p295.
36. J. Cronin, *New Labour's Pasts*, p327, citing *Social Justice and Economic Efficiency* (London 1988).
37. P. Gould, *The Unfinished Revolution*, p84.
38. Labour Party Campaign Briefing 75 (special issue), June 1988.
39. Labour Party Campaign Briefing 75 (special issue), June 1988.
40. W. Thompson, *The Long Death of British Labourism* (London 1993), p153.
41. J. Cronin, *New Labour's Pasts*, p297.
42. T. Benn, *The End of an Era: Diaries, 1980-90* (London 1992), pp563/4.
43. W. Thompson, *The Long Death of British Labourism*, p153.
44. M.J. Smith, *The Changing Labour Party*, p28.
45. Labour Party, *Democratic Socialist Aims and Values* (London 1988), p3.
46. M.J. Smith, *The Changing Labour Party*, p223/4.
47. E. Shaw, *The Labour Party since 1945*, p103.
48. E. Shaw, *The Labour Party since 1945*, p105.
49. S. Crosland, *Tony Crosland*, p292.
50. J. Cronin, *New Labour's Pasts*, p33.
51. E. Shaw, *The Labour Party since 1945*, p106.
52. E. Shaw, *The Labour Party since 1945*, p107.
53. T. Blair, Labour Party press release, 7 April 1997.
54. R. Hattersley, 'Blair's Labour Party is not the Labour party I joined,' *The Guardian*, 17 October 2002.
55. J. Cronin, *New Labour's Pasts*, pp304, 312.
56. C. Hay, *The Political Economy of New Labour*, p59.

9. Labour, Modernity and 'Modernisation'

We looked in a previous chapter at the purpose and substance of the 'New Times' analysis associated with *Marxism Today*, and some of its influences on later New Labour rhetoric and practice. We need to look more closely now at its contemporaneous reception within the Labour Party, and specifically its relationship to the Policy Review and the tortuous process of Labour 'modernisation'. This in turn raises bigger issues about previous Labour attempts at modernisation, of both itself and the country, and about the relationship between Labourism – party, movement and ideology – and 'modernity'. This was a major subtheme of *Marxism Today* during this period, specifically that Thatcherism had 'constructed a dynamic new take on modernity' while the political left had lost touch with it; it therefore provides us with another thread of historical continuity.[1]

Most accounts of the origins of New Labour have acknowledged that 'New Times' was at least a contributory factor. Few have gone quite so far as Peter Mandelson in 1989, with his private remark to Martin Jacques that 'Without you (*MT*), we'd never have been able to do what we did', or have accepted on its own terms Charles Leadbeater's 'utopian post-capitalist vision', but most others accept that 'New Times' was part of the mix.[2] To this day the phrase occasionally pops up in New Labour rhetoric: for example, the declaration of ex-Labour minister ('man of the north' or 'heartlands candidate', and one-time Blair adviser) Andy Burnham that his 2010 bid for the Labour leadership aims 'to rebuild the party for new times'.[3] Hay characterises the use of 'New Times' within New Labour thinking as a pivotal transitional device, a primary conceptual feature of the specific historical context in which it found itself. As such, he thinks, it bears comparison with Attlee's post-war command socialism and Wilson's technocratic futurism as currents which define their eras: 'Where for instance the Keynesianism, quasi-corporatism, collectivism, egalitarianism, expansive welfarism and indeed socialism of Attlee or Wilson were appropriate to the post-war period, the fiscal conservatism, individualism, social (or even neo-) liberalism and, in Blair's terms, "social-ism" of New Labour are appropriate to new times'.[4]

So in this account, 'New Times' serves as a crucial stepping stone, alongside the contemporaneous Kinnockite party leadership and the Policy Review, between 'old' and 'new' Labour. Both enable a decisive shift from a self-declared and recognisably socialist variety of Labourism associated with previous generations of Labour leaders – with at least some rhetorical commitment to 'public ownership' and 'the redistribution of wealth' – to a newer form which has adjusted to the fundamental social, cultural and economic shifts wrought by Thatcherism. This is presented as a necessary adjustment, electorally essential if internally politically risky – the left may be in decline but it is still strong and potentially troublesome within the party. New Labour recognised the nature of this challenge in its early years, while trying to establish its legitimacy and authority within the Labour Party, and attempted to square the circle, face both ways, by arguing that it represented 'traditional values in a changed world'.[5] This has also been the gist of virtually every significant speech by John Prescott, Blair's deputy and symbolic point of contact with 'old' or 'real' Labour.[6]

The parliamentary-electoral ramifications of 'New Times' were, for Cronin, that Labour should:

> … move towards the political centre in order to attract votes from the expanding ranks of white-collar workers and professionals, particularly those living in the suburbs and the more prosperous southern part of the country. Labour should therefore distance itself from the rhetoric and policies of the past and abandon nostrums like nationalisation, in which few people believed but which scared away potential voters. This would remodel Labour by making it less socialist, less collectivist and less hostile to property ownership and private enterprise.[7]

This process was already well under way before the term 'New Labour' was coined and popularised; Cronin concludes 'This was basically the Kinnock agenda'.[8] He goes on to describe 'New Times' as 'a call for innovation' over and above electoral adjustments, and to observe that it was guaranteed a receptive audience amongst the (then) Labour parliamentary opposition. After all, 'politicians fearful of their political futures did not of course need left-wing intellectuals to tell them that the Labour Party needed retooling, rethinking and repositioning'.[9]

Themes within the Policy Review borrowed freely from the contemporaneous debate going on in *Marxism Today* about 'New Times'. There was indeed a striking convergence and cross-fertilisation between the Kinnock leadership and the latter-day Euro-communists (as there was between Labour and the CPGB, for all their mutual mistrust and antipathy, throughout their shared history).[10] The Labour Party report produced on the outcome of the 1987 general election, 'Labour and Britain in the 1990s', which served as an analytical preliminary to the Policy Review, reads like a contribution to the 'New Times' debate. It was produced by a team of media and marketing professionals comprising Peter Mandelson, Phillip Gould, Deborah Mattinson, Roger Jowell (Director of British Social and Community Planning Research), Paul Ormerod (Director of the Henley Centre for Forecasting) and Andrew McIntosh (IFF Research Ltd).[11] It differed radically from previous Labour Party reports of electoral behaviour, Shaw observes, in that, in its exploration of the mental picture of the party held by voters, far more attention was given to the questions of 'values, perceived economic competence and trustworthiness' than to traditional concerns with policies, issues and leader's image.[12] The application of new market research methods – tried and tested within the new, more consumer-sensitive capitalism identified, disparaged and/or celebrated by 'New Times' – to political analysis and strategy was evident.

The report's content also rehearsed arguments made some years before by, among others, Eric Hobsbawm in his seminal 1978 'Forward March of Labour Halted?' *Marxism Today* article; a clear example of the phenomenon noted by Martin Jacques of Labour belatedly 'coming round' to *MT* thinking, in this case a full nine years later, though as always the focus is on electoral implications.[13] According to 'Labour and Britain in the 1990s', Labour's 'habitual voters … were falling because of a number of major social trends', primarily the passing of the age of Fordist production, 'with its huge industrial plants organising masses of workers engaged in repetitive, alienating tasks and often living in nearby socially homogeneous council estates.' More recently, the report went on, Thatcherism had appealed to the material interests and aspirations of key sectors, especially 'skilled workers residing in the South and the Midlands ... Most of these subsequently remained loyal to their new (Tory) allegiance'.[14] This was very close to Stuart Hall's conception, derided widely on the left as heresy when it first took shape in the late 1970s, of the appeal of Thatcherite ideology to the material interests of the British working class. By now, it had achieved the force of 'common sense', and not only on the political left. 'Labour and Britain in the 1990s' calculated that 'about 6 per cent of the 13 per cent loss of support [for Labour] since 1964 could be accounted for by structural social change'.[15] This (remarkably precise) 'structural' percentage loss in itself could very nearly account for at least two of the momentous Labour election defeats to Thatcher, in 1979 and more recently in 1987. Labour had finally, it seemed, understood that its forward march had halted.

Shaw draws directly from the 'New Times' debate in *Marxism Today* to explain Labour's fading core support, summarising NT/*MT* contributor Charlie Leadbeater's analysis of 'the loss of trust in the state's ability to act as the guardian of collective social interests; the decay of traditional sources of solidarity and common identity forged through work; the growth in the importance of individual choice in consumption, the revolt against centralising sameness, the pursuit of diversity'. Later, in his account of the obsolescence of Croslandite social democracy by the 1980s, Shaw quotes a slab of hard capitalist realism – 'Companies are not in business for social purposes, they are not even in business to make products, they are in business to make profits' – by a *Financial Times* journalist who turns out to be, in professional day-job mode, none other than Charlie Leadbeater.[16]

Shaw argues persuasively that the key instrumental changes under Kinnock occurred in the first four years of his leadership, 1983-87, when the party was effectively cowed into submission, the prestige and power of the Leader's office was substantially boosted (not least by a massive increase in state funding for the parliamentary parties), and the broader political left was cast into headlong flight by the Falklands war, the miners' strike and Thatcher's attacks on the 'loony left' in local government.[17] The Policy Review was, on this account, simply a next stage in the defeat of the left, in Labour's accommodation with Thatcherism, and in the formation ultimately of New Labour. Shaw also draws important distinctions between the expectations placed upon the Policy Review by, respectively, the soft left (of which he was, via the Labour Coordinating Committee and its Executive Committee, a member) and the leadership group around Kinnock who would later provide the core personnel for New Labour.[18] There are the beginnings here of a split that would seriously undermine the effectiveness of New Labour in government: 'The soft left wanted an open-minded, critical scrutiny of Labour's programme, with no preconceived notions as to what the final outcome would be', whereas Kinnock's entourage wanted 'a considerable lightening of the party's traditional ideological freight'.[19]

Shaw also describes two distinct phases to the Policy Review. The first produced 'Meet the Challenge, Make the Change' in 1989, which constituted the review's most extensive statement 'but not the more ruthless expunging of existing policy that the leadership wanted'. By the time of 'Looking to the Future' (1990) and 'Opportunity Britain' (1991), the Kinnock leadership was able to shape the Party's programme more emphatically and constructively, with policy initiatives beyond the Policy Review's formal duration.[20] The report of the Commission for Social Justice, drafted by David Miliband and published in 1994, completes the transition: its central argument is that:

> Inequalities in individual opportunities are rooted in the stock – or lack – of individual skills and abilities, and the environment within which such abilities can be enhanced and used … competition and capital mobility in the new global economy create a demand for investment in new labour skills and flexibility. Governments may no longer have the power to manage demand to boost employment, but they can shape the supply side of the economy in such a way as to make the country more attractive to international investors and individuals more employable at higher rates of pay.[21]

This represents the full adjustment by Labour to the 'post-Fordist' realities of 'New Times', with more than a residual hint of the older Labourist emphasis on personal improvement.[22]

The Commission on Public Policy and British Business, launched in April 1995 and reporting in January 1997, was the very final piece in the Policy Review/'New Times' jigsaw, now firmly under the New Labour brand. Its membership was drawn almost wholly from business, with only TUC General Secretary John Monks from the 'other side' of industry and very little other 'public' representation. Its conclusions wholeheartedly endorsed the Tory market liberalisations of the 1980s and promoted a set of distinctively New Labour adjustments summarised by Anderson and Mann as 'a (low) minimum wage, tougher competition policy, improvements in education and training, investment in the transport infrastructure, tax incentives for long term investment and strict adherence to a tight fiscal and monetary regime'.[23] Without the sudden lurch or jolt of the Policy Review and the background noise of 'New Times', such frankly non-socialist policies would have been inconceivable. Blair and Brown's takeover of the party and open embrace of business would have been that much more difficult, or at least compromised.

The Policy Review and Labour 'modernisation'

The final consideration of the Policy Review is its proper place in the historical process of Labour 'modernisation', the point where Labour's internal procedures and sub-cultural values (what Drucker terms its 'ethos') meet the changing realities – circumstances and 'events' – of the wider world.[24] Successive Labour leaderships, drawn mainly but not only from the right, have set out to 'modernise' the party. Almost every positive change to the party's policies, perspectives, structures and procedures has to be described as 'modernisation', and their advocates cast as 'modernisers'. In the internal codes of political Labourism, 'modernity' is the counterpart to 'tradition', a signifier of broader differences of perspective and allegiance, and usually of social origin and class affiliation. As always, we need to be careful with terms. Heffernan insists that Labour's embrace of the word modernisation began only in the early 1990s.[25] The point is well made, but earlier, similar, currents in the Labour Party had clearly aimed for forms of 'modernisation'; the Fabians applying 'science' to the management of the state, the revisionists attempting to align Labour with cultural changes in broader society, Wilson briefly taking on the whole society and economy. Though the terms used may have differed, there has been a strand advocating modernisation since the 1950s.

The contemporary Labour Party took shape in the 1950s, following what was its most successful (and certainly most fondly remembered) experience of government, between 1945 and 1951. As Cronin points out, 'Old' Labour was not really very old; it was 'a

204

product of the achievements of the 1940s'.[26] Attlee's government inherited the revived sense of national purpose and cohesion that derived from a successful war effort, and applied many of the instruments and policies of the wartime command economy to post-war reconstruction. Its most important and cherished achievement was the National Health Service, but this was the centrepiece of a broader welfare state encompassing education and social security as well. Measures to nationalise and centralise transportation and utilities and particular ailing industries gave the state a much bigger role in the economy than ever before, though it stopped well short of the 'full-blooded socialism' the more radical members of the party and government would have liked. This 'loss of nerve', symbolised most famously by Chancellor Stafford Cripps' austerity programme of 1947/8, is often cited as the cause of the disillusionment that beset this particular Labour government, but arguments about Britain's orientation towards the post-war superpowers were arguably more debilitating (just as Iraq finally did for New Labour).[27]

At the 1951 general election, Labour achieved its highest ever vote, 13,948,605, roughly a quarter of a million more than the victorious Tories.[28] Because of the vagaries of Britain's first-past-the-post constituency-based electoral system, which does not distribute parliamentary seats in proportion to votes, Labour found itself cast into opposition. The party spent the 1950s looking for new approaches and directions, and ways of regaining a parliamentary majority and government power, broadly divided between the two poles of Aneurin Bevan's state socialism and the social-democratic revisionism associated with Anthony Crosland and Hugh Gaitskell. Throughout this period, it continued to enjoy ostensibly solid and reliable support from its 'core vote' in the tribal heartlands of the industrial north and midlands of England, central Scotland and South Wales, though political affiliations were nothing like as regionally marked as they would become under Thatcher. In the 1950s, the Conservatives still had numerous and well-established MPs in the English north, Scotland and Wales, and a substantial presence among councils and councillors right across the country. Pan-British 'popular Toryism' – with its roots in late nineteenth-century working-class 'empire' Conservatism – was another barely remarked upon victim of Thatcher's 'authoritarian populism'.

The post-war Labourist social alliance was made up of the still numerous and intact manual working class and elements of the urban intelligentsia, especially those employed in the burgeoning public sector and the nationalised industries, who had a clear vested interest in state intervention and services. Labour's popular vote at general elections remained around twelve and a half million throughout the 1950s, still within reach of its 1951 historic high. This was never enough to displace the governing Tories, but sufficient to demonstrate widespread popular support for the post-war social-democratic consensus, otherwise known as 'Butskellism', after the Tory Chancellor R.A.B. Butler and the Labour opposition leader Hugh Gaitskell. The Tories were able to continue in office partly because their programme took cognisance of the wider consensus.

The social-democratic consensus of the postwar period in fact included a deep 'modernising' impulse, and it was the nearest the political left has ever come to any kind of Gramscian 'hegemony' in Britain – its depth demonstrated by successive Conservative governments' general acquiescence. But as is the way with political currents that attempt to latch onto the slippery concept of 'modernity', it required constant 'revision' and adaptation to new and emerging forms of 'the modern' in surrounding society.[29] As the 1950s and 1960s proceeded, the Labour Party and associated political commentators were much exercised with the effects of rising prosperity among the general population, and subsequent re-stratification between and fragmentation within the major social classes.[30] They saw new levels of comfort and contentment as the country recovered from the privations of the war and government slowly abandoned such aspects of the command economy as rationing and state control of supplies and services. Alongside this, working class people were supposedly adopting higher aims and ambitions for themselves and their children, in particular through the opportunities offered by reformed and much expanded state education. This was at odds with the old 'cloth cap' image of traditional Labourism.

In the approach to the 1964 general election, campaigning against a visibly tiring and scandal-beset Conservative government, Harold Wilson attempted to project Labour as the party of the future. He espoused a kind of scientific Labourism encapsulated in the oft-quoted slogan 'the white heat of the technological revolution'. This was not so far removed from the technocratic 'expertism' of the 1920s Fabians – the most notable earlier 'colony' of intellectuals within the labour movement – but in the genuinely 'young country' of the 'baby boom' and its demographic after-effects, hungry for social and cultural change and material and economic advancement, it struck a real popular chord. At least to begin with, Wilson had a sure touch for the public mood. He also had a very modern, populist sense of his own public image. The Gannex mackintosh coat, the northern accent and the pipe were mostly affectations by an Oxford academic and professional economist and long-time southern resident, but were nonetheless astutely chosen and deployed. For the Labour heartlands in the north of England, Wilson remained 'our man' until the onset of the post-industrial devastation of the 1970s.

In a Labour historiography which delights in drawing parallels between politicians of different eras, Wilson is now plainly the nearest historical equivalent to Blair (Phillip Gould would no doubt demur; he says 'Wilson appeared modern, but was in no sense a moderniser', without ever spelling out his own idea of the difference).[31] Both came to power after long, debilitating periods in opposition, which their predecessors (Gaitskell and Kinnock) had spent in defeating the left. They were self-styled 'modernisers' who consistently defied efforts to 'fix' them within the politics of the Labour Party, and somehow managed to rise above any fixed allegiances of their own, or any easily identifiable ideological or factional 'position'. As a result, they were each able to draw upon the conditional support (if not undying loyalty) of the various wings and sections of the labour movement, in return for a message and appeal to the broader public which promised parliamentary revival and electoral success. They both positioned themselves carefully to take advantage of the deaths of established, respected and popular party leaders – Gaitskell in 1963 and Smith in 1994 – who had already gone some way to making Labour 'electable' again. And both fell from grace and party favour rapidly, once their political 'magic' had evaporated and viable successors emerged.

Wilson's 'modernisation' was arguably a more serious and broadly based project than Blair's, but it foundered on the deep and long-term problems and inadequacies of the British economy. The immediate cause of retrenchment and loss of popular support was the 'balance of payments crisis' of 1966, but this was symptomatic of a much deeper decline in relative productivity.[32] Britain did not make as much and as well as other comparable countries. This indeed was what Wilsonism had set out to redress, but it was very quickly overwhelmed by the scale of the problem. Wilson's primary modernising instrument, the 'National Plan' overseen by the short-lived Department of Economic Affairs (itself conceived as a 'modernising' counterweight to the Treasury), was the most notable casualty. DEA official Roger Opie's epitaph for the National Plan ran: 'conceived October 1964, born September 1965, died (possibly murdered) July 1966'.[33] Compared to Western European and North American competitors, the British economy was archaic, inflexible and technologically backward. What's more, the taproot of Labourism – the proportionately largest and most culturally cohesive manual working class in the world – was beginning to fragment and disperse, not least because of different levels of involvement in and commitment to 'modernisation'. They were mostly its 'objects' rather than 'subjects', and as such largely resistant to its appeal. The 'cultural revolution' of 1968 was, at least in Britain, a relatively transient and marginal phenomenon, largely confined to university campuses; its underlying impulses of personal liberation and social diversity have always been contested, not least by the much deeper and more durable social conservatism of the British working class. The institutional manifestations of the 'permissive society' in the legal reforms customarily associated with Roy Jenkins' time at the Home Office – the 1960s-liberal litany of homosexual, divorce and abortion law reform – have likewise never been wholly secure (which is why Thatcherism was able to mobilise ideological hostility towards them).

By the mid-1970s, deeply troubled by continuing economic crisis and tensions with its industrial wing in the trades unions, Labour was losing any clear sense of historic mission, 'modernising' or otherwise. The American historian Samuel Beer's judgment, of a country 'blighted by plural stagnation, class decomposition and a revolt against authority', would with differences of emphasis, have been accepted across the political spectrum.[34] Faced with a resurgent Thatcherite Conservatism, 'old' Labour had very little left to offer, other than a slightly softer landing from the collapse of the social-democratic consensus, rather like New Labour in the credit crunch/deficit recession thirty years later.

Yet another economic crisis, with profits collapsing and inflation as high as 26 per cent in 1975, confronted Labour with a historically familiar quandary: how to manage a capitalist recession from within a nominally socialist political framework? How to maintain a welfare state, the essential settlement that had secured working-class acquiescence to an intact capitalist economy, when 'market forces' were refusing to continue to pay for it? How to keep faith with 'one-nation socialism', still sacred to the urban intelligentsia that supplied much of Labour's activist core, when the international capitalist system within which the domestic economy was increasingly enmeshed rejected all its nostrums? Above all, how to maintain the historic purpose of Labourism, the protection of working-class economic interests within the purview of the nation-state, which had seen it through right from its founding moment.[35]

The Wilson government's answer in 1975/6, to go 'cap in hand' to the International Monetary Fund for massive financial assistance in return for swingeing cuts in public spending, did much to finally destroy the traditional basis for mass, 'tribal' Labourism. By 1979 and the 'winter of discontent', Labour – now under the leadership of James Callaghan – was exhausted and incapable of resisting a resurgent Conservative Party under Margaret Thatcher. Labour's 1979 general election vote, 11,532,148, was actually 100,000 up on its victorious result in October 1974, but with a substantially increased total poll, the Tories secured 43.9 per cent and a comfortable parliamentary majority. Regional disparities in votes were now becoming especially marked, with a 7 per cent swing to the Tories in southern England, compared to a national average of 5.2 per cent and a swing in Scotland of less than 1 per cent.[36] These disparities would deepen under Thatcherism, leading commentators as politically diverse as Tom Nairn and Simon Heffer to posit the 'break-up of Britain'.[37] After an apparent but temporary reversal in the 1997 'landslide' election, when Labour MPs were returned to parliament from such unlikely constituencies as Edgbaston, Winchester, Enfield Southgate and Hove, contrasting regional concentrations in party support remained a major feature of the electoral landscape under the New Labour adaptation. At New Labour's reported demise in 2010, with its failed 'suburban populism', Labour's concentration in its geographical heartlands was more marked than ever (and its vote was only one percentage higher than its worst-ever general election, under Michael Foot in 1983).

Ultimately, New Labour was very like those earlier Labour 'modernising' projects, from the Fabians to the revisionists, in aim and composition and practical function if not necessarily in political substance and character. Desai argues that they all consisted of surprisingly small, established and well-placed groups of intellectuals, lured by 'the promise of political influence' and granted privileged positions in the higher echelons of the Labour Party and broader movement; from here they devised and offered philosophical and strategic direction to its industrial and local sections – a very particular application of traditional British patterns of division and deference.[38] These were members of several overlapping and mutually supporting elites. Desai argues persuasively that the Social Democratic Party, one of New Labour's primary sources, was not so much an 'attempt to break the mould of British politics' as a backward-looking and ultimately 'vain attempt to preserve a political mould in which intellectuals had occupied a central place'.[39] New Labour might thus be seen as a kind of 'intellectuals' revenge' on a party which, since the death of Crosland and then the SDP defection, had grown decidedly cool towards its traditional cadre of ideas-merchants.

Desai and others have also argued that revisionism was demoralised and ultimately discredited by the experience of the first Wilson governments (1964-70), which – as we have seen – started out with high ambitions to 'modernise' central aspects of British life, most notably but not only its economy. Partly because of the continuing difficulties of the British economy, but also because of its own internal tensions, Wilsonian modernisation ended in rancour and failure, and a loss of support beyond its own parliamentary base. In particular, in the fiasco around 1969's 'In Place of Strife' Wilson failed to reconcile the demands of the trade unions with the broader 'national interest', the sharp horns of Labourism's historical dilemma. This always seems to be what eventually does for Labour 'modernisation': the failure to engage and maintain substantial and sustained support from broader society, or in Gramscian terms to construct anything like a hegemonic 'historic bloc' around itself. And when Labour has achieved permanent legislative change, it has always been within a climate of broader social, cultural and ethical change: the NHS in 1945/51, for example, or late-1960s legal reforms on abortion, divorce and homosexuality.

By contrast, the economic and industrial policies of revisionism were based on narrowly consumerist concepts of affluence and aspiration (reflecting the essentially 'top-down' view of what working-class ambition and self-reliance look like to an alarmed upper and middle class). This, combined with an instrumentalist politics whose aim was to enable individuals and families to realise their personal goals – giving people 'what they want' – is the kind of economic populism which has always been a current within Labour thinking. There is a striking convergence between the rhetoric of late-1950s Labour revisionism and the anxious contemporaneous theoretical 'modernism' of McLuhan and Marcuse. They even deploy some of the same imagery in their sketches of 'modern life'– 'The people recognise themselves in their commodities; they find their soul in their automobiles, hi-fi sets, split-level homes, kitchen equipment', as Marcuse put it.[40] And there is in both forms of modernism an ultimately gloomy, fatalistic view of human natures and appetites.

Political postmodernism

For Marshall Berman, in a widely influential survey published in the early 1980s, political post-modernism is a tawdry, materialistic distortion of the original nineteenth century impulses of modernism in Marx and Nietzsche and Baudelaire, whose 'visions and revisions of modernity were active orientations toward history, attempts to connect the turbulent present with a past and a future, to help men and women all over the contemporary world to make themselves at home in this world'.[41] The repudiation of these earlier, expansive, optimistic and idealistic, fundamentally and radically democratic conceptions of modernity – the 'loss of faith' which came to characterise the moral climate of the later twentieth century – gave rise to 'the mystique of postmodernism, which strives to cultivate ignorance of modern history and culture, and speaks as if all human feeling, expressiveness, play, sexuality and community have only just been invented – by the postmodernists – and were unknown, even inconceivable, before last week.' In this historical context, New Labour is not so much a 'modernising' project as a prime example of the wilful 'great forgetting' of postmodernism, the triumph of elite despair and cynicism over popular hope and idealism.[42]

Like other initially successful forms of Labourism, New Labour was remarkably adept, almost promiscuous, in its appropriation and deployment of theoretical and rhetorical devices from non-Labour traditions, movements, institutions and intellectual currents. It was very much a 'pick'n'mix' politics, a constantly adaptable 'brand'; this is another feature of its postmodernism. But in political practice and personnel, it has been a relatively small and localised phenomenon, almost Leninist in its compact core; as Rawnsley observes, 'the progenitors of this all-embracing self-styled People's Party were tiny in number'. [43] They were 'a tightly-knit group of politically motivated men' (a clever redeployment of Harold Wilson's comments on the 1966 docks strike); but in this case career parliamentarians instead of communist militants. [44] This helps to explain why its approach to government has been so generally cautious and occasionally timid. For all its grand visions and 'big ideas', most famously the 'Third Way', New Labour has lacked a broad constituency of support, and the instruments with which to flesh out its policies and give them genuine intellectual substance, let alone practically implement them. As a political 'agency', New Labour has failed to enlist the active support or involvement of very many people beyond the upper echelons of the Parliamentary Labour Party and the party organisation, and its outriders in the media and public affairs. This explains why it has had such little lasting impact of its own on British society, and why Tony Blair left office with such a meagre positive 'legacy'. Almost all New Labour's 'achievements' have taken the form of withdrawal of government from the economy – from the independence of the Bank of England to the use of the Private Finance Initiative to fund massive public sector building programmes. On the other hand, many of its 'actions' – from sending inspectors into failing schools and hospitals to the nationalisation of Northern Rock – have involved reluctant, 'last resort' state intervention.

So, even if New Labour willed the modernisation of Britain as a worthy end, it denied itself the means with which to bring it about, not least as a result of what Neal Lawson calls its 'hollowing out' of the Labour Party. [45] This is why so much of its social policy has been reduced to the hectoring of individuals, families and other small local groups and institutions about personal conduct and misconduct. In this New Labour was tapping into the Party's strong moralistic streak, derived from its early origins in non-conformist religion and cooperative solidarity, and the community and trade union disciplines of the industrial proletariat, the determined 'levelling down' of the back street and the shop floor. Indeed, this is one of the historical burdens which have complicated Labour's response to free-wheeling, irreverent and always individualistic modernism and modernity. And when it is unattached to any broader transformative politics, socialist or social-democratic or otherwise, such moralising simply becomes finger-wagging: judgmental, unattractive and profoundly un-'modern'.

This failure is a major part of the explanation for the repeated inability on the part of Labour, in its old and new guises, to 'modernise' itself and British society and economy. Again, there is a close and illuminating parallel with postmodernism, which purported to supersede previous forms of modernism, but in the end simply expressed a profound loss of faith in the whole concept of modernity. Britain – and beneath the New Labour gloss Labour too – remains resolutely unmodernised. The most profound shifts in the way the country is run have taken the form – as Jonathan Meades has argued from a 'cultural' perspective and Simon Jenkins from a rather more orthodox 'political' one – of centralisation, a concentration of power, prestige and resources on the central state and the region, London and the south east, where most of its premises and personnel are located. Ultimately, this has represented a consolidation of elite power rather than a modernist call to arms.

> Harold Wilson … that most under-appreciated of prime ministers, effected the centralisation of Britain. The politicisation of newness was on its way.
>
> Jonathan Meades, *At Seal House*[46]

Notes

1. C. Leadbeater, 'Thatcherism and Progress', *Marxism Today*, October 1988.
2. M. Jacques, personal interview, 14 December 2003; C. Leadbeater, *Living on Thin Air*, p167.
3. *Daily Mirror*, 20 May 2010.
4. C. Hay, *The Political Economy of New Labour*, p8.
5. T. Blair, *The Third Way* (London, 1998).
6. For example, J. Prescott, *Speech to Labour Party Conference*, September 1999.
7. J. Cronin, *New Labour's Pasts*, p305.
8. J. Cronin, *New Labour's Pasts*, p306.
9. J. Cronin, *New Labour's Pasts*, p308.
10. A. Pearmain, 'Labour's Critical Friends: The CPGB and the Labour Left', available from andrew.pearmain@ntlworld.com.
11. The Labour Party, *Labour and Britain in the 1990s* (London 1987); E. Shaw, *The Labour Party since 1979*, p81.

12. E. Shaw, *The Labour Party since 1979*, p81.
13. M. Jacques, personal interview, 12 December 2003.
14. E. Shaw, *The Labour Party since 1979*, p82.
15. The Labour Party, *Labour and Britain in the 1990s*, p24.
16. C. Leadbeater, *The Politics of Prosperity* (London, 1987), p4.
17. E. Shaw, *The Labour Party since 1979*, p202.
18. P. Thompson & B. Lucas, *The Forward March of Modernisation: A History of the LCC* (London 1998), p25.
19. E. Shaw, *Labour since 1979*, p84.
20. E. Shaw, *Labour since 1979*, p85.
21. L. Chadwick & R. Heffernan, *New Labour Reader*, p160.
22. S. Driver & L. Martell, *New Labour: Politics after Thatcherism*.
23. P. Anderson & N. Mann, *Safety First*, p40.
24. H. Drucker, *Doctrine and Ethos in the Labour Party* (Edinburgh 1979).
25. R. Heffernan, in *New Labour Reader*, p57.
26. J. Cronin, *New Labour's Pasts*, p49.
27. G. Foote, *Labour's Political Thought*.
28. H. Pelling & A. Reid, *A Short History of the Labour Party*, p100.
29. Cronin, *New Labour's Pasts*, p35.
30. R. Desai, *Intellectuals and Socialism*, pp86/93.
31. P. Gould, *The Unfinished Revolution*, p35.
32. J. Cronin, *New Labour's Pasts*, p76.
33. Cronin, *New Labour's Pasts*, p76.
34. S. Beer, *Britain Against Itself* (London 1982).
35. G. Stedman Jones, *Languages of Class*, p83.
36. H. Pelling & A. Reid, *Short History of the Labour Party*, p160.
37. T. Nairn, *Break-up of Britain* (London, 1981); S. Heffer, 'Farewell UK', *Sunday Times*, 12 April 1983.
38. R. Desai, *Intellectuals and Socialism*, p5; see also Ross McKibbin, *London Review of Books*, 8 November 2007.
39. R. Desai, *Intellectuals and Socialism*, p8.
40. H. Marcuse, *One Dimensional Man* (London 1964), p9.
41. M. Berman, *All That Is Solid Melts Into Air* (London 1985), p33.
42. The term 'great forgetting' was coined by the American sociologist Fred Bloch to indicate the strategic obliteration of left-wing activities, experiences and traditions from the historical record. As such it represents a kind of retrospective hegemony.
43. A. Rawnsley, *Servants of the People*, p270.
44. A. Rawnsley, *Servants of the People*, p270.
45. N. Lawson, personal interview.
46. J. Meades, in *London: City of Disappearances*, ed. I. Sinclair, (London 2007), p511.

10. What New Labour Took from the Left

Placing New Labour

Most analyses of New Labour, including much of my own up to now, have dwelt upon what New Labour took from the right. These include its abandonment of social and material equality, of the Labourist holy grail of full employment, and of the redistribution of wealth and power as primary policy objectives; its accommodation with Thatcherism and the process of neo-liberal capitalist expansionism undertaken from the mid-1970s onwards; its disavowal of traditional Labourist mechanisms and methods of state planning and strategic intervention in the workings of the market economy; its favouring of 'business' over any other corporate interest, including those of its own labour movement backers (who continued to stump up around £9m per annum, fully 73% of the party's cash donations);[1] and its 'marketising' reforms and punitive micro-management of public services. In recent years the argument that New Labour represents a shift to the right has entered the mainstream of British political discourse, alongside enthralled accounts of New Labour's leading personalities, their daily doings and interactions. Thus the respected newspaper columnist and ex-editor Simon Jenkins, himself an anti-Thatcher 'old' Tory, writes: 'Tony Blair's celebrated "project", guided by Phillip Gould, dismantled the rambling coalitions that formed the Labour coalition and turned Labour into whatever the leader wanted it to be. Even, in Blair's case, a continuance of Thatcherism.'[2]

Then there is New Labour's social conservatism and professed distaste for the liberal/humanitarian concerns of the 'urban intelligentsia', more colloquially known as the 'chattering classes' and associated with readership of *The Guardian* newspaper. For much of the party's history, especially after the Second World War, what

Crewe and King call the 'educated middle class' formed a key element of the Labour social coalition, but New Labour – in a curious act of self-loathing by a government largely drawn from this social segment (which in turn reflects the British intelligentsia's complicated feelings towards itself) – has had no qualms about dismissing its concerns.[3] This distaste has verged at times on outright authoritarianism, and drawn openly on the centralising, top-down, deeply statist currents within Thatcherism, especially when articulated by successive Home Secretaries Jack Straw, David Blunkett and our ex-communist, self-styled Gramscian John Reid. But this is coupled with the more moralistic elements of 'old' 'respectable' Labourism, and explicitly decoupled from the expansive social ethos of liberal tolerance and egalitarianism of the 'revisionist' social democrats (who were by all accounts privately as well as publicly 'permissive'), to strike a wholly new note of intolerance and irritability.[4]

In this aspect – the admonishment and prosecution of deviant personal behaviour, albeit with new 'anti-social' targets – New Labour has remained persistently 'true to its roots' within the historically socially conservative moral nexus of the British working class. This Labourist residue is expressed through successive moral panics about crime and public disorder, binge-drinking, recreational drug use, and the extremes of sexual activity. In a further 'transformist' twist, a version of the social-democratic conception of the benevolent, malleable and amenable or at least neutral state enabled a higher level of surveillance and policing of civil society, social relations and personal life in Britain than most other countries would contemplate. Remarkably, Britain has proportionately more CCTV cameras pointing at its citizens than any other country in the world; even more remarkably, this has been accepted with barely a murmur of disquiet let alone active dissent beyond the already disaffected urban intelligentsia, and with no evidence that it has any direct impact on crime levels.[5] (Whether anybody actually looks at the resulting millions of miles of blurry CCTV footage is another matter; and, arguably, CCTV relieves individuals of the responsibility to look out for each other and so reduces public order and safety.)

Beyond these social and judicial elements of its 'governance', New Labour has been drawn steadily rightwards in its political image and message-making by the imperatives of parliamentary/electoral politics in a 'globalised' capitalist economy and in a stratifying, fragmenting and fractious society. In both Blairite and Brownite manifestations, New Labour persisted in its determination to occupy the 'centre ground' of British politics, simply because it had to in order to ensure continued success in Britain's sclerotic electoral system of 'first past the post' and customary single-party majority rule, in which a tiny shift in allegiance amongst the 'floating vote' – a few thousand people deciding to 'give the other lot a try' – can determine the outcome. This is the ultimate 'dead fact' of contemporary British electoral politics; the Con-Lib coalition will almost certainly prove a single-term historical aberration, an effective 'transitional' basis for renewed Thatcherite hegemony and Conservative government, but hardly a 'new mould' for British politics.

Even if the referendum on electoral reform that the Liberal Democrats extracted from the coalition agreement delivered the 'alternative vote' for Westminster elections, its practical affects would be limited. Proportional representation and other forms of procedural modernisation have previously been introduced in Assembly and European elections, with interesting (and faintly destabilising) results, but they remain marginal to the 'core business' of British government. For Raphael Samuel, they simply represented a further extension of the values of consumerism – of 'customer choice' – into the political arena.[6] The prevailing trajectory for electoral success in the greater nation remains within the narrow middle of a course drifting steadily rightwards, perhaps even more so for the new 'mould-breaking' Conservative-Liberal coalition than for New Labour.

Given all this, it is remarkable (and a tribute of sorts to its professional operatives) that Labour retains any 'core vote' at all. But it does, and thus retains a substantial if slowly loosening foothold in local and national electoral politics, even if only because many of its traditional supporters cannot quite bring themselves to vote for 'the other lot', especially at general elections. Labour 'loyalty' – which Drucker argues derives from trades union principles of defensive solidarity and 'unity is strength' in the face of exploitation, alongside generous helpings of British deference and the comforts of habit – persists, especially in the north British post-industrial 'heartlands'.[7] Indeed, one of the most effective tools of New Labour's continuing hegemony over the party was the highly traditional 'will to unity' under an established leadership, which Samuel identifies as the factor most important in stifling debate throughout its history.[8]

Away from the domestic politics which was always popular Labourism's primary concern, New Labour has maintained the traditional stance of modern British government – Labour and Conservative – in global affairs: a generally slavish attachment to US foreign policy. New Labour long ago abandoned any claim to be socialist, beyond Blair's attempt to coin a new 'social-ism' which was wholly compatible with liberal democracy, and seemed to indicate 'capitalism with a conscience'. As Smith pointed out, 'never before has a single hyphen been made to represent so great a disconnection'.[9] With the mid-1990s ascendancy of New Labour, Labour became a united *centre party*, no longer of the 'centre left', able to appeal to electors to its left and right.[10]

In European terms New Labour governed in the manner of (and on most significant matters of European Union social and economic policy aligned itself with) the centre-right clustered around Christian Democracy. In British political terms, the Blair government (and then, in areas where it really mattered, Brown too) could properly and suggestively be described as 'soft right', thereby indicating the political journey Labour has undertaken in the twenty years since the mid-1980s 'soft left' in which many prominent New Labour figures were involved. More recently, commentators have described New Labour's political approach as notably 'hard right', for instance in the May 2008 Crewe by-election, or two years later in Phil Woollas' ill-fated general election campaign in Oldham and Saddleworth, where it campaigned on an openly 'nasty' platform of xenophobia and populist class-prejudice.[11]

If we still accept the 'left/right spectrum' model of parliamentary politics, then, New Labour over its lifetime was increasingly and purposefully located towards the latter end. For all Blair's 'policy cross-dressing', Simon Jenkins is able to conclude that: 'In all his responses, values and body language, Blair was what an ordinary citizen would call right wing. He was a natural Tory.'[12] And in times of both boom and bust, Brown first as Chancellor then as Prime Minister was unerringly pro-business. These accusations have long been levelled by leftist critics. They now seem to have achieved the status of popular 'common sense', especially since New Labour abandoned the intellectual effort to cast itself, through 'the Third Way', as somehow 'beyond left and right'. The efforts to carve out a 'new political space' by the dwindling band of Blairite outriders like James

Purnell with his 'Open Left project', or the 'New Labour left' around Compass and the MP Jon Cruddas, seem somewhat plaintive and forlorn. They, like so much of the party's recent affairs, have more to do with post-defeat 'positioning' within the shrivelling confines of the Labour Party than some new inspiration for government or for the country.

New Labour and the left

Having listed its borrowings from the right, I want to focus these final chapters on what New Labour has taken from the left, usually without acknowledgement from either for reasons of mutual *post-partem* embarrassment. Furthermore, what it chose not to take – or rather which parts of a particular political articulation were detached and left behind – was often just as important, not least in neutralising any truly radical or even democratic edge. In this respect, New Labour has exercised 'triangulation' – the selective appropriation of your opponents' stances and rhetoric – to the left as well as to the right. New Labour's references to leftism are apologetic, disguised, cynical and oddly fey, almost an in-joke amongst its inner circle of devotees, trading on a particular set of caricatures and mannerisms of what 'being left-wing' involves, which are themselves largely derived from the experiences of defeat and disillusionment during the 1970s and 1980s. Back then amongst these particular individuals and their forebears there was a certain detached fascination with what the non-Labour left was up to. Such coded rhetorical flourishes as Gould's 'unfinished revolution' and Blair's 'permanent revisionism' or 'socialism', which have usually bemused the wider world, constitute an uneasy recognition of these sources.

Some elements of New Labour's neutralised (or 'centred') leftism are obvious. Above all, the narrower founding impulses of Labourism persist under New Labour – the pursuit of parliamentary representation and government office in the larger cause of 'fair shares' in the spoils of capitalism for the working class. But without the aim of socialism or any other broadly transformational principle or strategy, these are reduced to ritually invoked 'values' and 'traditions'. New Labour's relationship with what we might call the 'trappings' of Labourism has always been ambivalent. The demise of 'tribal' Labourism was the strand of the 1980s *Marxism Today* analysis that formative New Labour was most prepared to draw upon, especially in the halcyon days of 'high' Thatcherism, when it allowed the possibility of anti-Tory alliances or pacts with other non-Labour political groups and movements, especially the Liberal Democrats. But as soon as it became clear that such alliance politics were unsustainable because of residual Labourist resistance, or actually unnecessary because Labour had a realistic prospect of governing alone, the party reverted to its historically customary stance of insisting that prospective supporters and allies abandon their own independent political identity and apparatus and 'join the party'.

Even Labour's most broadly-based and expansive government, under Attlee between 1945 and 1951, had come to power in determined isolation, calculating (rightly as it turned out) that it could win a substantial majority on its own.[13] The Communist Party at that time, which also achieved its highest ever vote in 1945, had pledged to continue supporting Churchill's national coalition government into peacetime, 'trimmed of its more reactionary elements'.[14] Under Churchill, the coalition promised to sustain what Laybourn calls its programme of 'war socialism'.[15] The CP went so far in the spirit of unity as to withdraw established candidates who were standing against amenable Labourites (some of whom of course turned out to be 'crypto-communists'). When Labour proceeded to 'go it alone' under Attlee, the CP decided with considerable internal dissent to support the new government, but it had no effect on the bigger party's traditional hostility to electoral agreements.[16] Labour may be a 'broad church', but it is peculiarly enclosed and separatist, almost a mass sect, and has never embraced electoral ecumenism. This was the tradition New Labour – for all the tantalising dalliances with Paddy Ashdown and the Liberal Democrats – respected most assiduously.

In these circumstances – of a culturally residual, half-hearted Labourism shorn of its transformative socialist aims, combined with what Jenkins calls Blair's 'extraordinary ability to strip words of meaning yet load them with impressionistic effect' – New Labour's politics became largely a matter of style and presentation, technocratic managerial 'competence' and government 'trustworthiness'.[17] As Eric Shaw put it, redistributive policies challenging the existing spread of income and wealth could have no place in a political project seeking a secure niche in the radically changed landscape of Thatcherism.[18] The risk always was, as the industrial journalist Victor Keegan put it in 1994, that Labour would lose its soul.[19] Henry Drucker, writing fifteen years earlier, had also fretted that 'Shorn of a belief in any specific doctrine, the movement risks becoming a machine which wishes only for its own aggrandisement'.[20] Labour is reduced from a class to a party, and ultimately to an organisation whose primary concern is protecting the vested interests of its MPs and paid officials. As such, it offends the key Labourist moral principle of 'sacrifice'; Gordon Brown reportedly fretted in private that just such a fate has befallen Labour.[21] This is also surely why the moral or financial transgressions of Labour MPs are judged more harshly than those of the Tories, because Labourism has always set itself far higher moral standards, at least in public. Again, this kind of quasi-religious agonising appears to be a long-standing feature of the highly distinctive temperamental mix in Labour – the evangelical heir to Gladstone's 'party of conscience and reform' – and as such another deep strand of continuity in Labourism.[22] If a sense of high moral purpose is an important part of its ideology and culture, then so is a sense that it might be losing it.

The loss of evangelical purpose is also evident in Labour economic strategy. The revisionists attempted to shift the focus of Labourism from production to distribution, as befitted the new prosperity, stability and 'affluence' of the 1950s. Steady economic growth would guarantee increasing amounts of overall wealth. The political task then became its more equitable distribution'.[23] In this new age of plenty, the labouring masses were more concerned with what they might acquire than with what was taken from them in the process of making it. The obligation of 'democratic socialism' was to satisfy their aspirations and material requirements. But this approach presupposed steady, continuing growth. The gathering storm of capitalist crisis in the 1960s and 1970s, and its Thatcherite resolution, destroyed the economic basis of revisionism and any prospect it might offer of 'socialism'.

In similarly favourable economic circumstances to the 'age of affluence', New Labour has overseen a further strategic shift in the British economy, from distribution to consumption, and in the process abandoned altogether the traditional socialist concern with equality. As Chadwick and Heffernan argue, 'New Labour believes in redistribution, but only for poverty alleviation, not for the purposes of broader social equality'.[24] Peter Mandelson was famously reported as claiming that 'New Labour is intensely relaxed about people getting filthy rich'.[25] More recently, John Hutton MP eulogised the rich as social and economic leaders, and as such, patriotic role-models.[26] Will Hutton (no relation), one of New Labour's most trenchant and periodically influential critics, argued that the project fundamentally 'distrusts Keynesian political economy, preferring instead to trust the conservative political economy of its opponents'.[27] After ten years of New Labour government, according to separate reports published by the Institute of Fiscal Studies and the Office of National Statistics, Britain was a more unequal society than at any time since the Second World War.[28] The GINI coefficient – the standard measurement of income inequality – stood at 0.36, compared to 0.25 when Thatcher took office in 1979. Under New Labour, the growth in inequalities was slowed but nowhere near stopped. Social divisions based on income and wealth – the founding preoccupation of Labourism, the 'moral mission' which underwrote its more practical concerns with parliamentary representation and trade unionism – were more marked and evident than ever. New Labour's is a Labourism stripped of its historic purpose.

Beyond the fragments: feminism, Leninism and New Labour

I want to turn now to some rather less obvious left-wing themes and traditions New Labour has borrowed from and filleted; primarily the 'second wave feminism' of the 1970s and 1980s, which had a more profound effect on the practice and theory of the political left in Britain than any of the other strands of the emerging 'identity politics'. Alongside key late-1970s works by Hobsbawm and Hall already cited and examined, *Beyond the Fragments* by Sheila Rowbotham, Hilary Wainwright and Lynne Segal helped to shape the response of the left to the collapse of the social-democratic consensus and the emergence of Thatcherism.[29] Not that its authors consciously set out to do that at the time; they were more concerned to explore the possibilities of 'socialist feminism', the distinctive ideological coupling within which they had all been immersed for the previous momentous decade. Published in 1979, *Beyond the Fragments* was still operating within a strong sense of historical progress towards a socialised economy and an egalitarian society. In that respect it looked backwards, to the cultural upheavals and generational conflicts of

'1968' and ensuing 'arguments within English Marxism', rather than forwards to Thatcherite 'authoritarian populism' and 'regressive modernisation'.

At a certain profound level – and here resides its historic importance – *Beyond the Fragments* was also attempting reconciliation between Marxism-Leninism, with its deeply elitist conception of the 'vanguard' party, and the cultural revolutionism and radical egalitarianism of personal liberation. This was, as we have seen, an abiding concern of the left during this period, explored in the work of Althusser and others. It also of course underpinned the 'rediscovery' of Gramsci. This was the last significant, substantial dialogue between the new feminism and the old 'revolutionary socialism'; and as such, between the largest and most significant element of the new identity politics and the old politics of class.

Beyond the Fragments contained a powerful challenge to lingering British Leninism, primarily from a 1970s-feminist, women's liberation movement perspective, but also drawing from older democratic or libertarian, pre- or extra-Labour currents in socialist and communist politics. The influence of E.P. Thompson, as an historian of earlier waves of eighteenth and nineteenth century radicalism, a New Left/CND activist, and a contemporary advocate of what he called a new 'affirmative politics', is obvious and regularly acknowledged.[30] For example, the authors argued 'the idea of mutual self-help', central to the new feminism, has 'an ancient genealogy from the creation of friendly societies and cooperatives to the cycling clubs, Workers' Esperanto groups, nurseries and Socialist Sunday schools of the late nineteenth and early twentieth century [and] … the movement towards a Socialist Commonwealth'. *Beyond the Fragments* also deploys a number of clearly Gramscian perspectives and concepts, and makes several cautiously appreciative nods towards Euro-communism, especially in their shared critique of Leninism. The problem with Leninism, for *Beyond the Fragments*, was its haughty isolationism, its 'illusions about being omniscient'.[31]

So what does any of this have to do with New Labour? Jon Trickett MP mentioned very early in our discussion of 'democratic left' prospects his own involvement in the *Beyond the Fragments* discussions of the late-1970s; it clearly represented for him a source of personal insight and authority.[32] As Rowbotham (in the essay which forms the bulk of the book) notes of her own moment of induction into political activity, during a period of historical hiatus between the first and second New Lefts, 'in 1964 it seemed as if pressure on the left of the Labour Party was more realistic than the creation of an independent left movement'. 'But', she continues ruefully, 'we tended to underestimate the capacity of Labourism to exhaust left opposition'.[33] Henry Drucker noted in 1979 Labourism's 'basic force and weight to attract new and diverse adherents'.[34] Though *Beyond the Fragments* primarily addressed itself to the Leninist left, many of its concerns had relevance for the Labour Party – unsurprisingly since their traditions were historically interwoven and over-lapping. And indeed, one of the most curious of New Labour's accretions from the left can be seen as a form of Leninism strikingly similar to what *Beyond the Fragments* had set out to challenge.

Left-wing politics has always been hard work, with what Samuel calls its 'call to sacrifice' and 'moral vocation': 'Activity was a good in itself, irrespective of its outcome. "Struggle", whatever its particular object, was ennobling'.[35] Left politics tends to engage the whole person in a wide-ranging assault on received ideas and comforting wisdoms, their own and everyone else's, for distant, minimal and questionable rewards. Not surprisingly, most people get exhausted, and either drop out or devise their own survival strategies and personal defence mechanisms, including carapaces of cynicism and disillusionment. Alternatively they can set up a social enclave. As *Beyond the Fragments* put it:

> The stress on total solutions and the fears of co-option could give way to despair and disillusion when the world went on in its bad old course ... Breaking down all hierarchy and denying all skills could become an in-turned and moralistic network which excluded people. The alternatives [to capitalism] could seem like the lifestyle of a sub-culture, almost a fashion coming out of an anti-fashionable stance.[36]

If they wish to continue in active politics, activists learn to hide their real feelings or express them in authorised, pre-determined, essentially harmless and ritualistic forms. These are often built upon mythologised and sentimentalised bases, such as the Labourist tradition abounds in; and these in turn help sustain the long haul of what we might call, after the weary old song with which sizeable Labour Party meetings are still sometimes concluded, 'Red Flag' politics. Coupled with the imperatives and rewards of professional career politics, they combine to create a powerful motivational complex.

New Labour's Leninism

In a nutshell, New Labour took a large part of the political practices of Leninism from the declining, exhausted left, what *Beyond the Fragments* called its 'grindingly manipulative ways of doing politics', and merged them with aspects of the more outward-looking, forward-thinking theoretical analyses derived from *Marxism Today* and 'New Times' (though these borrowings were disassociated from the democratic/Euro-communist current within the British communist tradition, which was itself by then a long way into the process of disbandment and dispersal; and even more so from the aspects of feminism that the whole of the left had been forced to some extent to accommodate). New Labour's inner core, its largely self-selected 'vanguard' – several with experience of communist and Trotskyist politics – proceeded to apply the whole heady brew to its takeover of a dispirited, enfeebled, disorientated Labour Party, in what Phillip Gould (in his customary unintentionally revealing way) describes as a 'quest for Leninist simplicity'.[37]

Others have noted quite how small New Labour's 'vanguard' was: in compiling their *New Labour Reader,* Chadwick and Heffernan confess to being struck by 'how few substantive primary ideological statements we could locate which had not been delivered by, or published in the name of Blair and Brown':

> Even though background personnel – in particular figures like Alastair Campbell, Jonathan Powell, David Miliband, Andrew Adonis, Ed Balls, Phillip Gould and Geoff Mulgan – have played some role in honing the New Labour message (particularly Campbell and Powell), they have done so by working as agents of the party leadership; the party's *public* presence since 1994 has been very much the product of Tony Blair and Gordon Brown.[38]

More recently, David Runciman described Brown's closest ministers as 'men who once worked as juniors in his office, having been hand-picked at a very young age'.[39] New Labour's inner core has been a very small, tight and exclusive hierarchy, built on personal dedication, group loyalty and discipline, and a type and level of drive bordering on the obsessive, not to say autistic. Brown's entourage in particular were expected to submit to punishing work-schedules and regular 3am phone calls from the boss to discuss his 'latest idea'.[40] There are also obvious commonalities of background amongst New Labour's underlings: the two Milibands, Balls and Cooper, Jacqui Smith, Ruth Kelly, James Purnell all went to Oxford and read PPE, and have had very little other life experience. New Labour is socially and culturally very narrow as well as politically exclusive. Their takeover of the Labour Party was a less blatant and formal 'entryism' than various Trotskyist *groupuscules* have attempted at various times in the party's history, but it was a kind of entryism nonetheless. As Jenkins notes of Blair's purposeful assault on the party immediately after assuming leadership in 1994, 'Blair seemed at the time hardly a Labour Party member at all, rather an alien political force employing the "entryist" tactics once confined to the hard left'.[41]

In the process, New Labour also brushed aside the kinds of changes to the traditional left advocated by those influenced by 'second-wave feminism' of the 1970s Women's Liberation Movement and the arguments of *Beyond the Fragments*, which had been taken on board by some currents within Euro-communism, the remnants of early 1970s 'libertarian Marxism' and the other new impulses of 'personal/identity politics'. In particular, the critical and crucial insights into how you do politics were discarded – what Rowbotham calls 'how a socialist should behave' and what an earlier generation (following William Morris) had called 'the making of socialists'. [42] We might sense faint echoes of feminist practice in New Labour's informal 'networking' style – what was described in the Butler enquiry as 'sofa government' – but it is directed towards entirely traditional ends, and over-determined by its other components, including an unabashed laddish machismo. This was most evident in Alistair Campbell's published diaries: the crass 'blokey-ness' of Campbell and Blair's relationship, with its mannered swearing and ogling of passing females. Reviews of the feature film *In the Loop*, whose central character Malcolm Tucker is broadly based on Campbell, frequently picked up on the coruscating anger and utterly unapologetic male aggression of New Labour's inner life, if not necessarily on its 'hard-core' Leninism.[43]

After socialist feminism

Since the 1970s the position of women and the nature of the women's movement have changed massively. And these complex changes have interacted with other economic and cultural developments, and with Labour and left politics, sometimes with curious effect. *Beyond the Fragments* assumed that the 'extraordinary power' of second-wave feminism would carry this 'new social movement' forward. The hope of socialist feminists was that women's liberation would reinvigorate the left. Sisterhood had assumed the sense of grand historic purpose, if not outright 'inevitability', that had motivated earlier generations of the socialist, social-democratic and communist 'brotherhood'. In this they shared in the optimism of the 1970s.

But for some years, it did indeed look like the women's movement was in a far healthier state than the political left. Waves of equal opportunities legislation, backed by subsequent case law and on occasions industrial action, improved women's earnings, prospects and status at work (these were what we might call the 'economistic' or 'professional' concerns of women's liberation, in which socialist-feminists in and around the Labour Party and the Communist Party were heavily involved). Changes in social policy and family law strengthened women's personal and domestic positions, and offered some measure of new protection from male oppression, exploitation, abuse and violence. Women continued to expect and exercise greater choice over conception and reproduction, what Rowbotham called 'birth control over and above workers' control'. This expectation was materially supported by the introduction of the Pill and legal abortion on the NHS in the 1960s, which (Rowbotham again) 'represented a most dramatic break with the past experience of women of their bodies'.[44] Women began to enjoy rather than mistrust their femininity, to investigate rather than deploy it. Though always (and to this day) under attack from the religious right, these battles gave the women's movement a series of highly effective and educative causes to rally round. Even the overwhelmingly male and interconnected preserves of the law, parliamentary politics and the professions have absorbed increasing numbers of women. Girls and young women began to outperform their male peers at every level and in pretty much every subject in education.[45]

This was the 'respectable' face of feminism, steadily and up to a point successfully working its way through the institutions of British society with a broadly 'reformist' agenda. 'Radical' or 'revolutionary' feminism took a rather different course, with much stronger and more explicitly 'separatist' tendencies, determinedly 'anti-men' if not stereotypically 'bra-burning', and substituting gender for class as the primary historical category. It also, as the socialist-feminist Rowbotham noted, contained strange echoes of overbearing political leftism – 'the feminism of the women's liberation movement can be presented as the consciousness of women in general' – and of crude, elitist Leninism: 'Under a "false" non-feminist consciousness sits a "true" natural feminism in every woman'.[46] Radical or separatist feminism's most public *cause celebre,* the Greenham Common Peace Camp, was established in 1981 and became a semi-permanent settlement until the end of the Cold War and the 'peace dividend' gave it a local, inadvertent (and possibly unwelcome to its inhabitants) victory.[47]

But alongside this more 'political' manifestation, a distinctive subculture – often lesbian, and culturally (if problematically) aligned with the much more visible and resourceful 'new social movement' of gay men – emerged and spread to most parts of the UK. By the 1990s, it had become one of a number of 'enclaves' based around features of 'identity politics'; separate, self-sufficient, self-reflexive and increasingly disconnected from any broader traditional political purpose. Like the various 'gay villages', certain places acted as magnets: Brighton and Hebden Bridge for example. The more 'established' these enclaves became, and the more comfortable and fulfilling individual lives within them, the less overtly 'political' their outlooks and activities, requirements and preoccupations. The Women's Liberation Movement suffered the same disabling split – between matters of identity and lifestyle on one side, and legislation and procedure on the other – that afflicted and weakened pretty much all the post-1968 British left. The personal ceased to be political, actually went beyond it, by becoming – for most people, increasingly disgusted with 'politics' – far more important and congenial.

This complicated process – not so much 'Beyond' as 'Back to the Fragments' – was taking place against a backdrop of ideological and political reaction, the steady privatisation and marketisation of the global economy, and the acquiescence of successive British governments to deepening neo-liberal hegemony. The domestic or household economy was affected as much as manufacturing industry or finance capital; the reassertion of 'the family' as the primary, self-reliant and isolated unit of social relations was a central element in the ideological onslaught of Thatcherism. (This helps to explain women's much faster and surer progress at work than at home; men may be more individually inclined to accept a female boss if their 'equal opportunities employer' tells them they have to, but recent research suggests that most of them are not much more inclined than their fathers were to play a bigger role in the private spheres of childcare and housework.[48])

New Labour has been globalisation's most enthusiastic observer, supporter and 'enabler', but gender has also played a key role. The shift from productivism to consumerism has privileged women, who have been historically more involved in the spheres of consumption than production. In the process they have 'feminised' capitalism. What remains at its heart a ruthlessly efficient machine for generating profit has cultivated some frilly edges. The shift from manufacturing industry to an economy based on services, distribution and retail has put women in a pivotal position as workers, shoppers, consumers and propagandists for 'retail therapy'. Most men have a more distant, marginal and much less comfortable relationship with consumption and consumerism; apart, that is, from the male elite who remain firmly in overall control.[49] For the left there is a deep historical irony in this, because its own exclusive preoccupation with production was a relatively recent phenomenon; as Rowbotham notes, 'the shift to the organisation of production ... had not been present in libertarian forms of Marxism like the Socialist League (associated with William Morris) in Britain in the 1880s or the Anarchist-Communism of Emma Goldman in America'.[50] These earlier and largely forgotten pre-Labour political movements (which, for all their retrospective glamour, were always wilfully marginal), with their concerns for 'whole lives' and for the social dynamics of homes and neighbourhoods as well as factories and offices, were much more open to women and women's perspectives.[51]

The 'post-feminist' political era reflects the reconfiguration of economic categories in the late twentieth and early twenty-first centuries. Women voters are targeted as a 'key demographic' by the political marketers – albeit as passive consumers or receivers of political messages, sources of opinion and reaction in political market research, and exercisers of regular if strictly limited electoral choice.

Political leaders cultivate and display their 'feminine' – or at least less formal and buttoned-up – sides. They regularly summon the families they otherwise spend very little time with to photo-opportunities, and moistly reference their children and parents in their 'family man' speeches. The political parties worry about their 'accessibility', sensitivity and appeal to women, and ponder forms of positive discrimination to draw them into membership and public office. New Labour's make-over of Labour into a 'virtual party', with a mass membership which 'buys into the brand' with its subscription fees but otherwise takes little active role (beyond leadership postal voting under One-Member-One-Vote), has been justified as a form of 'positive discrimination' favouring women, as well as an extension of democracy within the party and outwards to 'the people'.[52] But the functionaries, office-holders and leaders of 'the political class' remain overwhelmingly male. They constitute the parliamentary-political wing, albeit with sharply declining relative rewards, prestige and status, of the largely intact male elite of 'UK Plc'.

New Labour is not exempt from this general pattern of 'cosying-up' to women, but its most noteworthy feature for our purposes is how closely it resembles Rowbotham's feminist caricature of Leninist organisation. It represents the 'politics of a chosen elect', 'professionals concentrating above everything upon the central task of seizing power', practicing 'the tactic of entryism ... the covert control of front organisations ... the use of smear tactics to defeat any opposition', pushing 'the line' and 'one way to truth'. 'They are untouchable and apart', not least because their isolation in Westminster and their disavowal of Labourism, however superficial, have released them from the 'informal cultural correctives to this process in the labour movement', primarily working-class scorn for the 'jumped-up' and 'hoity-toity'.[53] Labour's old leaders had to gain their supporters' trust and respect, primarily through personal sacrifice and dedication, and displays of humility. New Labour leaders and ministers demand a more untrammelled deference, a wholly modern version of what Drucker calls the party's 'traditional tenderness to its leaders'.[54] At the same time, the relaxation of traditional disciplines, as well as the loss of unifying purpose in 'socialism', creates an atmosphere of poisonous rivalry and back-biting.

The self assurance of New Labour also smacks of Leninism: 'they have a surface coherence, they argue about brass tacks and hard facts.

They claim history and sport their own insignia and regalia of position. They fight dirty, with a quick sneer and the certainty of correct ideas'.[55] Indeed, the theoretical basis for Leninist vanguardism – the masses within capitalist society labouring away in 'false consciousness' and the enlightened, 'scientific' intelligentsia providing clear-sighted leadership – exists right across the left, including the various shades of social democracy. One of the high priests of reformism, Karl Kautsky, had persuaded Lenin of the necessity of such adjustments to the conceptions of political agency found in Marx – who was much less enamoured of 'the party'.

Above all, there is in New Labour's world view a similar sense of individual or group passivity in the face of the tides of history: towards socialism and communism for classical Leninism, towards global capitalism for New Labour. Any signs of dissent or 'weakness' or even doubt are frowned upon. This in itself favours certain character-types, cultural and social identities, psychological and professional formations, and perhaps above all a certain kind of man. As Rowbotham put it:

> Membership of this elect will for a start be predominantly male, for if it attracts a minority amongst men, it fits even fewer women. Left to carry the burden of a higher consciousness, members of this elect will tend to see the people around them as, at worst, bad, lazy; at best ignorant, needing to be hauled to a higher level. In the hauling the faint-hearted fall by the wayside, the cuddly retire into cosiness and all the suspicions of the elect are confirmed. Being an elect they can rely on no one and … they have to do everything. And always the weight of the burden of responsibility, the treachery and insensitivity of everyone else is bearing down on them.[56]

This passage could be describing, albeit twenty to twenty-five years early, the frenetic, punishing and debilitating (and ultimately highly destructive of people and relationships) atmosphere within the higher echelons of New Labour.[57] Its moral undertow – of asceticism, self-denial, blind faith – also reminds us of the religious undercurrent within Labourism, which Blair and a number of his acolytes subscribed to via the small but surprisingly influential Christian Socialist Movement.[58] It doesn't matter that these individuals don't adhere to these standards and values in their own personal private lives; Leninist leaders, like authority figures in any largely male hierarchical order, were notoriously exploitative of their followers. And five minutes in the company of any member of New Labour's elite will demonstrate Rowbotham's dictum that: 'A sure sign of a leader of a Leninist political group is a tendency to look past your eyes and over your head when they talk to you'.[59]

There are also elements, in New Labour's most macho forms, of the much-vaunted backlash against feminism, which has run alongside the incorporation of women's needs and wants into the imperatives of consumer capitalism, and the exemplary breakthroughs of some women. This backlash – evident in persisting domestic violence and abuse, the extraordinary internet-driven global expansion of sexual exploitation and pornography, and the contradictory mutual expectations and troubled interactions of most 'ordinary' men and women – expresses, amongst many other things, the resentment of those men who have been left behind in the increasingly competitive spheres of work, education, their families and communities. Women can also feel severely 'conflicted' about their roles and expectations. As Rowbotham put it thirty years ago, 'We can oppose men's control politically and then feel deserted when it is not asserted in our own lives. We can resist being treated as an object and yet still want to be desired in this way, as this remains our means of valuing ourselves'.[60] Women of her outlook and generation – another 'transitional' cultural group, rejecting the 'submissive' femininity of their mothers and in turn rejected for their feminist 'stridency' by their daughters – would carry these unresolved conflicts through the rest of their lives.

But for our purposes, the simpler truth is nearer this: that the leaders and central operatives of New Labour managed to insulate themselves against feminism, largely through their formative membership and (in most cases) heavy involvement in the Labour Party through the 1970s and 1980s heyday of women's liberation. The Labour Party, with its overwhelming preoccupation with procedure and structure and 'policy' – for Samuel, 'that constitutional nit-picking which is the bane (or delight) of a Labour (constituency) General Management Committee' – is notoriously uncomfortable with any element of 'the personal is political', and arguably the broadly political in any form.[61] Part of its distinctive 'ethos' is its proceduralism. As Drucker observes, 'for just about every level of the party there is a formal "rule-book" procedure ... its own self-contained quasi-legal rule-system'). And there is also its 'manifesto-ism' (a politics of 'demands' which may or may not cohere, and may or may not be realisable). All this is a long way from the consciousness-raising, focus on feeling, and the centrality of sexuality of the Women's Liberation Movement.[62]

For all their protestations of modernity and inclusivity, most leaders of New Labour learnt to 'do politics' and were politically 'made' in the arcane settings of Labourism: the ward or council meeting room, the Labour club bar or 'regular' pub, the Sunday afternoon or weekday evening suburban front room, the compositing and caucusing jamborees of 1970s/1980s Labour Party conferences that they condemn and fondly recall in virtually the same breath. When their time came, with Brown and Blair's 'Granita pact', they took their Labourist habits into the appropriately gentrified and domesticated settings of 'secret cabals in Islington kitchens'.[63] These people were not 'touched' by feminism, challenged and excited, undermined and 'reconstructed', in the way that others were through involvement in non-Labour left-wing organisations and activities. They were thus well equipped for a career in the House of Commons, experienced by many women as 'a strange blend of boy's public school common room and seedy gentlemen's club.' [64]

New Labour's discomfort with the themes of personal liberation and identity politics has on occasions been made explicit. Blair told the executives of Rupert Murdoch's News Corp in 1995 that 'during the sixties and the seventies the left developed ... a type of social individualism that confused liberation from prejudice with a disregard for moral structures ... it appeared indifferent to the family and individual responsibility'.[65] This formulation in itself indicates that Blair was relatively immune to the challenges of feminism, which were largely about forcing men to come to terms with their 'individual responsibility', but as so often his opaque generalities were signalling a rather different political message. The notion that the 1960s 'permissive society' went too far was a pivotal ideological instrument of Thatcherism – primarily addressed to those who felt they had no part in the 'sexual revolution' – and Blair and other New Labour luminaries have made regular use of it.

In the larger historical sweep, the conflict between socialist organisations and 'autonomous movements' like the WLM – which so exercised Rowbotham in the middle and latter parts of *Beyond the Fragments* – was resolved by the prior demise of the political left. 'Wimmin' (perhaps the most memorable formulation of radical feminism) became, within the framework of hegemonic neo-liberalism, another niche market; arguably the largest and most lucrative of them all (women do after all constitute a majority of the population), but a niche nonetheless, elevating the chore of shopping into a leisure pursuit, a mass hobby, and for some a dangerous and expensive compulsion; 'retail therapy' indeed. In practical, organisational reality the women's liberation movement, with its conferences and newsletters and networks and even widely recognised if always informal 'leaders', ceased to exist at around the same time the New Labour project was taking shape, at the back end of the 1980s, a decade or so after *Beyond the Fragments*. The WLM's real organisational forms, its material existence, its historical agency are now little more than fond memories for an older generation of feminist activists. They often complain that their efforts are little appreciated by younger 'post-feminist' women, who take for granted the rights and opportunities that were so hard-won, and use them for their own personal and professional purposes. Older gay men and black activists make the same complaint; a curious inversion of the conflicts across the 'generation gap' that their younger 'baby-boomer' selves fought in the 1960s and 1970s.

'Second-wave' feminism 'prefigured' a resurgence of capitalism not socialism, and a thoroughgoing restoration of bourgeois hegemony, refreshed rather than subverted let alone transformed, by its 'feminine side'. The Leninists, in ways they could never have imagined or truly understood, turned out to be right in their condemnations of 'bourgeois feminism'. And surely one of the reasons was that, in the crucible of late-1970s and early-1980s left-wing politics, feminism was a much more attractive option (for many men as well as women, *cf* the curious phenomenon of 'men's groups' which aped feminism in their concentration on feeling and communality) than the mind-numbing, soul-destroying, hard graft of Leninist militancy. Anti-sexism was something that could be done in the here and now: at home and in personal relationships, in the kitchen and the bedroom. It could offer ready and substantial rewards: for women in enhanced self-esteem and the solidarity of 'sisterhood', for men in relief from the burdens (as well as benefits) of masculinity – and in (looking at it a little cynically) the warmly appreciative embraces of feminists. Its objectives and enemies were close at hand, and often amenable to immediate change, even if only at the surface levels of language and behaviour. As Rowbotham put it, 'Consciousness-raising, therapy and self-help imply that we want change now'. She added, somewhat hopefully, that such feminist practices 'are involved in making something which might become a means of making something more'; herein lay their 'pre-figurative' potential. But she also acknowledged how difficult this might turn out to be: 'Our consciousness of ourselves in fucking cannot be neatly transferred to our activity in a union branch'.[66] Sex and left-wing politics, it seems, do not make very good bedfellows.

Notes

1. *Sunday Times*, 30 December 2007.
2. S. Jenkins, 'The Leader's Cheerleaders', *London Review of Books*, 20 September 2007.
3. I. Crewe & A. King, *SDP*, p126.
4. S. Crosland, *Tony Crosland* (London 1982).
5. *New Statesman*, 29 October 2005.
6. R. Samuel, *Island Stories*, p262.
7. H. Drucker, *Doctrine and Ethos in the Labour Party*, p12.
8. R. Samuel, *The Lost World of British Communism*, p15.
9. C. Hay, *The Political Economy of New Labour*, p53; P. Smith, *Millennial Dreams* (London 1997), p177.
10. A. Chadwick & R. Heffernan, *The New Labour Reader*, p18.
11. J. Harris, *The Guardian*, 16 May 2008.
12. S. Jenkins, *Thatcher and Sons*, p274.
13. H. Pelling & A.J. Reid, *Short History of the Labour Party*, p87.
14. K. Morgan, *Against Fascism and War*.
15. K. Laybourn, *The Rise of Socialism in Britain*, p138.
16. E. Upward, *The Rotten Elements* (London 1979), one of several semi-autobiographical novels about the CP in this period, depicts the process of dissent and discipline over this particular change in 'the party line'.
17. S. Jenkins, *Thatcher and Sons*, p217.
18. E. Shaw, *The Labour Party since 1979*, p225.
19. V. Keegan, *The Guardian* 31 May 1994.
20. H. Drucker, *Doctrine & Ethos in the Labour Party*, p87.
21. J. Trickett MP and PPS to Gordon Brown, private conversation, 21 November 2007.
22. R. Samuel, *The Lost World of British Communism*, p2.

23. H. Drucker, *Doctrine & Ethos in the Labour Party*, p47.
24. Chadwick & Heffernan, *New Labour Reader*, p9.
25. A. Rawnsley, *Servants of The People*, p213.
26. *Daily Telegraph*, 12 November 2007.
27. W. Hutton, *Observer*, 13 December 1998; P. Anderson & N. Mann, *Safety First*, p38.
28. Institute of Fiscal Studies, 2005; Office of National Statistics May 2007.
29. S. Rowbotham, H. Wainwright, L. Segal, *Beyond the Fragments* (London 1979); see also S. Rowbotham, *Dreams and Dilemmas* (London, 1983).
30. E.P. Thompson, interviewed by Terry Illott, 'Recovering the Libertarian Tradition', *The Leveller* no. 22, January 1978, p20.
31. S. Rowbotham et al, *Beyond the Fragments* (London 1980), p22.
32. J. Trickett MP, private conversation.
33. S. Rowbotham, *Beyond The Fragments*, pp23, 26.
34. H. Drucker, *Doctrine & Ethos in the Labour Party*, p68.
35. R. Samuel, *The Lost World of British Communism*, pp56/57.
36. S. Rowbotham et al, *Beyond the Fragments*, p30.
37. P. Gould, *Unfinished Revolution*, p242.
38. Chadwick & Heffernan, *New Labour Reader*, p4.
39. D. Runciman, 'Brown and Friends', *London Review of Books*, 3 January 2008, p27.
40. N. Lawson, personal interview.
41. S. Jenkins, *Thatcher and Sons*, p219.
42. S. Rowbotham, *Beyond the Fragments*, p29; K. Laybourn, *The Rise of Socialism in Britain*.
43. A. Campbell, *The Blair Years* (London, 2007); A. Iannucci, *The Thick of It* (BBC TV) and *In the Loop* (feature film 2009); see for example P. Bradshaw in *The Guardian*.
44. S. Rowbotham, *Beyond the Fragments*, p124.
45. *The Guardian*, 12 May 2005.
46. S. Rowbotham, *Beyond the Fragments*, p105.
47. www.greenhamwpc.org.uk.
48. *The Guardian*, 3 April 2006.
49. K. Soper, in *Soundings* 35, 2007.
50. S. Rowbotham, *Beyond the Fragments*, p92; E. P. Thompson, *William Morris: Romantic to Revolutionary* (London 1977); Emma Goldman, *Living My Life* (London 2006).
51. B. Taylor, *Eve and the New Jerusalem*.
52. *New Statesman*, 12 October 2008.
53. S. Rowbotham, *Beyond the Fragments*, pp37, 75, 28, 130.
54. H. Drucker, *Doctrine and Ethos in the Labour Party*, p1.
55. S. Rowbotham, *Beyond the Fragments*, p148.
56. S. Rowbotham, *Beyond the Fragments*, pp68/69.
57. See such insider accounts as L. Price, *The Spin Doctor's Diary*.

58. Jenkins reports how in 1992, 'The small band of Christian Socialists found themselves overwhelmed not just by (John) Smith but by Blair, Brown, Jack Straw and David Blunkett', none of them previously known for their religious convictions, *Thatcher and Sons*, p215.
59. S. Rowbotham, *Beyond the Fragments*, p130.
60. S. Rowbotham, *Beyond the Fragments*, p129.
61. R. Samuel, *The Lost World of British Communism*, p80.
62. H. Drucker, *Doctrine and Ethos in the Labour Party*, pp16, 92.
63. S. Jenkins, *Thatcher and Sons*, p222.
64. *The Guardian*, 20 February 2005.
65. T. Blair, speech to NewsCorp Leadership Conference, 17 July 1995.
66. S. Rowbotham, *Beyond the Fragments*, pp140/1.

11. What New Labour Left Out: the 'Gramscian' Left

> There is no real left in the Labour Party.
>
> Denis Healey, BBC Radio 4, 26 September 2010

By the end of the 1980s, Gramsci was rarely read or even discussed on the British left. The 'definite "Gramscian" traces' which Eley detected in 1982 – in 'the left intellectual discussion oriented towards the Labour Party since the Conservative electoral victory of 1979 … the launching of the *New Socialist* and the Socialist Society, some intellectual cross-currents around Tony Benn, and talk of promoting "a general ferment of socialist ideas"' – had largely dissipated.[1] In the whole eleven-year heyday of *Marxism Today* Gramsci only featured substantially three times. The terms 'Gramscism' or 'Gramscian' had not yet been clearly ascribed to any distinct political or theoretical perspective. The group gathered around *Marxism Today* were far more likely to be called and to call themselves 'Euro-communist' or 'Euro' or simply 'Marxism Today'. For the historian Raphael Samuel in 1985, even this didn't get to the bottom of it: 'the "fragments" analysis of *Marxism Today*' more properly constituted a species of 'Right Wing Communism', with its 'undercurrent of anti-trades unionism' and 'fantasies of rebirth'.[2] According to Samuel, 'The name of Gramsci is invoked to dignify their project' – but without the Italian's deep sense of communist principle, popular history, Marxist theory and class politics.

The 1991 'farewell issue' of *Marxism Today* would make only passing reference to 'imbibing Gramsci' as a step along the route of factional formation, alliance building and brand development, alongside 'going euro-communist, breaking with Stalinism, taking feminism seriously'. One of the final controversies provoked by *Marxism Today* involved 'imbibing' of a rather different sort, when

237

the magazine marketed its own-brand wine as well as filofaxes. The *Daily Mail* even carried a feature articles about 'Yummies', young upwardly mobile Marxists. For Samuel, the latter-day magazine-format *MT* seemed increasingly drawn to 'the frisson of the forbidden'.[3] This was a long way from the cool rigour and painstaking 'absolute historicism' of the *Selections from Prison Notebooks*. The initial intellectual thrill for the political left of discovering Gramsci had well and truly worn off.

Gramsci was more likely by now to feature on the reading lists of cultural studies courses in the more adventurous universities and (still) polytechnics – Eley's 'Gramsciology' – than in debates about the future of the left.[4] If the 'Gramsci reception attained academic respectability', it was often at the price of historical accuracy and political point: 'while a certain kind of knowing reference has become very fashionable, most Gramscian uses can remain very unreflected and casual.'[5] As the resurgence of the right impacted upon intellectual fashion – and, for what remained of the left intelligentsia, the wilful insularity and uncertainty of postmodernism seemed to sweep all before it – Gramsci fell out of academic as well as political favour. As Eric Hobsbawm wrote ruefully in his introduction to the 2000 edition of *The Gramsci Reader*, by 'the 1990s ... former leftists transformed into neo-liberals no longer cared to be reminded of anything that recalled old enthusiasms'. [6]

Hobsbawm clearly failed to spot the sporadic references to Gramsci by figures within New Labour – Britain's very own group of mainly 'former leftists transformed into neo-liberals' – perhaps because he was reluctant to share the 'peculiar responsibility' for the project which Stuart Hall owned up to in 1998.[7] But even Hall was not above changes of emphasis over time. In his 1989 introduction to *The Hard Road to Renewal*, Hall declared the political topography of 'right, centre and left ... conventional and now outdated divisions'.[8] This 'beyond left and right' argument has of course been a central part of and a critical moment in New Labour's formation and abiding rhetoric. As recently as July 2006, Blair told yet another Newscorp conference that 'cross-dressing is rampant; the era of tribal political leadership is over'. Fifteen years after his initial encomium for the 'right/left' spectrum model of politics, Hall was rather less sure of the death of the left or the political topography it was traditionally part of. It may be a central feature of our debased political culture, and of popular loss of confidence in it, that its basic categories are constantly disputed and confused.

'Gramscism' without Gramsci

What I want to look at here is how New Labour was able to make use of certain concepts within 'Gramscism' without challenge from people with a truer and broader grasp of what Gramsci had actually said and written. To some extent, the use (and abuse) of isolated concepts for immediate political and rhetorical purposes has always been Gramsci's fate, even within his own country and party. There have been, as Carl Levy puts it, 'many seasons of Gramsci'.[9] As Anderson argued in 1976, and Hobsbawm acceded in 1999, 'several of the issues most hotly debated in Italy were not so much arguments about Gramsci as arguments for (or more usually against) some phase of the policy of the PCI'.[10] There is a fine line between contemporary practical application, which all prominent Gramscians from Tom Nairn to Stuart Hall have attempted, and wilful conceptual distortion, which will usually take the form of simplification for popular purposes. In his Gramsci introduction Hobsbawm went on to make the complaint, which he accepted might seem trivial that 'an Anglo-Saxon reference work can – I quote the entry in its entirety – reduce him to a single word: "Antonio Gramsci (Italian political thinker, 1891-1937) see under HEGEMONY" (A. Bullock and O. Stallybrass (eds), *The Fontana Dictionary of Modern Thought*, London 1977)'. In attempted consolation, Hobsbawm observes that 'the acceptance of a thinker as a permanent classic is often indicated by just such superficial references to him by people who patently know little more about him than that he is "important"'.[11] Perhaps this is also the way we should understand the references to Gramsci by New Labour figures like John Reid, or the use of the term 'hegemony' by Phillip Gould to indicate a workable parliamentary majority – as a kind of back-handed compliment.

But it is clear that certain elements of New Labour's political practice owe something to other 'Gramscian' concepts and preoccupations. Some are more obvious than others. A much diminished conception of 'war of position' for instance can be used to justify the politics of positioning, where the stance you take within the political spectrum (still here, for all the talk of 'beyond left and right', an important analytical tool) is more important than the substance of your policies and arguments. At a push, the practice of 'Clintonian triangulation', where you appropriate the 'best' or most popular of your opponents' policies in order to neutralise their political challenge, can look like an attempt to forge a new 'historic bloc' of social allies under your political leadership (even if in reality it simply means the very much more limited objective of 'occupying the centre ground'); this was how New Labour understood its 1997 landslide general election victory. And at an even bigger push (a 1980s Labour left-style 'one big heave for socialism'?) these accretions of 'policy' can look like a 'pre-figurative' attempt to construct elements of a 'progressive' movement, which might just one day amount to a new or 'good' society. This is the current perspective of the 'New Labour left' around the lobby group Compass.

The problem with this, rather like the 'pre-figurative' potential of feminism and identity politics, is one of historical context. Gramsci always understood that political manoeuvre, even Leninist-style manipulation and repression, could only be justified in the service of a larger objective – the construction of a socialised economy and an egalitarian, ultimately communist society – and as simply one aspect of mass democratic politics, in which a growing body of people assume responsibility for the conduct of a widening range of the various aspects of their lives. We might describe this in contemporary terms as 'decentralisation', 'localism' or even Mouffe and Laclau's 'radical democracy'. However, within a context of declining democracy and popular participation, widening inequalities and social tensions, and deepening neo-liberal hegemony exercised by a realigned, refreshed ruling historic bloc (in the broader, fuller sense of a deeply rooted 'epochal' shift across the whole of society) – such as we have witnessed through the 1980s, 1990s and into the new century – these political methods become little more than the small-scale wheezes, fixes and intrigues in which Labourism (in all its left and right shades) has always abounded. The debate on 'localism' is a case in point; utterly unobjectionable in principle, but in practice just another set of think tank 'proposals' and broadsheet comment columns.

At best, these 'initiatives' represent a kind of *sovversismo* (Gramsci's term) or 'alternativism', isolated pockets of 'progressive' politics, all too easily accommodated within the established order and tending towards fixed social 'enclaves' and 'niche-markets'. The people who understand and accept them congratulate themselves on doing so, while those who don't just let them pass by. No minds are changed, and the whole shouting match just moves on. At their very worst, they are merely a kind of rhetorical theft, assuming a certain historical legacy for wholly opportunistic purposes. As such, the 'unreflected and casual' use of Gramscian concepts fits quite comfortably alongside the other, much more commonly derided 'dark arts' of New Labour such as 'spin' and 'negative briefing'. By neutralising dissent and disarming criticism, the practised politician's smile in response to scorn, they serve the broader political/administrative purpose of yet more disenfranchisement and marginalisation, and further centralisation of the British state and public services.

Other Gramscian themes

I want now to look at other, perhaps less obvious, 'Gramscian' themes within the politics of New Labour, and see whether Gramsci might offer some critique rather than support for them; the beginnings, perhaps, of a rigorously Gramscian or 'absolute historicist' assessment of the New Labour years. Firstly, there is New Labour's abiding fascination with new technology, which underwrites its awed acquiescence to 'globalisation'. Computerisation, we have been frequently told, is revolutionising the way the world does business; it is the contemporary equivalent of the early nineteenth-century industrial revolution which supposedly shaped the modern world. This is above all the leitmotif of New Labour operative and ex-*Marxism Today* writer Geoff Mulgan, with his spectral 'supercomputers the size of a grain of sand', and his visions of a world modelled on Silicon Valley.[12] This theme has recurred regularly in the writings and speeches of Tony Blair – on 'Technological advance and the rise of skills and information as key drivers of employment and new industries' – and Gordon Brown, with the shift from 'location, raw materials and indigenous capital as sources of national competitive advantage to skills, knowledge and creativity'.[13] New Labour's technophilia underpins its central and ultimately fatalistic conception of how liberalisation and deregulation have eliminated all alternatives to neo-liberalism.[14]

The Soviet Bolsheviks of the 1920s and 1930s were similarly fascinated by the new 'scientific' techniques of industrial management pioneered by the Ford motor company in the USA, and attempted to apply Fordist production and 'Taylorist' organisational methods to their own programmes of industrialisation. Gramsci attributed this, in 'Americanism and Fordism', to the common challenges posed by 'the contradictory conditions of modern society', whether capitalist or socialist, confronted with 'the inherent necessity to achieve the organisation of a planned economy'.[15] This is the point, familiar to anyone involved in running something, where strategic direction elides into operational management, with similar quandaries whatever the bigger economic context. The neo-liberal capitalist aversion to the 'planned economy' is a relatively recent, politically driven and rhetorically 'anti-corporatist' development in US-style capitalism, the novelty in its neo-liberalism and the freedom in its free enterprise obscuring a quasi-anarchist bridling against 'management' of any kind. Until the 1980s, when the radical deregulation and privatisation programmes of 'Reaganomics' took hold, the ethos of American capitalism was still firmly and unapologetically corporatist; even today, the 'fiscal stimulus' in response to the banking crisis indicates a residual 'technical' statism.

It was also this 'corporate/scientific' element of Soviet Communism which most impressed the Fabians and other advocates in the British Labour Party of 'planning': 'as a fulfilment of their dream of a well-ordered and harmonious society run by a benevolent elite', and on a scientific-technocratic basis.[16] This was the point at which pre-Second World War Labour politics came closest to communism. As Ralph Samuel comments, 'centralised discipline was the master idea of the Third International' – all in the cause of 'the planned economy, rational society, science-based industrialisation, a future of material abundance':

> The Russian 5-year plans had a more immediate impact on Fabians than on (British) Communists. Labour leaders were making their pilgrimage to Russia in 1932-3 while the CPGB was still engrossed in unemployed agitations, rank-and-file movements and class-against-class.[17]

Harold Wilson took up the theme in the 1960s, with his 'white heat of technological revolution'. As Michael Kenny demonstrates in his study of the New Left, many socialist intellectuals were initially carried along by that too.[18] 'Scientific' socialism, with its promise of technical, objective grounds for social progress – somehow above the messy human business of politics and ideology, morality and culture – has always had a certain seductive or consolatory power, especially for politicians who sense the ideological force and the socio-cultural base of their own politics faltering or slipping away.

Gramsci detected the same sense of awed technophilia in Bukharin's *Manual of Popular Sociology*, and linked it to a mechanistic conception of economic development. In the section of the Prison Notebooks headed 'Problems of Marxism', he mounted a sustained critique whose ferocity – in the light of Bukharin's show-trial and execution at the behest of Stalin in 1938 – now feels somewhat disproportionate. But it attests to Gramsci's contempt for forms of Marxism that substitute 'social mathematics' for 'the development of social relations', and that fail to understand that 'the philosophy of praxis is precisely and specifically a theory of history'. Their economism amounts to a 'primitive infantilism', and their reductionism to a quest for 'the single ultimate cause ... (and as such a wholly un-Marxist) search for God'. For Gramsci the absolute historicist, 'the struggle for objectivity ... is the same as the struggle for the cultural unification of the human race'.[19] In other words, it is a matter of social analysis, political action and historical contingency, with a clear view towards a socialised economy, a democratic politics and an egalitarian society; or, following political defeat, away from them.

Following Gramsci, we might regard our contemporary IT 'revolution' – in raw human practice, the isolation of individual workers in front of screens, linked if at all to each other and their 'customers' through 'virtual networks' – as the de-socialisation of the processes, means and social relations of industrial production. As such, it represents a reversal of the historical trend of capitalism towards social aggregation, which previous generations of socialists had hoped would germinate the seeds of capitalism's own destruction; and an extension back into the productive process itself of the disabling anomie, alienation and atomisation which Weber, Marcuse et al had primarily located within consumption and civil society. As Gramsci always insisted and the political left has repeatedly failed to grasp, capitalism is well aware of its own self-destructive potential – its 'inhuman face' – and where necessary quite capable of taking steps to avert, override, disguise, justify or supersede it, in pursuit of profit and sustained control. The cause of social disaggregation, as much as greater technical 'efficiency', helps to explain the resources, personnel and political power deployed by capitalism in the cause of 'computerisation'. No doubt Gramsci would have been as baffled and amazed, in roughly equal measure, as the rest of us by personal computers, email, the internet and the rest of it; but he would never have lost sight of the people in front of and behind it all.

In an interesting aside, Gramsci ponders the value of Marx and Marxism to capitalism and to capitalists as a means of understanding their own economic system, in just the way its more confident and thoughtful practitioners felt able to do in the 1990s with the end of the Cold War and the apparent demise of any real live Marxism. A special edition of *The New Yorker* in October 1997 billed Marx as 'the next big thinker, with much to teach us about political corruption, monopolisation, alienation, inequality and global markets … Marx was really a student of capitalism'.[20] Thirteen years later, at the opposite 'bust' end of the trade cycle, 'insider' analyses of recession and prognoses for recovery show the lessons have been well learnt: Richard Jeffrey, chief investment officer at Cazenove Capital Management, argues 'We needed far more pain from the recession … Recessions should always be an economic cleansing process, washing away the excess of the previous upswing. At its hardest that translates into companies collapsing, jobs lost and families forced to leave their homes. This is part of the process of getting the economy back into balance.'[21]

Gramsci recalls an opinion piece in *La Stampa*, wondering 'whether in their heart of hearts the more intelligent industrialists were not convinced that *Capital* contained very good insights into their affairs and whether they do not take advantage of the lessons thus acquired …', and observes that 'this would not be in any way surprising, for if Marx has analysed reality exactly then he has done nothing other than systematise rationally and coherently what the historical agents of this reality felt and still feel'.[22] Indeed, a recent biography of Karl Marx revealed how he supplemented his irregular income with occasional dabbling in the stock market; informed by close study of 'the complexity of the political situation', he wrote to an associate, 'it's worthwhile running some risk in order to relieve the enemy of his money'.[23] If Marx could make productive use of capitalism, capital can make similarly productive use of Marxism;

though, with its rather different class basis and interest, it's hardly surprising that its insights are distorted, disordered and put to unintended uses. Similarly – *vide* Leadbeater and Mulgan – capitalism can easily accommodate compliant, intelligent and entertaining 'Marxists'.

Caesarism

The next Gramscian concept I want to look at in relation to New Labour is 'Caesarism', which I have already ascribed in larger form to Thatcherism, and which Stuart Hall ascribed in smaller form to the SDP. The concept enabled one of Gramsci's most incisive examinations of Italian fascism. We have become used to studies of fascism which focus on its demagogy, brutality and authoritarianism, exemplified by the image and style of Mussolini; or, more profoundly, on the social base of such movements amongst the aggrieved, reactionary and marginal sections of a population.[24] Gramsci identified these, in an Italian setting, as 'peasants and petty bourgeois intellectuals'. Elsewhere he used the more colourful epithets of 'the pettifogging lawyer', 'monkey people', or most startlingly 'the scum of society' he had observed hanging around the squares and bars of Cagliari when he was a student.[25]

Within the rhetoric of twentieth-century liberal democracy, the nearest equivalent to 'Caesarism' would be the profoundly ideological construct of 'totalitarianism'. But Gramsci is more concerned with the historical circumstances which give rise to particular movements and regimes, and as such his analysis has a far wider and more suggestive historical application, drawing in both inspiration and theme on Marx's *Eighteenth Brumaire of Louis Bonaparte*, which analysed the reactionary backlash following the failed 1848 revolutions. He clearly has Italian fascism in mind as a prime example of Caesarism, though he was concerned not to over-aggrandise Mussolini. *Il Duce* was all too happy to draw historical parallels of his own with Julius Caesar, who 'transformed Rome from a city-state into the capital of the empire … By implication Mussolini had (by his own estimation) effected a similar transformation in the status of modern Italy'.[26] But fascism is not the only example of Caesarism, and it shares distinct and unsettling features with other political movements, including (uncomfortably for communists) what Samuel calls 'the cult of

Stalin'. Samuel makes the connection even more uncomfortable for Gramscians by, quite plausibly, portraying Stalin as 'the Modern Prince' of 1930s and 1940s communism (or rather, in a gloriously telling misprint in the 2006 Verso edition of his *The Lost World of British Communism*, 'the Modern Price'!).[27]

Caesarism is, for Gramsci, a characteristic outcome of situations of historical stalemate, when 'forces in conflict balance each other in a catastrophic manner [that] can only terminate in their reciprocal destruction … A 'crisis of authority' is spoken of: this is precisely the crisis of hegemony, or general crisis of the State.' At this point, 'a third force intervenes from outside, subjugating what is left of both' original contending forces. For Gramsci Caesar and Napoleon I are examples of 'progressive Caesarism', and Napoleon III and Bismarck of 'reactionary Caesarism'.[28] The phenomenon can bring about quite different historical outcomes. It has historically occurred as a response to the conditions and demands of war, but more recently has been prompted in particularly acute phases and sites of international capitalist competition ('war by other means', to paraphrase Clausewitz). It typically calls forth 'charismatic men of destiny', such as Winston Churchill, whose 'wartime socialism' government might be regarded as an example of 'progressive Caesarism'; for Gramsci, 'every coalition government is a first stage of Caesarism'.[29] The Con-Lib coalition in Britain, with its determination to reduce the post-New Labour deficit by shrinking the public services, is clearly the beginnings of a project to 'break the logjam' in the established configuration of the British economy, with its supposed imbalances towards public spending and benefits. There is space within this 'Caesarist' resettlement for 'progressive' impulses, most obviously in measures advanced by the Liberal Democrats to mitigate the impact of cuts on the very poor. At the same time, there is no disguising the broader 'regressive' direction of coalition government policy determined by its senior Conservative partners.

We have another clear example of Caesarism close to hand, of a plainly reactionary character. The protracted economic crisis in Britain of the 1960s and 1970s involved apparent stalemate between an outmoded and scarcely profitable capitalist system and an entrenched but deeply defensive labour movement; the stalemate was exemplified by the welfare state, 'unaffordable' for capitalism and 'indispensible' for Labourism. This was 'an equilibrium of forces

heading towards catastrophe', best illustrated by soaring inflation rates
and the shrivelling of capitalist profitability to near-zero on the one
side, and the abandonment of Labourism's historic objective of full
employment   amid rancorous wage-militancy on the other.
Thatcherism broke this stalemate, following Heath's failed attempt to
resolve the 'crisis of authority' (which culminated in the 'Who
Governs Britain?' general election of February 1974, when the
electorate responded 'Not you Ted'). In the process, the
welfarist/productivist, 'Butskellite' post-war settlement between
corporate Labourism and 'one-nation' consensual Toryism was
destroyed. Thatcher's confrontational style also fits Gramsci's model
of 'modern Caesarism', albeit within a parliamentary-democratic
framework, as 'more a police than a military system'.[30] The conduct
of the police during Thatcherism's decisive moment of the 1984/5
miners strike came close to military occupation of parts of the
country, but Thatcher stopped just short of overt deployment of the
armed forces, which would have offended the historical British
'received opinion' that you don't use the army against your own
people.[31]

Gramsci cited other, earlier British examples: 'The "Labour"
governments of Ramsay MacDonald were to a certain degree
solutions of this kind; and the degree of Caesarism increased when the
[National coalition] government was formed [in 1931] which had
MacDonald as its head and a Conservative majority'.[32] Stuart Hall,
in one of his early 1980s essays for *Marxism Today*, attempted to
apply the concept (not entirely successfully) to the 'little Caesars' of
the newly-formed Social Democratic Party, who would turn out
nothing like as important as they (and Hall) thought they were. Hall's
1981 analysis of the SDP was predicated on the apparent early
faltering of Thatcherism, with soaring rates of unemployment and
still-high inflation, so that the 'Gang of Four' et al represented a kind
of proxy version, 'British capitalism's last political ditch'. But the
'doctrinaire decentralisers' of the SDP 'went up like a rocket and came
down like the stick'.[33] The social base of the SDP was very much
narrower and less dynamic than Thatcherism's, a demographic
segment rather a 'historic bloc', heavily concentrated on the 'public
sector salariat' part of the 'progressive, educated middle class'. They
were far more conscious of what they had to lose than gain from neo-
liberalism, and rapidly retreated from their earlier grander visions into

their own genteel sectionalism.[34] Hall eventually identified the primary function of these 'little Caesars' as stiffening Thatcherism's resolve and warding off any final possibilities of socialism: 'An old-style Labour government, succeeding in its third rotation in power (after Attlee and Wilson), would certainly neutralise socialism for a very long time to come. That after all may be what Social Democracy is really about.'[35] And, we might now add, this would prove a central function of the New Labour project (and for all its declarations of novelty, 'old-style Labour government') into which much of the extant SDP would dissolve.

The Owenite, post-Lib Dem merger, 'purist' rump of the SDP was especially enamoured of the 'free market', which it attempted to couple with traditional social democratic formulations in the concept of the 'social market', which survives under the aegis of the Social Market Foundation think tank. More recently under New Labour, this has mutated into 'social enterprise' and enabled the decidedly 'Caesarist' imposition of 'business practice' – through the covertly ideological dictates of 'income generation' and 'performance management' – onto the public and voluntary sectors, alongside further coercive measures to force the benefit-dependent into paid work. These are also the elements of New Labour's adapted Thatcherism which the Con/Lib coalition government has adopted (and will further adapt) with greatest enthusiasm. But without an understanding of Thatcherism's deeper economic purposes and ideological thrusts, the 'reactionary' ('regressive' in Hall's formulation) elements of its Caesarism could easily be underestimated or missed altogether, while its 'progressive' elements could be overstated. This is one of the ways in which New Labour – with its wilful myopia towards the historical realities of capitalism and studied ignorance of the play of ideologies and cultures – has justified its accommodation with Thatcherism; and which underlies repeated references in its rhetoric to the basic technical 'necessity' of its industrial, economic and legislative adjustments. Thatcherism is on balance a predominantly 'reactionary Caesarism'; but an element in New Labour's accommodation with it, of its grudging or sneaking admiration, is actually to imagine it is predominantly 'progressive'.

In the 1930s Gramsci was ready to acknowledge the 'progressive' elements of Italian fascism:

[such] modern historic-political movements … are certainly not revolutions but are not entirely reactionary either – at least in the sense that they shatter stifling and ossified State structures in the dominant camp as well, and introduce into national life and social activity a different and more numerous personnel … they indicate that there were effective forces latent in the old society which the old leaders did not know how to exploit.[36]

This helps to explain the rhetorical anti-statism of Thatcherism, its contempt for the consensual, quasi-social-democratic corporatism of 'One-nation' or 'wet' Conservatism, and its fostering of a new 'entrepreneurial' spirit, supposedly across all classes but heavily focused ideologically on the lower and non-professional middle class. These 'effective forces latent in the old society', revived and emboldened – the people of 'business' who had been sidelined by the post-war social-democratic consensus, even demonised as 'spivs' – were key elements in Thatcherism's project of 'regressive modernisation'.

The question now arises of how Caesarism might apply to New Labour itself. Blair and Brown quite clearly saw themselves as 'charismatic men of destiny', and there was some recent flurry of controversy over whether New Labour was itself fascist.[37] We have to be careful here, not least to avoid what Stuart Hall called 'facile name-calling' when Thatcherism was being equated with fascism by some on the left in the early 1980s, thereby profoundly missing the point of its distinctively British, late twentieth century, historical novelty. We are in the presence of ghosts and ghouls; fascism has taken on monstrous connotations from the experience of the Second World War and the Holocaust, which makes identification of elements it might share with other political phenomena especially fraught. The left is further haunted by two particularly uncomfortable historical facts. Firstly, fascism and Nazism arose from pretty much the same social, cultural and ideological maelstrom as socialism and communism, before, during and immediately after the First World War. They articulated a lot of the same grievances and solutions; they shared and exchanged personnel, including most famously Mussolini, who was editor of the Italian Socialist newspaper *Avanti!* until deciding to break away and support the war effort in 1915. Recent German historiography has stressed the 'socialist' component of

National Socialism, and the ways in which the *Volk* were enlisted into it – in a classically Gramscian combination of 'coercion and consent' – by generous public and welfare spending (of which at least a quarter was funded by the expropriation of European Jews), as well as street thuggery and systematic victimisation.[38] Secondly, the 'Third Period'/late 1920s Communist International 'class against class' policy of denouncing social democrats as 'social fascists' – because of their supposedly common social bases, 'class collaborationist' strategies and similarly 'neutralist' and corporatist conceptions of the capitalist state – casts a long shadow over the history of the political left and relationships within it, and was arguably in part responsible for the ascendancy of fascism and Nazism in the 1930s (as well as obscuring the essentially Russian-nationalist character of Stalinism).

If recent British history has undergone a definitive moment of 'Caesarism' – what Gramsci called a 'permanent and formally organic political and social ideology' dedicated to 'the halting of the fundamental organic [social class] struggle' – it is surely Thatcherism.[39] New Labour's ultimate 'tragedy' is that it has had to operate in the shadow of this far larger historical, 'epochal' phenomenon, just as it has had to respect the neo-liberal economic terms of Thatcherism's passive revolution and operate strictly within them, as at most a 'modernising' or 'updating' adaptation. If New Labour is a new development of a fundamentally Caesarist project, its leading characters are – just like those of an earlier 'centre-left' attempted accommodation with Thatcherism, the SDP – notably 'little Caesars'. New Labour's function remains subserviently 'transformist', humbly consolidating Thatcherism's epochal shift and its newly constituted 'historic bloc' of social and political forces, normalising its reconfigured civil society and its redirected state, driving the imperatives of consumer capitalism ever deeper and wider into our lives, selves, social relations and civil institutions.

Class politics without class

Finally, I want to consider Gramsci's conception of the social base of political movements, and how it might relate to New Labour. Here, for all Gramsci's openness to other traditions and the flexibility of his Marxism, he remained convinced that politics was a conflict between 'fundamental social groups'; albeit in permanent flux and creative realignment, and in multiple layers of alliance within and beyond the various historic blocs, absorbing or repulsing variously 'subaltern groups' identified not just by their economic function but by their shared experiences, ideologies and cultures. Politics also featured all sorts of 'accretions' and adjustments at the level of 'the superstructures', shifting and sometimes tenuous connections to the established political parties, which in circumstances of crisis 'are no longer recognised by their class (or fraction of a class) as its expression'. His analyses were always concrete and rigorously 'historicist', and as such able to accommodate premonitions of future development and leftovers from previous epochs.

This can include, I would argue, much of what we still identify as the primary elements of British politics: Conservatism, Labourism and the political current they both overcame, that is fragmented (and never entirely supplanted) 'free-trade' Liberalism; 'every historical phase leaves traces of itself in succeeding phases', especially in a parliamentary system which is wilfully arcane. This will include echoes and symbols of anachronistic configurations of social class. But there are always 'the major social classes (bourgeoisie, proletariat) defined in strict Marxist terms by (their constantly shifting) position in the fundamental relations of production'.[40] In this, Gramsci remained rigorously and consistently Marxist, and far closer to Lenin than to any variety of liberalism – political, social, economic or neo – all of which subscribe in some way to what Adam Morton calls a 'sanitised view of global governance ... global capitalism with a human face'. [41] Peter Thomas goes so far as to describe Gramsci as 'Lenin's Italian translator', 'translating' Bolshevik perspectives and political culture into Italian circumstances, but always rigorously Marxist and 'historical materialist'.[42] This was so much more than 'class politics', but it was a politics with social class at its core.

This returns us to the question of political agency that has bedevilled 'Gramscism' since at least the 1970s. This is what Adam Morton recently called 'the grimly comic riddle of hegemony': with the dispersal of the industrial proletariat and the political defeat of its various loosely defined 'parties', what are the prospects for a new 'modern prince'?[43] The failure of what remains of the political left in Britain and elsewhere to provide any kind of compelling answer to these questions has enabled the emergence of forms of 'Gramscism' almost wholly divorced from Gramsci as a real historical figure:

'cultural' rather than political, populist rather than democratic, liberal rather than Marxist, idealist rather than materialist, 'pluralist' rather than revolutionary; a name to drop and very selectively quote rather than read and comprehend and apply. Writing in 1982, Eley warned how easily the potential value of Gramsci's concept of hegemony could be misconstrued. 'without a necessary familiarity with both the texts of the *Notebooks* themselves and the larger Marxist discussions that have recently come to surround them'.[44] He had in mind rightist critiques that equated hegemony with straightforward ideological domination in a 'totalitarian' sense', but he might just as well have been discussing more recent reductions of Gramsci's 'master concept'.

Labourism without the left

New Labour is what happens when you remove the left from the equation of British politics. This argument seems to me startlingly obvious, but I have not so far come across it in any of the academic or journalistic commentaries, critical or otherwise, on 'the project'. Most of these have focused on New Labour's debt to Thatcherism, and whether New Labour is or is not itself Thatcherite. This seems to me to confuse the political subject with the political setting, and as such only constitutes part of the story. The epochal meaning of Thatcherism – its Gramscian 'passive revolutionary' character, its 'Caesarist' power, its 'extra-parliamentary' reach – is precisely that it radically changed the social, economic and ideological setting within which British politics is conducted. It is so much more than the period in which Margaret Thatcher was in office, or even the way in which her government operated from day to day. In hegemonic triumph – and this is the neglected but equally important part of the early *Marxism Today* analytical couplet – it delivered a crushing, arguably, fatal blow to the political left.

Although *Marxism Today* consistently pointed to the decline of the left in the 1980s, it conducted surprisingly little detailed analysis of how, when and why it was happening, perhaps for fear of being seen 'looking in on itself', a perennial habit of the British left. Beyond veiled criticism of general political strategy – for example, the conduct of the miners' strike – and a general sense that the left was out of touch with the thrust of 'New Times', you will look in vain for the kind of hard data and analysis on party or group membership figures, finances, political impact and so on that abounds in histories of the Labour Party ('the left' was admittedly always a more diffuse body of people, culturally as much as politically self-identified, and not easily quantified in terms of MPs and other office-holders). Most labour history has been written by Labour-affiliated academics like Pelling, Drucker or Shaw, or by others outside the party political framework altogether; all these had a primarily and often primly academic interest. They might pop up occasionally in *New Socialist* or *Tribune*, but never in *Marxism Today,* which as Raphael Samuel noted was always 'singularly bereft of historical articles'.

Those historians working from within the communist tradition, like Samuel, were also notably absent from the roster of *Marxism Today* 'contributors'. Its only famous historian was Eric Hobsbawm, whose contributions became increasingly 'topical' with the magazine. In this respect, *MT* was surprisingly 'ungrounded', and pre-figurative of New Labour's preference for journalists and think tanks over academics, prediction over history, trends over events, conjecture and controversy over scholarship. Perhaps *MT's* fastidious, almost amnesiac detachment is not surprising, given the perils of historical survey and political critique. It often exasperated its opponents by preoccupying itself with what they regarded as trivialities and irrelevances. When the magazine did carry direct criticism of left-wing and labour movement political practice, as in Tony Lane's September 1982 article about trades unions, it provoked a furious response from its own traditionalist critics; and as we have seen in a previous chapter, *MT* was strangely silent throughout about its own 'sponsor' the CPGB. Until the very end, the decline of the left was assumed rather than demonstrated, but it became a major element of the 'foundation mythology' of New Labour.

Tony Blair was notoriously dismissive towards the Labour left, which accounted for a large part of the party's active membership. His contempt was open and deliberate, especially in New Labour's first phases. He was being egged on by advisers like Phillip Gould, who found that 'without conflict, people are simply not convinced' that real change has taken place, but who also understood that a declining left made an easy target.[45] Under Blair, the party also shifted from a non-union income largely derived from voluntary membership subscription (whose 'dues collection' was, for Drucker, a crucial element of party activity, communications and culture; 'a face-to-face bond') to a murky web of debt, donation and siphoned-off public funds (including the labyrinthine system of MPs' expenses, which at least on the Labour side mainly support party organisation rather than lavish lifestyles). The Labour Party is now reportedly £20 million in debt; its first seventy years were characterised, according to Drucker, by a counter-productive, penny-pinching 'thrift', but it always remained solvent. If Britain was 'living on tick', in a year in which private indebtedness exceeded GDP for the first time ever (2007), so was its ruling political party.[46]

Raphael Samuel argued that Labour's historical achievement was the appropriation on behalf of the industrial working class of the British political tradition of radical Liberalism. In what McKibbin considers the most profound shift in modern British party politics, Labour supplanted the Gladstonian Liberal Party 'of conscience and reform', with its own 'master concept' of 'fair shares'.[47] From this, we can see how New Labour shrank the traditional purposes of Labourism. 'Conscience' became the more nebulous 'values', much less troubling and dictatorial, to be invoked rather than consulted, still less obeyed. 'Reform' is tightly focused on public services, things which the state does to itself and its associated utilities. 'Fair shares', with its over-tones of restraint and redistribution, becomes the more abstract 'fairness', and the working class itself becomes 'the many not the few'. The link with Labourism or even radical Liberalism cannot be wholly severed, but can only be hinted at with allusions and code-words.

The Labour Party leadership has for much of its history felt and acted upon a deep and abiding hostility to the communist, socialist and libertarian left. In the 1920s, Communists were prosecuted and imprisoned at the behest of Labour ministers.[48] In the 1940s and 1950s, the Labour Party spent much time and energy exposing and expelling communists and 'fellow travellers' from party, trade union and associated bodies, and under the provisions of 'bans and proscriptions' from public and civil service employment.[49] Fears of infiltration from the left have contributed substantially to the cultural and psychological formation of Labourism, and prompted periodic action against particular named individuals and groups. Labour has always policed its left flank far more assiduously than its right, and in the process became (for Samuel) 'progressively more monolithic'.[50] And the abiding theme of Labour foreign policy throughout the Cold War, in government and opposition, was its anti-communism.

More recently, attacks on the left were a central and recurrent element in the formative experience of New Labour, most obviously the expulsion of Militant and others, the revision of Clause IV and the adoption of OMOV (One Member One Vote) in party leadership elections. Several accounts associate this process with the mid-1980s attacks by the CP on its own Stalinists, grouped with various 'militant labourists' and hard left Bennites around the wayward *Morning Star*, and use it to suggest a new configuration of the political left. In 1991 Martin Jacques constructed a left-wing political geography of Bennites, CP Stalinists, the Trotskyist groups and conservative forces on one side, and *MT*, the euro-communists, the soft left and the Kinnockites on the other.[51] The CP's last National Organiser Dave Cook had asked in 1986: 'Does not the emerging realignment of the Left, to whose impetus we have already made an important contribution, now point an equally clear finger into the future?'.[52]

New Labour's own touchstones in Labour history usually involve some kind of fight within the party against left wing views or policies which might jeopardise its prospects of electoral success: Gaitskell and the 'fight, fight and fight again to save the party we love' from support for nuclear disarmament; the 'politically motivated men' who undermined the industrial policies of the first Wilson government; the 'bad old days' of the winter of discontent, and the subsequent resistance to Benn's deputy leadership campaign and anything else that would 'take us back to the 1970s'; Kinnock's expulsion of Militant, centralisation of party control and reining-in of the 'loony left'. Blair and Brown's takeover of the party, prior to the landslide victory in 1997, is largely cast in terms of defeating the left over Clause IV of the Labour Party constitution, and the substitution of 'the common ownership of the means of production' by 'a community in which power, wealth and opportunity are in the hands of the many not the few'.[53]

The original function of Clause IV had been to demonstrate Labour's 'continuous tradition of opposition to capitalism', as Drucker puts it. As such it served to differentiate it from the Tories, '*for* labour and *against* capital', during a period in which the Conservatives were generally happy to accept and maintain popular Labour initiatives like the NHS, council housing and full employment. But the Clause IV 'totem' was only ever an element of the Labour Party's 'ethos' rather than a worked-out and workable programme for socialism or even a 'theory of politics' (which Drucker argues Labour has never had, hence its general record of failure in government). Clause IV was thus more a tribal symbol and solidaristic instrument, with its religious verbosity and almost poetic metre, than a practical proposition. Clause IV's author Sidney Webb offered two versions, and himself preferred the much milder and more prosaic 'To secure for the producers by hand or brain the full fruits of their industry *by the Common Ownership of all Monopolies and essential Raw Materials*' (my italics). What Webb called the 'wild men' of Labour chose the longer version.[54]

New Labour's amendment of Clause IV was designed to reassure the electorate of Labour's 'trustworthiness' rather than to effect fundamental change in the party's organisation and culture, but it also quite genuinely served to illustrate and hasten the decline of the Labour left. The veteran Labour leftist MEP and renowned advocate of 'workers control' Ken Coates was quoted as saying that he 'could not live without Clause IV'.[55] Drucker (whose preface acknowledged the help of his PhD student Gordon Brown) implied in 1979 that Labour 'could not live without' its left, which 'performs an ideological task which is useful to the entire party... [upholding the belief] that supporting a Labour Party in the country and working for socialism in the House of Commons might succeed and are, in fact, given an intractable capitalist society, the most likely way to achieve its end'.[56] 'Parliamentary socialism' was what in turn differentiated the various strands and self-styled 'people's tribunes' of the Labour left from the 'extra-parliamentary' British left, even if only because the latter very rarely managed to win any seats.[57]

The wilful abandonment of any sense of transcendent historic mission goes some way to explaining the drastic decline in membership, activity, organisation and finances of the Labour Party under New Labour. There is very little reason for new people to join, especially the young, beyond narrowly careerist reasons. Careerism has always been an element within Labourism, but it was tempered by the party's sense of grander if ill-defined 'anti-capitalist' purpose, not to mention its typically British aversion to blatant personal ambition. By defeating the Labour left so thoroughly, New Labour has broken what Drucker called the 'tumultuous alliance of diverse parts' and Samuel 'a congregation of simmering doubts'; it was these that had generated the party's strength, adaptability and durability, and its capacity to absorb new energies, ideas and personnel from associated social forces and movements.[58] There is very little left of the 'idealism' which drew previous generations, with all their misgivings, into the nearest Britain has ever come to a 'mass party of the working class' or 'People's Party'. It remains to be seen whether the 'virtual party' some New Labour luminaries are reportedly quite comfortable to lead and represent is able to maintain any of Labour's historic purpose – or, as it has so far signally failed to do, discover a new one.

In historical reality, the left has always been a marginal, ineffective force in British politics. At best it has helped to condition the actions of Labour governments, to act as a counterweight to the right and to the inherent social conservatism of Labourism, which itself reflects the prevailing 'subaltern mentalities' of the British people. It has sometimes managed to latch onto a wider 'progressive' or liberal climate of public discourse and opinion, usually around matters of personal morality and private behaviour, where the traditionally British individualist refrain of 'live and let live' and suspicion of an overbearing state can be brought to bear. On only two occasions has the left come anywhere near centre stage in public political life. In the few years after the Second World War, Communist MPs and councillors sat in parliament and council chambers, and a left-inclined Labour government enacted the key elements, instruments and provisions of the welfare state. Twenty years later the counter-cultural upheavals of '1968' had considerable impact on the social relations of Britain (though limited when compared to continental Europe, or even the USA), but made little lasting difference to our political arrangements, other than (arguably) to furnish ideological fuel to the Thatcherite backlash against 'the permissive society' and 'the sixties'.

Apart from that, the British political left has been almost wholly ineffectual, if often busy and occasionally noisy. With the possible exception of a few tolerated celebrities and self-appointed 'commentators', its members and advocates have been driven back, isolated and silenced. If they remain active or at all influential, it is within cultural spheres or 'lifestyle groups' which, in the context of consumer capitalism, have largely changed from transformative, pre-figurative projects into niche-markets. In the more recent period, from 1979 onwards, the left has relentlessly declined, to the extent that it now barely organisationally exists at all on any measure:

electoral, membership figures, or the far less tangible 'influence'. This, it seems to me, is the central, largely undocumented and barely commented upon, historical fact of contemporary British politics, which should be a concern for anyone interested in the health of our democracy. It explains, almost tautologically, the much-vaunted 'shift in the centre of political gravity' to the right which conditions almost every aspect of life in Britain in the twenty first century, and which, Jon Trickett MP reported, was 'deeply depressing' for Labour's last Prime Minister.[59]

Notes

1. G. Eley, 'Reading Gramsci in English', *European Historical Quarterly* vol. 14, 1984, pp444/445.
2. R. Samuel, *The Lost World of British Communism*, pp16/18/19/25.
3. R. Samuel, *The Lost World of British Communism*, pp31/39.
4. G. Eley, 'Reading Gramsci in English', p445.
5. G. Eley, 'Reading Gramsci in English', p444.
6. E. Hobsbawm, in *The Gramsci Reader*, ed. D. Forgacs, p10.
7. S. Hall, 'Wrong', *Marxism Today* Special Issue 1998.
8. S. Hall, *Hard Road to Renewal*, p14.
9. C. Levy, *Gramsci Conference* London, 28 May 2010.
10. P. Anderson, 'The Antinomies of Antonio Gramsci', *New Left Review 100*; E. Hobsbawm, *The Gramsci Reader*, pp11/12.
11. E. Hobsbawm, *The Gramsci Reader*, p13; a similar fate has of course befallen Hobsbawm.
12. G. Mulgan, *New Times*, p388.
13. T. Blair, *The Third Way*; G. Brown, Speech at Mansion House June 2001.
14. C. Hay, *The Political Economy of New Labour*, p30.
15. A. Gramsci, *SPN*, p279.
16. G. Foote, *The Labour Party's Political Thought*, p32.
17. R. Samuel, *The Lost World of British Communism*, p116.
18. M. Kenny, *The First New Left*, passim.
19. A. Gramsci, *SPN*, pp430, 398, 431, 407, 437, 445.
20. F. Wheen, *Karl Marx*, p5.
21. *Times*, 1 October 2010.
22. A. Gramsci, *SPN*, pp391/2.
23. F. Wheen, *Karl Marx*, p268.
24. E. Nolte, *Three Faces of Fascism* (London 1966) is the classic study of this type (and makes some use of Gramsci).
25. A. Gramsci, *SPN*, pp210, 93, 316.

26. A. Gramsci, *SPN*, p219 ft.9.
27. R. Samuel, *The Lost World of British Communism*, p133.
28. A. Gramsci, *SPN*, p219.
29. A. Gramsci, *SPN*, pp210, 220.
30. A. Gramsci, *SPN*, pp219, 222.
31. D. Peace, *GB84* (London 2004); this is a fictional treatment of recent historical research.
32. A. Gramsci, *SPN*, p220.
33. I. Crewe and A. King, *SDP*, pvii.
34. A. Pearmain, 'Hatless to Work: The Social Democratic Party and the 'Dream of Classlessness'', available from andrew.pearmain@ntlworld.com.
35. S. Hall, *The Hard Road to Renewal*, pp60, 65, 66, 67.
36. A. Gramsci, *SPN*, p223.
37. L. Britt, 'Fascism Anyone?' *Free Inquiry* Spring 2003; the 'political scientist' Britt concluded a 'comparative study' of authoritarian regimes based on '14 characteristics of Fascism' with the finding that New Labour was '67 per cent fascist'.
38. G. Aly, *Hitler's Beneficiaries – Plunder, Racial War and the Nazi Welfare State* (London 2007).
39. A. Gramsci, *SPN*, pp216, 221.
40. A. Gramsci, *SPN*, pp210, 409, 5, ft1.
41. A.D. Morton, 'The Grimly Comic Riddle of Hegemony: Where is Class Struggle?' in *Politics:2006*, Vol. 26 (1), p63; J. Sanmartin, 'Gramsci & The Idea of Freedom', paper to University of East Anglia conference on *Gramsci in History*, 19 July 2006. Sanmartin demonstrates Gramsci's persistent, thoroughgoing Marxism in relation to his friend Piero Gobetti's 'revolutionary liberalism'.
42. P. Thomas, *Gramsci Conference*, London, 28 May 2010.
43. A.D. Morton, 'Grimly Comic Riddle', *Politics 2006*, p62.
44. G. Eley, 'Reading Gramsci in English', p464.
45. P. Gould, *Unfinished Revolution*, p263.
46. *Guardian*, 18 September 2007); H. Drucker, *Doctrine and Ethos in the Labour Party*, p16.
47. R. Samuel, *Island Stories*; R. McKibbin, *Ideologies of Class*.
48. H. Pelling & A.J. Reid, *Short History of the Labour Party*, p54.
49. H. Pelling & A.J. Reid, *Short History of the Labour Party*, p93; K. Morgan, *Against Fascism and War*; F. Beckett, *Enemy Within*, p121; H. Pelling, *The British Communist Party* (London 1958).
50. R. Samuel, *The Lost World of British Communism*, p98.
51. M. Jacques, 'The Last Word', *Marxism Today*, December 1991, p29.
52. D. Cook, cited in R. Samuel, *The Lost World of British Communism*, p138.
53. H. Pelling & A.J. Reid, *Short History of the Labour Party*, pp39 & 191.
54. J. M. Winter, *Socialism and the Challenge of War* (London 1974).

55. *Times*, 19 September 1994.
56. H. Drucker, *Doctrine & Ethos in the Labour Party*, p69. This encapsulates neatly Tony Benn's political perspective, such as it is, expressed in his diaries and his *Arguments for Democracy* (London 1981); a rather less subtle variation is to be found in one-time communist and wary Bennite Eric Heffer MP's *The Class Struggle in Parliament* (London 1980).
57. R. Miliband, *Parliamentary Socialism*, represents a classic critique of the Labour left's political practice, while (in common with much of the *Socialist Register/Merlin* stable) underestimating the social and cultural roots of Labourism.
58. H. Drucker, *Doctrine & Ethos in the Labour Party*, p68; R. Samuel, *The Lost World of British Communism*, p6.
59. J. Trickett MP, private conversation.

Postscript: Gramsci, History and New Labour Revisited

Gramsci had very little to say about the future, or even the present, at least in the mature reflections of the prison notebooks. All we could know with any confidence was the past, and even then it was subject to constant re-examination and reinterpretation. All else was at best 'mere speculation', and at worst a quasi-mystical search for baseless consolation and stubborn certainty and finally God. After some initial sympathy towards the futurism of 'Marinetti the Revolutionary' and his artistic companions, Gramsci was eventually dismissive of these 'truanting schoolboys who whooped it up in the woods before being escorted back to school before the policeman's stick' (unsurprisingly the futurists were mostly absorbed into the cultural edifice of fascism).[1] His writings were imbued with a determined 'absolute historicism', a restless investigation of what had already happened, a quest for both the grand themes of history but also its telling detail, for both the consequences of ignorance but also the accumulated wisdom of human experience.

On this basis alone, he would surely have been as scornful of New Labour as he was of the futurists (if I can be forgiven some transhistorical speculation of my own), with their constant injunctions to look 'forward not back'. The working atmosphere of the project's inner core has also had more than a little of the schoolboy gang about it, of 'naughty boys' thumbing their noses at their elders and forebears, with their bullying and smirking and ogling and knowing in-jokes; and above all, their refusal to engage seriously with the past. Even now, Brown's protégé and successor Ed Miliband remains determinedly neophyte, dodging honest and informed discussion of Labour's history, for fear (I would suggest) of accountability for its generally inglorious failings and of the inevitable conclusion that the

261

party was a barely suitable vehicle for real political change in the twentieth let alone twenty-first century. I would also suggest that Labour's wilful amnesia is a major current factor in its drift towards political irrelevance, in a time and society which is hungry for historical explanation, and fiercely – perhaps too much so – obsessed with its past. The British people know that Labour has failed, but are offered no convincing account of why and how this happened from the party itself.

For all these reasons we should be wary of gazing into the future. As New Labour found to its eternal cost, there is nothing quite so ridiculous as predictions which don't come true. But in amongst the general retrospective scorn towards this 'coalition of losers', there is a real danger of missing what was honourable and genuinely progressive in the New Labour project: a search to find some new basis for left-wing politics in Britain that could transcend the tired materialism, tribal sectionalism, broken corporatism, cynical economism, repressive social conservatism and overbearing statism of 'old' Labour. They went looking for ideas and support in the right social class – the 'educated middle class' or professional 'salariat', the 'people like us' they themselves belonged amongst – but in their narrow electoralism and parliamentary careerism, their overwhelming obsession with shifting focus group 'opinion' and 'voting intention', they chose to pander to the wrong sub-section. New Labour pitched themselves towards Mondeo Man and Winchester Woman, the people with money and no class, the Thatcherite nouveaux riches, the comfortably philistine, the irritably complacent, the heirs to Gramsci's 'monkey people'. This was the social base of Gould's 'suburban populism'; of Mandelson's 'intense comfort with the filthy rich', which he calculated the not-so-filthy rich would find somehow endearing and uplifting; of Blair's courting of Murdoch and the tabloid press that these anxious people glanced at on their way to work and business. In political economy terms, New Labour was a pitch to the grasping affluence and hungry aspirationalism that Crosland's revisionism had acknowledged in the 1950s, but without his leavening social conscience and libertarian morality, let alone the 'industrial muscle' of the organised labour movement that underwrote it.

The big issue of our time is climate change. Much of the damage is already done, after two hundred years of industrial production, technological innovation and relentless 'growth'. In technical terms, the realistic challenge is to mitigate and limit the worst effects of human-induced global warming. Reductions in the rate of increase by fractions of a degree can make a huge difference to the lives of millions of people, to whole countries and regions, and to the eco-systems and life-chains of the natural world we all inhabit. Substantial reductions might avert catastrophe altogether. This is well understood and, beyond the cranks and fools and hired hands of climate change denial, generally accepted. The big problem is what we can do about it. The established political parties are too bound up in the politics of consumerism, pitching their own tarnished 'brands' to an ever more weary and uninspired electorate. Environmentalism only ever features as a modish adjunct to their manifestos, a wink to the habitual recyclers and little more than a nudge to everybody else.

Labour, the party of productivism and the weekly wage, is especially hamstrung by its dual historical perspectives of perpetual growth and immediate gratification. Even now, Gordon Brown is advocating 'a growth pact for a global New Deal', perhaps (as disenchanted ex-Blairite Robert Harris puts it) as his own 'extended job application for the World Bank or the IMF'.[2] But whatever else remains of the British left is unable to do very much about the environment either. Despite wholly favourable political circumstances, the Green Party and wider green movement remain wilfully marginal, a refuge for the anti-social and downright cranky, totally unsure where to place themselves in the political spectrum to which most people still look for their own reference-points, let alone within the broader philosophical currents of modernity and urbanism. One minute the Greens are supporting the un-reconstructed 'militant labourism' of Bob Crow and the RMT, the next they are equating animal with human rights. One day they are 'pounding the pavements' in the curiously anti-political 'community politics' of electoral routine, 'getting out the vote' just like any other party machine; the next they are condoning violent and illegal 'street protest'.

Environmentalism takes us back to the future; on that basis it is not easily amenable to Gramsci's 'absolute historicism'. It requires us to imagine, negatively, what the world is going to look like if we carry on as we are. This also conflicts with all our previous models of 'progressive politics', especially socialism and communism, which depended heavily on the prospect of 'a better world' which people could consciously and collectively create. It's also surely why it's proving so hard to devise an effective green politics, the hard graft of changing people's minds and actions, because we are asking them to take responsibility for the far future, and for averting something of which none of us can have any clear conception beyond an amorphous dread. For all the 'utopian visions' of socialism and communism, it was also a politics securely rooted in present hard reality; that was almost the entire point of 'scientific' Marxism. All we have in contemporary environmentalism are visions of dystopia, prophecies of doom, and a wilful anti-humanism which posits as a 'final solution' for nature the casual self-destruction of the human race. We need above all a green *social* politics, that isn't just a guilt-trip or even the paler version of Labour leftism currently espoused by the Green Party, but a means of constructing a new 'historical bloc' around the increasingly 'hegemonic' common sense that we cannot go on consuming the earth's resources as if there is no tomorrow – because if we do there truly won't be. But the message must also be positive: to stress the advantages of 'de-cluttering', of ridding our bodies, lives, relationships, homes, settlements and countries of all that extraneous 'stuff' which we only acquired because capitalism told us to. To take an analogy from public health, we need to abandon unsustainable growth on the same basis that many of us (myself included) gave up smoking: that it was a stupid thing to do in the first place.

We also have to reach beyond the already converted, the bike-riding, train-travelling, composting, recycling, high fibre feeding, low energy lighting and heating, scarf glove and extra jumper-wearing cognoscenti (myself included again), whose zealotry can so easily look like self-satisfaction. Real and lasting 'progressive' political change in Britain, and quite probably anywhere else, has always come about as a result of active alliance between the 'liberal intelligentsia' and the organised working class. The dispersal of the industrial proletariat is a well-attested historical fact; what is less well-documented is the insti-tutionalisation and marginalisation of the 'educated middle class', perhaps because undertaking that kind of analysis might look like unattractive navel-gazing. That precious education, and the advantages it confers under capitalism, has proved the marker of key social and cultural divisions in modern Britain: the islands of 'culture' and intellect around the universities and professions on one side, the small-minded and hard-headed zones of business and commerce on the other, with an ocean of the befuddled and blinkered all around.

One aspect of our social separation is the codification of a certain set of habits and mentalities into a distinctive and exclusive 'lifestyle', fastidiously and smugly 'green', in charge of the daily routines of personal consumption, production and waste in a way only those rich in Bourdieu's 'cultural capital' (not to mention time and space to think) can be. This is where Gramsci comes back in, with his peerless conception of 'organic intellectuals', thinking and cultivated individuals emerging from amongst the 'popular masses', who understand both where people are coming from but also where they might want to go and how to take them there; and crucially *remaining* there with them, rather than being carried ever upwards and apart by the hydraulics of social mobility, patronage and cultural segregation. In this sphere, we have probably gone backwards in the last hundred years; there were almost certainly a lot more 'organic intellectuals' among the working classes in Britain in 1900 than there are now, all those autodidacts and free-thinkers, with their evening classes and shelves of precious books. With the destruction of the political organisations of the sensible class-conscious left – first the Communist Party by its own hand, and now (more slowly but surely) the Labour Party – there are very few places where those organic intellectuals (the backbone of Gramsci's 'Modern Prince') might learn their political craft and their moral code. So, to a very great extent, we are having to start again, just like Marx and Engels in the 1870s, or Togliatti and (in spirit) Gramsci in post-war Italy.

Thinking afresh 'in a Gramscian way' is not just about what we should do, but also about what we should *not* do. In the second volume of her autobiography, written with a heavy dollop of post-communist hindsight, Doris Lessing records her own growing weariness as long ago as the mid-1950s with the empty rituals of left-wing politics: the marches and demos, the petitions and letter-writing campaigns, the interminable meetings, above all the passing-off of individuals' personal desires and formations and of groups' neuroses and prejudices as collective political objectives, and finally the sheer and utter futility of it all.[3] It's not just that it all begins to seem pointless; you also become increasingly aware of how off-putting it seems to most ordinary people. Successive generations of left-wing activists, including my own in the 1970s, have had to find their own way to disillusionment. It is especially painful to watch our own children go through it, as in the quite bizarre 'protests against tuition fees' of late 2010, in reality media-orchestrated demonstrations of naked and ill-informed self-interest by the already better-off segments of a generation entirely formed within the hegemonic framework of consumer capitalism. Young people are understandably angry at the recession being resolved at their expense, but without our clear guidance are condemned to repeat our mistakes. With each successive historical re-enactment, the politics of 'protest' becomes ever more farcical.

Gramsci insisted that the political left had to immerse itself in popular experience if it was to make any kind of difference. This would be a process of mutual enrichment, which would create new forms of thought and action on all sides. That's what the best of the left was trying to do in the 1960s and 1970s; we still have the cultural evidence in our CD and DVD collections and bookshelves, not to mention the improvements in social standing of previously oppressed and marginal groups. But our achievements were only ever partial, easily contained and always vulnerable to 'transformist' absorption by the 'hegemonic historic bloc', as it used them to revitalise itself through the 1980s and 1990s, so that in most cases they lost their transformative charge and ended up as niche-markets. One of the smallest but most significant tragedies of that era, which I hope I've fully outlined in this book, was the way in which the highly original and creative thinking that underlay the *Marxism Today* debates about 'The Forward March of Labour Halted?', 'The Great Moving Right Show' and 'New Times' was taken apart, rearranged and expropriated by New Labour for its own much narrower purposes in the political marketplace of neoliberal hegemony. I've tried to explain how and why that happened and how, in the necessarily uncertain future we face, we might avoid it happening again. Maybe next time it'll all turn out a lot better; 'optimism of the will, pessimism of the intellect'.

Notes

1. A. Gramsci, *Cultural Writings,* p23.
2. G. Brown, *Beyond the Crash* (London 2010); R. Harris, *Sunday Times,* 12 December 2010.
3. D. Lessing, *Walking in the Shade* (London 1997).

Bibliography

Books and Pamphlets

M. Abrams, *Must Labour Lose?* (London 1960)

W.L. Adamson, *Hegemony and Revolution* (Los Angeles 1980)

L. Althusser, *Reading Capital* (London 1970)

G. Aly, *Hitler's Beneficiaries* (London 2007)

P. Anderson, *Considerations on Western Marxism* (London 1976)

Paul Anderson and N. Mann, *Safety First: The Making of New Labour* (London 1997)

G. Andrews et al, *Opening the Books* (London 1995)

G. Andrews, *Endgames and New Times* (London 2004)

R. Archer et al. (eds.), *Out of Apathy – Voices of the New Left* (London 1989)

P. Baker, *Polari: the Lost Language of Gay Men* (London 2002)

J.G. Ballard, *Super Cannes* (London 2001)

R. Barker, *Education and Politics 1900-1951: A Study of the Labour Party* (Oxford 1972)

J. Baudrillard, *Selected Writings* (London 1988)

S. Bayley, *Labour Camp* (London 1998)

F. Beckett, *Enemy Within: The Rise and Fall of the British Communist Party* (London 1995)

R. Bell and S. Gunn, *Middle Classes* (London 2002)

S. Beer, *Britain against Itself* (London 1982)

R. Ben-Ghiat, *Fascist Modernities* (Berkeley 2004)

T. Benn, *Arguments for Democracy* (London 1981)

T. Benn, *The End of an Era; Diaries 1989-90* (London 1992)

A. Bennett & K. Hahn-Harris, *After Subculture* (London 2004)

M. Berman, *All That Is Solid Melts Into Air* (London 1985)

M. Bevir, *New Labour: a Critique* (London 2005)

H. Beynon et al (eds.), *Digging Deeper – Issues in the Miners strike* (London 1985)

L. Black, *Coercion or Consent?* (Cheltenham 2001)

T. Blackwell and J. Seabrook, *The Politics of Hope* (London 1988)

T. Blair, *Let us face the Future* (London 1995)

T. Blair, *The Third Way* (London 1998)

J. Bloomfield (ed.), *Class, Hegemony and Party* (London 1977)

D. Blunkett, *The Blunkett Tapes* (London 2006)

C. Boggs, *Gramsci's Marxism* (London 1976)

G. Bridges & R. Brunt (eds.), *Silver Linings* (London 1981)

B. Brivati and R. Heffernan, *The Labour Party*, London 2000

C. Buci-Glucksmann, *Gramsci and the State* (London 1980)

Lord Butler, *Review of Intelligence on Weapons of Mass Destruction* (London 2004)

C. Calhoun, *The Question of Class Struggle* (Chicago 1982)

J. Callaghan, *The Far Left in British Politics* (Oxford 1987)

J. Callaghan, *The Retreat of Social Democracy* (Manchester 1995)

A. Callinicos, *Althusser's Marxism* (London 1976)

J. Cammett, *Antonio Gramsci and the Origins of Italian Communism* (Stanford 1967)

A. Campbell, *The Blair Years* (London 2007)

B. Campbell, *Iron Ladies: Why do women vote Tory?* (London 1985)

S. Carrillo, *Eurocommunism and the State* (London 1977)

J. Carvel, *Citizen Ken* (London 1984)

A. Chadwick & R. Heffernan (eds) *The New Labour Reader* (Cambridge 2003)

Clarke, *Gary's Friends* (Brighton 2007)

C. Clarke and D. Griffiths, *Labour and Mass Politics – Rethinking our Strategy*, Labour Co-ordinating Committee 1982

P. Chatterjee, *Nationalist Thought and the Colonial World* (London 1986)

A. Clarke, *Diaries* (London 1993)

D. Coates, *The Labour Party and the Struggle for Socialism* (Cambridge 1975)

R. Cockett, *Thinking the Unthinkable* (London 1994)

R. Cook, *The Point of Departure* (London 2004)

P. Cozens, *Twenty Years of Antonio Gramsci: A Bibliography of Gramsci and Gramsci Studies, 1957-77* (London 1977)

Communist Party of Great Britain, *The British Road to Socialism* (London 1977)

I. Crewe and A. King, *SDP: The Birth, Life and Death of the Social Democratic Party* (London 1995)

Crick, *In Defence of Politics* (London 2005)

M. Crick, *Militant* (London 1984)

J. Cronin, *New Labour's Pasts* (London 2004)

Crosland, *The Future of Socialism* (London 1957)

Crosland, *Can Labour Win?* Fabian Tract 324, (London 1959)

R. Crossman, *Labour and the Affluent Society*, Fabian Tract 324 (London 1959)

A. Davidson, *Antonio Gramsci: The Man, his Ideas* (Sydney 1968)

Davidson, *Antonio Gramsci: Towards an Intellectual Biography* (London 1976)

J. Denham, *How the Labour Party – and the Left – Can Win*, Labour Co-ordinating Committee, 1984

R. Desai, *Intellectuals and Socialism* (London 1994)

I. Deutscher, *Heretics and Renegades* (London 1969)

I. Deutscher, *Stalin – a political biography* (London 1961)

I. Deutscher, *Trotsky – The Prophet Unarmed, 1921-29* (London 2003)

P. Devine, A. Pearmain, D. Purdy (eds.), *Feelbad Britain* (London 2009)

H. Dewar, *Communist Politics in Britain* (London 1976)

Donoughue and G.W. Jones, *Herbert Morrison* (London 2001)

S. Driver and L. Martell, *New Labour: Politics after Thatcherism* (Cambridge 1998)

S. Driver and L. Martell, *Blair's Britain* (Cambridge 2002)

H. Drucker, *Doctrine and Ethos in the Labour Party* (London 1979)

D. Eisenbach, *Gay Power: A History of Gay Liberation* (London 2006)

R. Elms, *The Way We Wore* (London 2006)

G. Elliot, *Labourism and the English Genius* (London 1993)

S. Engel, *The Unfinished Revolution* (Cambridge 2001)

F. Engels, *Socialism: Utopian and Scientific* (London 1892)

F. Engels, *The Origins of the Family, Private Property and the State* (Moscow 1978)

A. Etzioni, *The Spirit of Community* (London 1993)

N. Fairclough, *New Labour New Language?* (London 2000)

F. Fanon, *Black Skin, White Masks* (London 1986)

J. Femia, *Gramsci's Political Thought: Hegemony, Consciousness and the Revolutionary Process* (Oxford 1981)

O. Figes, *A People's Tragedy* (London 1996)

Fine & R. Millar, *Policing the Miners' Strike* (London 1985)

A. Finlayson, *Making Sense of New Labour* (London 2003)

G. Fiori, *Antonio Gramsci Life of a Revolutionary*, trans. T. Nairn (London 1970)

K. Flett and D. Renton (eds.), *New Approaches to Socialist History* (London 2003)

G. Foote, *The Labour Party's Political Thought* (London 1985)

N. Frazer, *Justice Interruptus* (New York 1997)

F. Fukuyama, *The End of History and the Last Man* (New York 1992)

J. Fyrth (ed.), *Labour's Promised Land?* (London 1995)

A. Gamble, *The Free Economy and the Strong State – The Politics of Thatcherism* (London 1988)

S. Garfield, *The End of Innocence: Britain in the Time of AIDS* (London 1994)

E. Genovese, *Red and Black; Marxian Explorations in Southern and Afro-American History* (New York 1971)

A. Giddens, *The Third Way: The Renewal of Social Democracy* (Cambridge 1998)

I. Gilmour, *Dancing with Dogma* (London 1992)

P. Ginsborg, *Italy and its Discontents* (London 2006)

E. Goldman, *Living My Life* (London 2006)

A. Gorz, *Division of Labour* (New York 1976)

A. Gorz, *Farewell to the Working Class* (London 1982)

P. Gould, *The Unfinished Revolution* (London 1998)

A. Gramsci, *The Open Marxism of Antonio Gramsci*, Carl Manzoni ed. (New York 1957)

A. Gramsci, *The Modern Prince*, ed. and trans. L. Marks (London 1957)

A. Gramsci, *Workers' Control and Revolution*, trans. S. Boddington (Nottingham 1968)

A. Gramsci, *Selections from Prison Notebooks*, edited and translated by Quintin Hoare and Geoffrey Nowell Smith (London 1971)

A. Gramsci, Special Issue, *New Edinburgh Review* (Edinburgh 1975)

A. Gramsci, *History, Philosophy and Culture in the Young Gramsci*, ed. P. Cavalcanti and P. Piccone (St Louis 1975)

A. Gramsci, *Selections from Political Writings 1910-1920*, trans. John Matthews, selected and edited by Quintin Hoare (London 1977)

A. Gramsci, *Selections from Political Writings 1921-26*, trans. and ed. Quintin Hoare (London 1978)

A. Gramsci, *Letters from Prison*, selected and translated by Lynn Lawner (London 1975)

A. Gramsci, *Further Selections from the Prison Notebooks*, trans. and ed. D. Boothman (London 1983)

A. Gramsci, *Selections from Cultural Writings*, trans. W. Bollhower, ed. D.

Forgacs and G. Nowell Smith (London 1985)

A. Gramsci, *The Gramsci Reader*, selected and edited by D. Forgacs (London 1988)

A. Gramsci, *Prison Letters*, selected and translated by Hamish Henderson (London 1996)

I. Grewen & C. Kaplan, *Scattered Hegemonies* (Minneapolis 1994)

R. Griffiths, *Was Gramsci a Eurocommunist?* (London 1984)

T. Griffiths, *Occupations* (London 1972)

S. Gunn & R. Bell, *Middle Classes* (London 2002)

S. Hall & T. Jefferson (eds.), *Resistance Through Rituals* (London 1976)

S. Hall, *The Hard Road to Renewal* (London 1989)

S. Hall, *Critical Dialogues in Cultural Studies* (London 1996)

S. Hall & M. Jacques (eds.), *New Times* (London 1989)

C. Handy, *The Empty Raincoat: Making Sense of the Future* (London 1995)

C. Handy, *The Hungry Spirit: A Quest for Purpose in the Modern World* (London 1998)

C. Harman, *Gramsci Versus Reformism* (London 1983)

D. Harris, *From Class Struggle to the Politics of Pleasure* (London 1992)

T. Harrison, *V* (Newcastle 1985)

C. Hay, *The Political Economy of New Labour* (London 2000)

F.A. Hayek, *The Road to Serfdom* (London 2001)

F.A. Hayek, *The Constitution of Liberty* (London 2006)

D. Hebdige, *Subculture: the Meaning of Style* (London 1979)

E. Heffer, *The Class Struggle in Parliament* (London 1980)

R. Heffernan and M. Marqusee, *Defeat from the Jaws of Victory* (London 1992)

S. Hibbin (ed.), *Politics Ideology and the State* (London 1978)

B. Hindess and P. Hirst, *Pre-capitalist Modes of Production* (London 1975)

E. Hobsbawm, *The Forward March of Labour Halted?* (London 1981)

E. Hobsbawm, *The Age of Extremes* (London 1983)

E. Hobsbawm, *Politics for a Rational Left* (London 1989)

R. Hoggart, *The Uses of Literacy* (London 1957)

S. Holland, *The Socialist Challenge* (London 1975)

Hollingsworth, *The Line of Beauty* (London 2005)

N. Hornby, *Fever Pitch* (London 1992)

W. Hutton, *The State We're In* (London 1996)

S. Imlach, *My Father and Other Working Class Football Heroes* (London 2005)

P. Ives, *Language and Hegemony in Gramsci* (London 2004)

M. Jaggi, R. Muller, S. Schmid, *Red Bologna* (London 1977)

S. Jenkins, *Thatcher and Sons* (London 2007)

K. Jefferys, *Leading Labour* (London 1999)

Jerome, *The New Media* (London 1993)

B. Johnson, *Have I Got Views for You* (London 2006)

R. Johnson, *Working Class Culture: Studies in History and Theory* (London 1980)

J. Joll, *Gramsci* (London 1977)

N. Jones, *Sultans of Spin: The Media and the New Labour Government* (London 1999)

T. Jones, *The Dark Heart of Italy* (London 2003)

M. Kenny, *The First New Left* (London 1995)

D. & M. Kogan, *The Battle for the Labour Party* (London 1982)

The Labour Party, *Labour and Britain in the 1990s* (London 1987)

The Labour Party, *Democratic Socialist Aims and Values* (London 1988)

The Labour Party, *Social Justice and Economic Efficiency* (London 1988)

J. Lacan, *Ecrits: a Selection* (New York 1977)

E. Laclau & C. Mouffe, *Hegemony and Socialist Strategy* (London 1985)

P. Lambert, *The Concept of Class* (London 1982)

J. Lawrence, *Speaking for the People: Party, Language and Popular Politics in England 1867-1914* (Cambridge 1998)

N. Lawson (ed.), *New Maps for the Nineties – A Third Road Socialist Reader*, Labour Coordinating Committee 1990

N. Lawson, *Dare More Democracy* (London 2004)

K. Laybourn, *The Rise of Socialism in Britain* (London 1997)

C. Leadbeater, *The Politics of Prosperity* (London 1987)

C. Leadbeater, *Living on Thin Air* (London 1998)

C. Leadbeater, *Up the Down Escalator* (London 2002)

V.I. Lenin, *Left Wing Communism: an Infantile Disorder* (Moscow, 1921)

R. Limbaugh, *The Way Things Ought To Be* (New York, 1993)

S. Ludlam and M. Smith, *New Labour in Government* (London 2001)

J-F. Lyotard, *The Post-Modern Condition* (Minnesota, 1984)

J. Major, *The Autobiography* (London 1999)

E. Mandel, *Introduction to Marxism* (London 1982)

P. Mandelson & R. Liddell, *The Blair Revolution* (London 1996)

H. Marcuse, *One Dimensional Man* (London 1972)

D. Marquand, *The Progressive Dilemma* (London 1999)

D. Marquand, *The Decline of the Public* (London 2004)

F. T. Marinetti, *Manifesto of Futurism* (Paris 1909)

D. Massey, *London: World City* (London 2007)

R. Mabey (ed.), *Class* (London 1967)

J. McGuigan, *Cultural Populism* (London 1992)

D. McIntyre, *Mandelson and the Making of New Labour* (London 1999)

D. McKnight, *Beyond Left and Right* (Sydney 2005)

Meyer, *DC Confidential* (London 2005)

R. Miliband, *Parliamentary Socialism* (London 1961)

L. Minkin, *The Labour Party Conference* (London 1978)

L. Minkin, *The Contentious Alliance* (Edinburgh 1991)

J. Mitchell, *Psychoanalysis and Feminism* (London 1975)

K. Morgan, *Against Fascism and War* (Manchester 1989)

K. Morgan, *Harry Pollitt* (Manchester 1993)

K. Morgan, G. Cohen and A. Flinn, *Communists and British Society 1920-1991: People of a Special Mould (*London 2005)

C. Mouffe (ed.), *Gramsci and Marxist Theory* (London 1979)

M. Mowlem, *Momentum* (London 2003)

T. Nairn, *Break-up of Britain* (London 1981)

D. Nolan, *Confusion* (Church Stretton 2007)

E. Nolte, *Three Faces of Fascism* (London 1966)

F. O'Connor, *The Habit of Being* (New York 1980)

G. Orwell, *The Lion and the Unicorn* (London 1941)

L. Panitch & C. Leys, *The End of Parliamentary Socialism* (London 1997)

F. Parkin, *Middle Class Radicalism* (Manchester 1968)

D. Peace, *GB84* (London 2004)

H. Pelling, *The British Communist Party* (London 1958)

H. Pelling, *Origins of the Labour Party* (London 1965)

H. Pelling & A.J. Reid, *A Short History of the Labour Party* (London 1996)

B. Pimlott, *Harold Wilson* (London 1992)

K. Polanyi, *The Great Transformation* (London 1944)

N. Poulantzas, *Classes in Contemporary Capitalism* (London 1975)

A. Pozzolini, *Antonio Gramsci: An Introduction to his Thought*, trans. A. Showstack, (London 1970)

L. Price, *The Spin Doctor's Diary* (London 2005)

M. Prior & D. Purdy, *Out of the Ghetto* (Nottingham 1979)

A. Rawnsley, *Servants of the People* (Harmondsworth 2001)

A. Rimbaud, *Illuminations*, A. Guyaux (ed.), (Neuchatel: La Baconniere 1985)

S. Riva, *An Introduction to Some Thoughts of Gramsci*, CPGB pamphlet (London 1976)

G. Robb, *Arthur Rimbaud* (London 2000)

S. Rowbotham, *Hidden from History* (London 1973)

S. Rowbotham, H. Wainwright, L. Segal, *Beyond the Fragments* (London 1979)

S. Rowbotham, *Dreams and Dilemmas* (London 1983)

E. Said, *Foucault and the Imagination of Power* (Cambridge, 1986)

R. Samuel, *The Lost World of British Communism* (London 2006)

R. Samuel et al (eds.), *The Enemy Within – Pit Villages and the Miners strike of 1984/5* (London 1986)

R. Samuel & P. Thompson (eds.), *The Myths We Live By* (London 1990)

R. Samuel, *Theatres of Memory* (London 1994)

R. Samuel, *Island Stories* (London 1998)

J. Seabrook and T. Blackwell, *The Politics of Hope* (London 1988)

L. Segal, *Making Trouble: Life and Politics* (London 2007)

A. Seldon, *Blair* (London 2004)

R. Sennett & J. Cobb, *The Hidden Injuries of Class* (New York 1972)

V. Serge, *Memoirs of a Revolutionary* (London 1963)

P. Seyd, *The Rise and Fall of the Labour Left* (London 1987)

P. Seyd & P. Whiteley, *Labour's Grass Roots: The Politics of Party Membership* (Oxford 1992)

E. Shaw, *The Labour Party since 1979* (London 1994)

A. Showstack Sassoon, *Approaches to Gramsci* (London 1982)

R. Simon, *Gramsci's Political Thought* (London 1982)

I. Sinclair (ed.), *London: City of Disappearances* (London 2007)

R. Skidelsky, *Politicians and the Slump: The Labour Government 1929-31* (London 1971)

R. Skidelsky (ed.), *Thatcherism* (London 1988)

Smith, *Moon Dust* (London 2005)

M. J. Smith, *The Changing Labour Party* (London 1992)

P. Smith, *Millennial Dreams* (London 1997)

P. Spriano, *Antonio Gramsci and the Party: The Prison years* (London 1979)

W. St Clair, *The Grand Slave Emporium* (London 2006)

Stedman Jones, *Languages of Class* (Cambridge 1983)

J. Steele, *Defeat: Why they lost Iraq* (London 2008)

P. Tatchell, *The Battle for Bermondsey* (London 1983)

B. Taylor, *Eve and the New Jerusalem* (London 1983)

D.J. Taylor, *Orwell – a Life* (London 2004)

E.P. Thompson, *The Making of the English Working Class* (London 1963)

E.P. Thompson, *William Morris: Romantic to Revolutionary* (London 1977)

E.P. Thompson, *The Poverty of Theory and other essays* (London 1978)

N. Thompson, *Left in the Wilderness* (London 2002)

P. Thompson and B. Lucas, *The Forward March of Modernisation*, Labour Coordinating Committee 1998

W. Thompson, *The Good Old Cause* (London 1992)

W. Thompson, *The Long Death of British Labourism* (London 1993)

A. Thorpe, *A History of the British Labour Party* (London 1997)

P. Togliatti, *On Gramsci and Other Writings* (London 1979)

E. Upward, *The Rotten Elements* (London 1979)

M. Waller et al (eds.), *Communist Parties in Western Europe* (Oxford, 1988)

B. Warren and M. Prior, *Advanced Capitalism, Backward Socialism* (Nottingham 1974)

J. Weeks, *Coming Out* (London 1977)

M. Westlake, *Kinnock: The Biography* (London 2001)

F. Wheen, *Karl Marx* (London 1999)

P. Whiteley, *The Labour Party in Crisis* (London 1983)

G.A. Williams, *Proletarian Order* (London 1975)

R. Williams, *Culture and Society* (London 1958)

R. Williams, *The Long Revolution* (Harmondsworth 1965)

R. Williams (ed.), *The May Day Manifesto* (Harmondsworth 1968)

P. Willis, *Learning to Labour* (London 1978)

J. M. Winter, *Socialism and the Challenge of War* (London 1974)

Newspaper, Journal and Magazine Articles

P. Anderson, 'Critique of Wilsonism', *New Left Review* 27, Sept-Oct 1964

P. Anderson, 'Origins of the Present Crisis', *New Left Review* 23, Jan-Feb 1964

P. Anderson, 'The Antinomies of Antonio Gramsci', *New Left Review* 100, Jan-Feb 1976

P. Anderson, 'European Hypocrisies', *London Review of Books*, 20 September 2007

E. Balls, 'Open Macroeconomics in an Open Economy', in *New Labour Reader*, eds, Chadwick & Heffernan

R. Bellamy, 'Gramsci for the Italians', *Times Literary Supplement*, 14 August 1992

P. Beresford, 'Whose Personalisation?' *Soundings* 40, Winter 2008

E. Berlinguer, 'Lessons from Chile', *Marxism Today*, February 1973

L. Bersani, 'Is the Rectum a Grave?' in *'AIDS: Cultural Analysis, Cultural Activism'* (ed) D. Crimp, London 1988 (MIT)

A. Bieler & A.D. Morton, 'The Gordian Knot of Agency-Structure in International Relations: A neo-Gramscian perspective', *European Journal of International Relations* 7 (1), 2001

R. Blackburn, *New Statesman* 18 July 1980

T. Blair, Back Page interview, *Marxism Today* July 1990

T. Blair, 'Forging a New Agenda', *Marxism Today* October 1991

Boccioni, Marinetti, Russolo, Piati, Carra, 'The Futurist Synthesis of War' (1914), featured in *Breaking the Rules*, British Library exhibition, Autumn 2007

British Social Attitudes Survey 2006, *The Times* 4 April 2007

L. Britt, 'Fascism Anyone?' *Free Inquiry* Spring 2003

M. Burawoy, 'For a Sociological Marxism: The Complementary Convergence of Antonio Gramsci and Karl Polanyi', *Politics and Society* vol. 31 no. 2, 2003

R.W. Cox, 'Social Forces, States and World Orders', *Millennium: Journal of International Studies* vol. 10, 1981

R.W. Cox, 'Gramsci, Hegemony and International Relations', *Millennium Journal of International Studies*, vol. 12 (2) 1983

A. Davidson, 'Gramsci and Lenin 1917-22', *Socialist Register* 1974

R. Debray, 'Schema for a Study of Gramsci', *New Left Review 59*, Jan-Feb 1970

T. Dodge, 'The Tikriti and the Sardinian: The Comparative Autonomy of the Middle Eastern State and Regime Change in Iraq', *paper to UEA conference on 'Gramsci in History'*, 19 July 2006

G. Eley, 'Reading Gramsci in English: Observations on the Reception of Antonio Gramsci in the English-speaking World 1957-82', *European History Quarterly* vol. 14, pp. 441-78

D. Forgacs, 'National-Popular: Genealogy of a Concept', in *Formations of Nation and People* (London 1984)

D. Forgacs, 'Gramsci and Marxism in Britain', *New Left Review 176*, July-Aug 1989

E. Genovese, 'On Antonio Gramsci', *Studies on the Left*, Vol. 7 (2), 1967

N. Geras, 'Post-Marxism?' *New Left Review* 163, 1987

D. Gitten, *Daily Telegraph* 24 October 2007

A. Gramsci, 'In Search of the Educational Principle', trans. Q. Hoare, *New Left Review 32*, July-Aug 1965

A. Gramsci, 'Soviets in Italy', *New Left Review 51*, Sept-Oct 1968

T. Griffiths, 'In Defense of Occupations', *7 Days*, 10 Dec 1971

S. Hall, 'A Sense of Classlessness', *Universities and Left Review* 1958

S. Hall, 'Rethinking the Base/Superstructure Metaphor', in *Class, Hegemony and Party*, ed. J. Bloomfield, London 1977

S. Hall, 'The Great Moving Right Show', *Marxism Today* Jan 1979

S. Hall, 'New Labour's Double Shuffle', *Soundings* 25, 2002

F. Jameson, 'The Cultural Logic of Capital', *New Left Review* 146, 1984

J. Harvey, 'Antonio Gramsci', *Marxism Today* vol. 11 no. 4 April 1967

J. Harvey, Review of Selections from Prison Notebooks, *Marxism Today* vol. 15 no. 12, Dec 1971

R. Hattersley, 'Blair's Labour Party', *The Guardian*, 17 October 2002

D. Hebdige, 'After the Masses', *Marxism Today* Jan 1989

S. Heffer, *Daily Telegraph*, 2 March 2007

P. Hirst, 'After Henry', *New Statesman and Society* 21 July 1989

Q. Hoare, 'What is Fascism?' *New Left Review 20*, July-Aug 1963

E. Hobsbawm, 'The Great Gramsci', *New York Review of Books* vol. 21 no. 5, April 1974

T.J. Jackson Lears, 'The Concept of Cultural Hegemony', *American Historical Review* 90(3) 1985

T.J. Jackson Lears, 'A Matter of Taste: Corporate Cultural Hegemony in a Mass Consumption Society', in L. May (ed.) *Recasting America* (Chicago 1989)

M. Jacques, 'Notes on the Concept of Intellectuals', *Marxism Today* vol. 15 no. 10, Oct 1971

M. Jacques, Introduction to online *Marxism Today* collection, www.amielandmelburn.org.uk/collections/mt/index_frame_r.htm

S. Jenkins, 'The Leader's Cheerleaders', *London Review of Books*, 20 Sept 2007

B. Jessop, 'The Gramsci Debate', *Marxism Today* Feb 1980

V. Kiernan, 'Gramsci's Marxism', *Socialist Register* 1972

J. Lanchester, 'Cityphilia', *London Review of Books* 3 January 2008

T. Lane, 'The Unions: Caught on the Ebb Tide', *Marxism Today* Sept 1982

J. Lawrence, 'The Myths We Live By', in *Labour's First Century*, ed. N. Tiratsoo et al (Cambridge 2000)

C. Leadbeater, 'Power to the Person', *Marxism Today* March 1987

M. Mann, 'The Social Cohesion of Liberal Democracy', *American Sociological Review* 35, 1970

D. Marquand, 'The Blair Paradox', *Prospect* May 1998

Marxism Today, special issue 'Wrong', 1998, ed. S. Hall & M. Jacques; articles by S. Hall, D. Held, G. Mulgan, T. Nairn et al

I. McKay, 'William Lyon McKenzie King and Hegemony', *paper presented* to '*Gramsci in History' seminar*, University of East Anglia, 19 July 2006

R. McKibbin, 'Pure New Labour', *London Review of Books* 4 October 2007

J. Merrington, 'Theory and Practice in Gramsci's Marxism', *Socialist Register* 1968

R. Miliband, review of 'Selections from Prison Notebooks', *Bulletin of the Society for the Study of Labour History* no. 25, Autumn 1972

A.D. Morton, 'Historicizing Gramsci', *Review of International Political Economy* Vol. 10 (1), February 2003

A.D. Morton, 'Structural Change and Neo-Liberalism in Mexico: 'Passive Revolution' in the Global Political Economy', *Third World Quarterly* 24 (4), 2003.

A.D. Morton, 'The Grimly Comic Riddle of Hegemony: Where is Class Struggle?', *Politics 2006* Vol. 26 (1)

G. Mulgan, 'Whinge and a Prayer', *Marxism Today Special Issue* 1998

R. Murray, 'Benetton Britain: The New Economic Order', *Marxism Today* Nov 1985

R. Murray, 'Life After Henry' (later published as 'Fordism and Post-Fordism' in 'New Times', ed. Hall & Jacques), *Marxism Today* Oct 1988

T. Nairn, 'The British Political Elite', *New Left Review* 23, Jan-Feb 1964

T. Nairn, 'The English Working Class', *New Left Review* 24, March-April 1964.

T. Nairn, 'The Anatomy of the Labour Party', *New Left Review* 27/28, Sept-Oct & Nov-Dec 1964

T. Nairn, 'Mucking about with Love and Revolution', *7 Days* 10 Nov. 1971

T. Nairn, *London Review of Books*, 7 Dec 2007

The New Yorker, special issue, October 1997

Nowell Smith, 'Gramsci and the National Popular', *Screen Education* 22, 1977

P.P. Pasolini, 'Gramsci's Ashes', in *The Faber Book of 20th Century Italian Poems*, ed. J. McKendrick (London 2004)

A. Pearmain, 'England and the National Popular', *Soundings* 38, Spring 2008

A. Pearmain, 'Pieces of Labourism and the "Fascist Possibility" in English Politics', available from andrew.pearmain@ntlworld.com

A. Portelli, 'Uchronic Dreams: Working class memory and possible worlds', in *The Myths We Live By*, ed. R. Samuel & P. Thompson, (London 1990)

Robinson, review of Togliatti's 'On Gramsci', *Marxism Today* May 1980

D. Runciman, 'Brown and Friends', *London Review of Books* 3 January 2008

M. Rustin, 'The Trouble with New Times', *New Left Review* 175, June/July 1989

J. Sanmartin, 'Gramsci and the Idea of Freedom', *paper to UEA conference on 'Gramsci in History'*, 19 July 2006

J. Saville, 'Marxism Today: an Anatomy', *Socialist Register* 1990

M. Shaw, 'The Making of a Party?' *Socialist Register* 1978

R. Shilliam, 'Hegemony and the Unfashionable Problematic of Primitive Accumulation', *Millennium: Journal of International Studies* 33 (1), 2004

R. Simon, 'Gramsci's Concept of Hegemony', *Marxism Today*, vol. 21 no. 3, 1977

F. Steward, 'Green Times', *Marxism Today* March 1989

L. Terry, 'Travelling the Hard Road to Renewal: A continuing Conversation with Stuart Hall', *Arena Journal* 8

G. Therborn, 'West on the Dole', *Marxism Today* June 1985

R. Thomson, 'Gramsci the first Italian Marxist', *Marxism Today* vol.1 no. 11, Nov 1957

E.P. Thompson, 'Recovering the Libertarian Tradition', interview by T. Illott, *The Leveller* 22, Jan 1978

J. Urry, 'The End of Organised Capitalism', *Marxism Today*, October 1988

G.A. Williams, 'The Concept of Egemonia in the Thought of Antonio Gramsci', *Journal of the History of Ideas*, Vol XXI, October-December 1960

S. Zizek, 'Resistance is Surrender', *London Review of Books* 15 Nov 2007

Television, Film and other Broadcasts

'Decision British Communism', Granada TV 1977

'Gramsci', Channel 4 Television, 1987, dir. Mike Alexander, script Douglas Eadie, narrator Brian Cox; studio discussion between Lidia Curti, Stuart Hall, Hamish Henderson and John Reid, chaired by Trevor Haylett

Neil Kinnock's Resignation, BBC News, 9 April 1992

'How to be Prime Minister', BBC2 1996

'The Battle of Orgreave', historical re-enactment directed by Jeremy Deller, 2001

'Goodbye Lenin', dir. Wolfgang Becker, feature film 2003
J. Reid, Radio 4 Today Programme profile and interview, March 2003
'The Queen', dir. Stephen Frears, script Peter Morgan, feature film, 2006
'Romanzo Criminale', dir. Michele Placido, feature film 2006
'The Lives of Others', dir. Florian Henckel von Donnersmark, feature film 2007
'The Culture Show', BBC2 27 Oct. 2007
'Dave Cameron's Incredible Journey', written and presented by Michael Cockcroft, BBC2 20 December 2007

Personal interviews:

Leighton Andrews, John Chapman, David Clarke, Hereward Cooke, Sally Davison, Pat Devine, Stuart Hall, Stephen Hopkins, Frank Howard, Martin Jacques, Alan Lawrie, Neal Lawson, Kate Markus, Peter Molyneux, Peter Oborne, Phillippa O'Neill, Mark Perryman, Mike Prior, David Purdy, Janice Robinson, Sue Slipman, Jane Taylor, Jon Trickett, Andy Wood.

(Methodological note: I make no claims for the 'representative-ness' of my interviewees. They were chosen from amongst people I know or have known, purely on the basis that I thought they might have interesting things to say about the subject and period under study, which they all did. Those few that didn't, whose names and views I have not included, were almost invariably serving politicians and journalists, who were either too guarded or plainly self-serving to say much I could use. At the same time, I was aware that those who did genuinely engage with the subject and honestly share their own views, feelings and experiences had occupied positions and roles of some influence and active responsibility in demo-cratic (mostly left but not always) politics; not exactly foot-soldiers, more like non-commissioned officers. While acknowledging my interviewees' un-representativeness, I would argue that the 'democratic left' perspective on this period and set of topics is under-represented in the historical record; to continue the military analogy, which always springs to mind in accounts like this, these people graciously admitted defeat and quietly retreated into the rest of their lives.)

Reported Speeches

T. Blair, speech to News Corporation Leadership Conference, July 1995

T. Blair, speech at the launch of report on Commission on Public Policy and British Business, 21 January 1997

T. Blair, speech to Labour Party Conference, September 1997

T. Blair, speech to Trades Union Congress, September 1998

T. Blair, speech to Labour Party Conference 2002

G. Brown, Mansion House speech 1998

G. Brown, Mansion House speech, 2001

J. Callaghan, speech to Labour Party Conference 1976

J. Cruddas, speech at University of East Anglia, 15 February 2007

J. Prescott, speech to Labour Party Conference 1999

J. Trickett, speech to Compass public meeting, 8 May 2007

Other Sources

'Modernism 1914-39', Victorian and Albert Museum exhibition, 6 April-23 July 2006

'Rodchenko and Popova', Tate Modern exhibition, November 2008-May 2009

'Futurism', Tate Modern exhibition, June-September 2009

Report on Gay Marketing Conference 2006

'Joe Guy', play by Roy Williams, Soho Theatre, November 2007

D. Marquand & S. Hall, seminar on 'Decline of the Public Realm', London 29 October 2004

'Gramsci in History' Conferences, University of East Anglia 2005, 2006

Gramsci Conference, Senate House, London May 2010

Select Index